Through Brown Eyes

PRAFULLA MOHANTI

Through Brown Eyes

Oxford   New York

OXFORD UNIVERSITY PRESS

1985

Oxford University Press, Walton Street, Oxford OX2 6DP

Oxford New York Toronto
Delhi Bombay Calcutta Madras Karachi
Kuala Lumpur Singapore Hong Kong Tokyo
Nairobi Dar es Salaam Cape Town
Melbourne Auckland
and associated companies in
Beirut Berlin Ibadan Mexico City Nicosia

Oxford is a trade mark of Oxford University Press

First published 1985 by Oxford University Press

British Library Cataloguing in Publication Data
Mohanti, Prafulla
Through brown eyes.
1. Great Britain—Social life and customs—1945-
I. Title
941.085'8'0924   DA588
ISBN 0-19-211784-X

Library of Congress Cataloging in Publication Data
Mohanti, Prafulla.
Through brown eyes.
1. Mohanti, Prafulla. 2. Artists—England—
Biography. 3. Architects—India—Biography. 4. England—
Social conditions—20th century. I. Title.
CT788.M568A35 1985 709'.2'4 84—29492
ISBN 0-19-211784-X

Set by Colset Private Ltd.
Printed in Great Britain by
St. Edmundsbury Press Ltd.
Bury St. Edmunds, Suffolk

Contents

CHAPTER 1
Arrival

I did not think the sun could shine so brightly in England.

It was a July morning in 1960. The P & O ship had anchored sometime during the previous night. When I woke up the ship was still. I realized we had arrived at Tilbury. I opened the porthole and saw hundreds of seagulls flying around. The water was muddy but the sun was glistening on it.

I ran to the upper deck. The sky was blue and the air fresh. I felt excited. I was in a new country, the country of my dreams. I had come to England for further qualifications and experience after graduating as an architect from Bombay University.

England was known as 'Bilayat' in Hindi. A Bilayati qualification was highly regarded in India. Everything Bilayati was considered superior to anything 'Deshi' (Indian). When I was studying architecture in Bombay most of my teachers had been educated in England. The students thought they were more important than the teachers with Indian qualifications. We were told that English architecture was the best. Architects with British qualifications were respected and got better jobs and commissions.

I heard the word 'Bilat', the Oriya equivalent of 'Bilayat', for the first time in my childhood in Nanpur, my village in Orissa. The village was totally isolated and I was not conscious of a world outside. When I was five years old my mother consulted the astrologer about my future. He was an old man with white hair and a long beard. Peering through a pair of steel-framed spectacles he carefully studied my jatak (horoscope), inscribed on a palm leaf. He drew diagrams on the mud floor with a piece of clay chalk and declared solemnly, 'This boy will go to Bilat.'

I was intrigued. I had heard names like 'Kalikata' and 'Kataka', where some of the villagers worked, but 'Bilat' was a totally new word.

As soon as the astrologer left I asked my mother what 'Bilat' meant. She told me it was the country where the Gora Sahibs lived. They were the Rajas of India.

'How do you go there?'

'By boat. There are seven seas to cross.'

It seemed a long way away.

'What language do they speak?'

' "Angrezi".'

'Would you like me to go to Bilat?'

She smiled. 'No. I don't want you to go anywhere. Those who go to Bilat lose their caste. They eat beef and drink alcohol. But I've heard that a boy from a poor family in Cuttack went to Bilat to study. He has come back and got a big job. But he didn't eat any beef.'

'So why don't you want me to go to Bilat? I promise not to eat beef or drink alcohol.'

'Where is the money? You must study well here. My only wish is for God to give you a long life.'

'Would you mind if I went to Bilat?'

She stroked my head. 'It is a different world.'

If I want to go to Bilat, I told myself, I must learn to read and write in English. There was a Brahmin in the village who sold books, papers, and writing materials from his house. I went to him and bought a book on how to teach myself English.

I asked my sister to help me. I told her, 'The astrologer says I'll go to Bilat.'

'But he also said the same thing to me,' she replied. 'He always says absurd things to please his jezmans (clients).'

I did not know then that my grandmother had forbidden her to go to school when she reached puberty. She was afraid my sister might become a 'Kirastani' (Christian).

In the years that followed I had forgotten the astrologer's forecast. I suddenly realized it had come true.

The Immigration Officer was polite. 'I hope you will be as happy in my country as I was in yours.'

I was in Bilat.

From Tilbury I came to Liverpool Street by train. Everything looked so clean. The trains in India were always crowded and the passengers had to fight to get into them. The seats were so dusty that they had to be wiped before sitting down. Here the seats were upholstered and travel seemed simple.

The excitement of arriving in a new country was overwhelming. I was so involved in my own thoughts that I was not aware of the other passengers or the view through the window.

When the train pulled into Liverpool Street station, the architecture reminded me of the Victoria Terminus in Bombay. But the atmosphere was quiet and orderly without crowds of coolies waiting to invade the compartments and haggle over the transport of baggage. Instead of brown faces there were white faces everywhere.

I was relieved to see Tom, who had been waiting for me on the platform. He was the only person I knew in England. He was a few years older than me and I had met him in Bombay where he was working for a British company. I had brought my three gods with me—small painted wooden figures of Lord Jagannath, an incarnation of Vishnu, his brother Balabhadra, and their sister Subhadra. They were my friends and protectors. I prayed and talked to them every day.

I climbed down from the train clutching my gods in one hand and my suitcase in the other. In my shoulder bag which I always carried with me were my painting and drawing materials—sketch pads, brushes, and paints.

Tom greeted me. 'Welcome to London.' He lived at Surbiton and we went there by taxi. To my surprise the buildings of central London resembled parts of Bombay. I had read so much about the River Thames that when Tom pointed it out to me I was terribly disappointed. It looked like an Indian canal. I was used to wide rivers with banks of clean white sand. The houses in the suburbs with their tiled roofs and neat little gardens seemed to continue for ever. After a while I was unable to distinguish one from the other.

Groups of people were sunbathing in the parks; half-naked young men and women kissed and cuddled. It was a strange experience for me. In India people always hide from the sun and there is no free mixing between boys and girls; kissing is even forbidden on the cinema screen.

Tom lived in a 1930s purpose-built block of flats overlooking a large private garden. When we arrived, his mother was waiting for us. I greeted her saying 'Namaste', joining my hands together as in prayer. Then we shook hands and she kissed me on the cheek, enquiring whether my journey had been comfortable. She had cooked a large meal specially for me, lamb curry and rice, English style. She was in her fifties and a widow. Her husband died when Tom was a small boy, but she did not marry again. She lived by herself in a small town in Sussex and from time to time came to London to stay with her son.

I gave her a handwoven silk stole I had brought from Orissa. It is an Indian custom to carry presents for the host. She examined it carefully, wrapped it round her shoulders, and went to look at herself in the mirror. She came back, kissed me again, and said 'Thank you'.

The flat had three bedrooms, a living room with a dining recess, a kitchen, two lavatories, and a bathroom. It was well-furnished with modern furniture, wall-to-wall carpeting, and patterned wallpaper.

My bedroom had a view of the garden. For the first time in my life I had a bedroom to myself. I had always shared rooms with other people, both in the village and in the hostel at Bombay. Suddenly I became aware of four walls and a ceiling and felt I was enclosed in a box. I looked through the window; it had started to rain. I sat staring at the grey sky, thinking about myself and my village.

I am the youngest son of a Karan family from the village of Nanpur. It is situated on the bank of the River Birupa in the Cuttack district of Orissa. The river gives Nanpur its identity. It provides a meeting place for the villagers, who use it for bathing, washing, and cleaning the cattle. The children love to swim in its clear blue water. In the monsoon the river overflows and the crops are often ruined. The whole area turns into a lake and the villages look like islands. In the summer the river dries up and provides a clean bed of silver sand for the children to play on.

My village has a population of about three thousand, living in six settlements separated by mango groves and paddy fields. Each settlement is mainly inhabited by one particular caste. Caste is the most important feature in the village. It defines a person's place and the work he is expected to do. Traditionally there are four castes—Brahmins, the priests; Kshatriyas, the warriors; Vaishyas, the businessmen; and Sudras, the servant class. The

Brahmins belong to the highest caste and only they can perform the ceremonies required by Hindu regligion. Over the years there have been many sub-castes relating to professions. Apart from the Brahmins there are Karans—the administrators, farmers, carpenters, astrologers, potters, jewellers, washermen; and Harijans—formerly called Untouchables. The Brahmins, Karans, and the Kshatriyas belong to the higher castes and are not expected to do manual work. The villagers are mainly farmers and craftsmen. Each craft is the property of a particular caste and provides a specialised family trade. Together they form the village community.

The villagers are Hindus. They believe in God, karma (fate), and the cycle of rebirth. For them God is everywhere—in a man, in a tree, in a stone.

Every village has a local deity. In Nanpur it is a piece of stone decorated with vermilion paste. It is called Mahlia Buddha. He sits under the ancient varuna tree protecting the village. The story goes that he was donated to the village by the barber's great-great-great-grandmother many generations ago. Since then the barber's family has the exclusive right to attend to the deity. Mahlia Buddha had a special power to cure smallpox and cholera, and people from the surrounding villages came to worship him. Although modern medicines have now brought the epidemics under control, the power of the deity has not diminished. People believe in him and worship him for everything, even for modern medicines to be effective. Clay animals are presented. It is believed that Mahlia Buddha rides them during the night and goes from place to place guarding the village.

Every villager has a jatak, which is a birth certificate inscribed on a palm leaf by the village astrologer. He is consulted for everything, whether the planets are favourable and the auspicious times for starting a journey. There is a saying, 'Tuesday night and Wednesday morning, wherever you go you receive good luck.'

The villagers live in joint families. Parents and sons live together with their families and share food cooked in a common kitchen. The houses are built of mud walls and thatched roofs with outside and inside verandahs. A central private courtyard provides shelter from the sun and is mainly used by the women. Every house has an altar containing the tulashi plant (sacred

basil). This herb is so valuable for its medicinal properties that it
is worshipped as a goddess. The joint family system ensures that
everybody is looked after. Because there is a great respect for old
age the old people are never neglected.

Marriages are arranged by parents, and the bride and bridegroom must belong to the same caste. The girl's father has to give
a dowry, and the bride must be a virgin. Widows are not allowed
to re-marry. They lead very austere lives. When their husbands
die they break their glass bangles and stop wearing the vermilion
spot on their forehead.

The role of a woman in my village is that of a mother. She has
the responsibility of managing the household. If she does it well,
she is compared to Lakshmi, the Goddess of Wealth, but if she
destroys its unity she is compared with Kali, the Goddess of
Destruction. Her duty is not complete until she has produced a
son, essential for the family to continue. A house is not a home
without a child.

The women in Nanpur worship Satyapir, a Hindu-Muslim
god, to bless them with sons. 'Satya' is the Hindu part, meaning
'truth', and 'Pir' in Islam means 'prophet'. There is a large
Muslim settlement two miles from Nanpur, and in a village on
the other side of the river, a single Muslim family lives among
Brahmins. The worship of a Hindu-Muslim god was a deliberate
attempt to bring the two communities together through religion.
In spite of Hindu-Muslim tensions in other parts of India, the
atmosphere around the village has remained tranquil.

My eldest brother died in childhood. Several years passed and
my mother did not have a son. She worshipped Satyapir every
day. My brother was born. He was named Fakir Charan, the Feet
of the Fakir, the Muslim holy man.

There are no Christians in the area, but the missionaries from
the city visit the market place from time to time to distribute
literature.

Religious fasts and festivals play a great part in the life of the
village. The most popular is the spring festival of Holi, when the
villagers throw coloured powder and water on each other as an
expression of love. It represents Krishna's love play with the
Gopis (milkmaidens). As the cuckoo sings, hidden among the
mango blossoms, welcoming the spring, the villagers carry
Gopinath (Krishna) in a palanquin around the village, singing

and dancing to the sound of cymbals, drums, and flutes.

All-night plays and concerts take place in the open air. Snake charmers, puppeteers, and wandering singers visit during the dry season. A wave of excitement goes through the children when they approach the village. There is no television but some villagers have radios; listening to film music is popular.

Time is measured by the sun. The day begins with sunrise, around six, and ends with sunset, twelve hours later. The pace of life is slow and nobody is in a hurry. Days become weeks, weeks turn into months, and months into years. Age has no specific meaning, and time and life continue after death. The saying, 'Time is money', has no significance in the village. There is plenty of time to gossip or do nothing and there is no boredom. The villagers discuss their personal problems with each other, sharing joys and sorrows. Life revolves around the children and the gods. Parents have no other interest.

My childhood was happy. We lived in a joint family. My father worked as a forester away from home and I was looked after by my mother, grandmother, and many uncles and aunts. In my great-grandfather's time there were about twenty in the family: my great-grandfather, his wife, their two sons, and their wives and children. They lived in six rooms and ate from a common kitchen. They all contributed to the running of the house and the children were treated equally.

After the death of my great-grandfather and his wife, my grandfather and his brother separated. All the properties were divided. My grandfather was the eldest and, according to the convention, got the eastern part of the house. My grandfather had two sons. His brother had no children and when his wife died he adopted my uncle, my father's younger brother.

The family house caught fire and was burnt down. Both the brothers built separate houses on their tiny plots of land. My grandfather wanted to make the house fireproof by using brick and lime mortar, but my grandmother objected. Brick was burnt earth and to her represented burning Vasudha, the mother earth. So the house was built with timber and a corrugated iron roof. My grandmother liked beautiful things and asked the carpenters to carve every piece of wood used in the building. But my grandfather died before the house was completed.

I played with my friends in the dust of the village path. We did

not have many toys to play with and we improvised games.
Nobody disturbed us; even the cows walked carefully by. During
the monsoon the village paths became small rivers on which we
sailed paper boats.

My mother told me a story to help me to count:
'This little finger said, "Mother, I'm hungry."
The next finger said, "Where can we get food?"
The middle finger said, "We'll borrow."
The first finger said, "How can we pay it back?"
The big thumb said, "We'll eat, drink, and leave the
village." '

Education was respected because it was the only means of
escaping from poverty. When I was three I was taken to the
chatshali, the nursery school held on a villager's verandah. I
remember my first day. My grandmother helped me to carry a
metal plate containing rice, money, and a coconut, which I
offered to the teacher. He blessed me by gently stroking my
outstretched palms with a cane. Then he took my right hand and
with a piece of clay chalk helped me to draw three circles on
the mud floor: Brahma the Creator, Vishnu the Preserver, and
Maheswar the Destroyer; the Hindu Trinity. I practised the circles
for several months. Now that I look back I find how profound it
was. The Oriya script is round and practising the circles helped
me to develop good handwriting.

I looked forward to religious festivals and ceremonies. They
were full of colour and movement. The characters in the all-night
plays intrigued me. The music and dancing inspired me to participate. I produced plays on the village path with other children,
using leaves and flowers as costumes and ash for make-up. Art
was a part of daily life. The villagers decorated the mud walls and
floors of their houses with rice paste. Brushes were made with
straw and occasionally coloured earths were used. The lotus was
the main symbol. At harvest festival it was used with stylized
footprints to welcome Lakshmi, the Goddess of Wealth. My
mother was a good painter and I followed her instinctively. I
became so good that I was invited by the villagers to decorate
their houses.

When I was seven, I went to the primary school. It was in
Kusupur, the next village, and I had to walk two miles to get
there. I carried my own mat made with palm leaves. The school

provided little desks, and the children sat cross-legged on the floor. I was taught to use my hands and make things. There were no manufactured materials available so we had to improvise. That gave me an incentive to create. There were no pens and I made quills from feathers. The school was an extension of the house.

I had already taught myself to read and write in English and was ahead of my classmates, who were just beginning to learn the alphabet. I had started with simple words: 'c–a–t', 'cat', 'd–o–g', 'dog'. Gradually I was able to read and understand. The first nursery rhyme I recited was:

'Pussy cat, pussy cat, where have you been?'
'I have been to London to see the Queen.'
'Pussy cat, pussy cat, what did you do there?'
'I frightened a little mouse under her chair.'

I had a little cat as a pet and used to ask her in English, 'Have you been to London to see the Queen?' My father had told me that London was the capital of England and the Bilati Queen lived there. I did not know what she looked like, but when I saw pictures of Queen Victoria in my school history books I thought she looked very motherly. The whole image of Queen Victoria, the cat and the frightened mouse made me feel close to her as if she was my grandmother.

My grandmother controlled everyone in the house, including my father. My mother was not allowed to join him in the forest. She had to stay at home to look after her. My grandmother would not allow my sister to continue her studies. She had to stay at home and receive training from her on how to become a good housewife.

My grandmother could not read or write. It was considered a waste of money for girls to receive education and my mother was not sent to school by her parents. After my mother married at the age of seventeen and came to the village, my great-grandmother arranged for her to read and write. She wanted my mother to read the puranas, the Mahabharata, and Ramayana aloud to her. There were public readings by a Brahmin, but my great-grand-mother did not want to depend on him. In the afternoons, when my mother had some spare time, she sat on the verandah reading the puranas and the village women gathered around her to listen.

The stories gave in detail imaginative descriptions of life and art.

Although my grandmother was very strict she was kind to everybody. The other villagers came to her for advice and she was always ready to help. She received them on the verandah, sitting on a straw mat. They sipped tea together, taking a little opium with it. I was her favourite and while my mother was busy in the house she looked after me.

In the primary school the Harijan children were not allowed into the classrooms. They sat on the verandah and got their lessons separately. But in the school playground we played together as friends. I was a good student and they used to come to my house for help. My grandmother warned me not to touch them. When the Brahmin priest came he was invited into the house as an honoured guest and given his special mat to sit on. The Harijans lived in separate settlements. They were mainly fishermen and basket weavers, and were originally called Untouchables. Later, Gandhi named them 'Harijans', Children of God. They were not allowed to enter the temples and if by chance a high-caste Hindu touched them he had to have a bath to purify himself.

The Harijans had no land of their own and worked as labourers. Even the land on which they had built their homes was loaned to them by the high-caste Hindus. They were the ryots (tenants) and had to provide some free service in return. The landlords harassed them and often took away vegetables from their gardens. Life was hard for them and some went to Calcutta to do manual work. Many got TB and died. So people from my caste, the Karans, never went to Calcutta to work because it was considered degrading. The villagers believed that the big cities destroyed people.

My class teacher took pride in his students and treated me like his son. He was very good at mathematics and helped me in mental arithmetic, explaining how to solve the problems in silence and give the answer. This helped me to concentrate and exercise my mind. He persuaded me to take part in village functions by giving dramatic recitals of poems. Although I produced plays with my friends in the village I felt so frightened at seeing a large audience that I forgot the lines. But my teacher told me not to be self-conscious.

We were taught to look after our health. My teacher told us that cholera was caused by contaminated water, flies carried germs, and smallpox was airborne. But the villagers believed that smallpox and cholera were evil goddesses and worshipped Mahlia Buddha for protection.

Mahlia Buddha could not help my grandmother when she had cancer of the mouth. I watched her suffer. There was no doctor in the village, and I did not know there were places called hospitals. She was treated by an ayurvedic practitioner who specialized in herbal remedies, and my mother nursed her. But my grandmother died.

I saw her body being carried by the male relatives to the cremation ground on a stretcher made of four pieces of bamboo. They chanted 'Ram nam satya hai; Hari nam satya hai'—'God is Truth.' My mother and other female relatives wailed, and I cried with them. The rituals continued for twelve days. On the tenth day my father and I had our heads shaved by the barber. When the ceremony was over the house seemed empty without my grandmother. When I asked my father where she had gone, I was told, 'To Baikuntha'.

Everybody in the village wanted to go to Baikuntha, the Land of the Gods. But only those with punya (piety) succeeded. So people spent their lives accumulating punya, which could be achieved by doing dharma. 'Dharma' means 'good work', like giving hospitality to strangers, respecting Brahmins, parents, and elders.

But I wanted to go to England. I read English stories like 'Red Riding Hood' and 'Goldilocks and the Three Bears'. They were illustrated with coloured pictures. Goldilocks looked beautiful with her golden hair and blue eyes but had a worried expression on her face. I thought England was full of forests and bears.

My image of England changed when I started reading English poetry in my school textbooks. There were two poems about daffodils, one by William Wordsworth and the other by Robert Herrick. Their attitudes to nature appealed to teachers and students. My English teacher used to show us small, funnel-shaped yellow flowers from the school garden and tell us that daffodils looked like them. I visualized England as a land of daffodils, like the yellow mustard fields along the bank of the river. The poem 'Leisure' by W.H. Davies was my favourite. 'What is this life if, full of care, we have no time to stand and stare.' It represented my own attitude to life.

I sat by the river looking at the sunsets. I wandered round the paddy fields and watched them turn from vivid green to golden brown. I saw the palm trees swaying in the wind. I lay on a mat in the courtyard looking at the moon play hide-and-seek with the floating clouds. I enjoyed the multicoloured birds, the sweet-scented flowers which opened out at night. It was magic. I felt at one with nature.

The high school was built by the villagers themselves without any government help and the students took part in its construction. There was a great sense of participation, and the students felt the school belonged to them. We planted coconut trees, grew flowers and vegetables in the garden. Apart from science and arts subjects we had a class in drawing. The students did not take it seriously as it was not a part of the examination syllabus. But the drawings had to be shown to the teacher and I was always asked by my friends to draw for them.

Every year two important festivals were celebrated at school. One was at the beginning of the academic year at the end of the summer, in honour of Ganesha, the God of Learning and remover of obstacles. The other was at the beginning of spring to worship Saraswati, the Goddess of Learning. Painted clay images were made and the students produced plays in which I always took part. There was no printing press and I edited the school magazine twice a year, writing it out in my own hand.

English history was one of our arts subjects, and we read about the Battle of Hastings and the Battle of Waterloo. That gave me the impression of England as a small island where people were aggressive and always fighting. Descriptions of battles frightened me. The Hindu epics, the Ramayana and the Mahabharata, were full of violence. In 261 BC Orissa was conquered by the Emperor Ashoka, and the battlefield was only sixty miles from the village. Ashoka was so repelled by the slaughter that he became a Buddhist and practised non-violence.

India became independent in 1947. We assembled in the school playground, hoisted the national flag, and sang 'Bande Mataram', 'We greet you Mother'. The headmaster made a speech telling us we were free. I did not know what he meant. I thought we were all free in the village; nobody controlled us. I had never seen a gora sahib.

My father's superior officers in the forestry department were

English. He used to talk about them as if they were gods. One year he arranged a Christmas party for four sahibs and four memsahibs in a remote part of the forest. An area had to be cleared and four cottages were built using timber and leaves. Each cottage was self-contained with a living-room, a bedroom, and a bathroom. A large tent was erected where the sahibs ate, drank, and danced at night. A twenty mile road was constructed for the motor vehicles and the villagers volunteered to work as labourers. They took pride in serving the sahibs. The village headman sent presents of goats, vegetables, fruits, and flowers. My father took the sahibs into the dense forest at night to hunt tigers. A male tiger was killed, which created a sensation. The next night its mate came looking for it and was also killed.

The officers enjoyed their holiday so much that they sent my father a wrist watch from Calcutta. It was a prized possession and he showed it to everybody. But when the local Raja found out he was displeased and warned my father not to do such a thing again. Only the Raja was entitled to such treatment.

Soon after Independence English history was taken out of the syllabus and replaced by Indian history. It was only then that we were taught how the British had occupied India and ruled for 250 years. But English still remained the first language at school.

For my matriculation I had two papers in English but only one in Oriya, my mother tongue and the medium of instruction. I usually translated my thoughts from Oriya into English and found English grammar difficult and complicated. The English teacher was an Oriya who had no training in phonetics. We never practised English conversation.

The examination questions were always set in English, even for the Oriya language paper. The question for the Oriya essay read, 'Describe the village well in the evening.' I thought it meant describe the village in the evening in a very good way. Luckily I included a short description of activities around the well and got reasonably good marks.

Cuttack was the centre for taking the matriculation exam. I was one of fifteen students from our school selected to appear. The village was so isolated that it took one day to reach the town, although it was only thirty miles away. We had to walk twelve miles to the nearest railway station along a mud track and there were two rivers to cross by boat. With only two trains a day, if you missed one there was a wait of twelve hours for the next.

Two teachers accompanied us and we took a cook from the village with our own supply of rice, dal, and vegetables. We stayed in the house of a relative of one of our students, and the teachers looked after us.

The reputation of the school depended on our results. When they were announced, seven had passed. Only a few students got first class in the whole of Orissa and I was one of them. The villagers offered a special puja to Mahlia Buddha to show their gratitude.

I felt I belonged to the village and the village belonged to me. I saw the sun rise in the east and set in the west. The moon appeared over the horizon like a huge golden plate and travelled upwards, getting brighter and brighter. The light was so bright that I could read by it. I called it 'Jahna mamu', 'Uncle moon', and watched it decrease in size and disappear. That night millions of stars came out shining like jewels. The next evening it reappeared, a thin curved line, and I watched it become full again. The jackals howled during the night at regular intervals. The owls hooted and the bats flew from tree to tree stealing fruit. When the mango tree blossomed I knew it was spring, and a yellow bird sat on a tree in our garden. My mother was always at home when I returned from school and I felt safe and secure.

But I was aware of darker sides of village life. My cousins did not have enough to eat and I gave them some of my food. Many of my friends died of cholera, typhoid, and diphtheria, and some were disfigured by smallpox. Terror went through the village when the epidemics struck and accidental deaths disturbed me.

I used to sit on the verandah with a hurricane lamp and study late into the night. The chowkidar, the night watchman, would come and sit beside me for a while and leave silently. One night he did not turn up. The next morning while I was going to the river to have my bath, a villager told me the chowkidar had been bitten by a snake and was being treated by a healer. Immediately I went to see him. The healer was trying to cure him and his wife and children were crying. I stood there helpless. I could not do anything. The chowkidar died. From then on I asked myself questions about life and death.

I wanted to be a doctor to help my village, but could not get into the medical school. I did not know how my father would have been able to pay for my studies; my mother had to pawn her bracelets to get the money for my matriculation fees. Although I thought of myself as an artist and writer I did not know there were professional artists and writers who earned their living by selling their work. The aim of education was to get a secure office job and there was nobody to advise us on the choice of a career or the opportunities open. By chance I saw an advertisement in an Oriya newspaper about a course in architecture in Bombay. There was a small scholarship attached to it. I applied without knowing what an architect was. To my amazement I was accepted.

Bombay was fifteen hundred miles away by train from the village. I was eighteen and it was my first visit to a large city. The time of my departure was fixed by the village astrologer and my mother put a pot of water with a twig from the mango tree at the entrance to the house. It was considered lucky to see a full pot when starting a journey. A man must put his right foot forward when leaving the house and a woman her left; the air must flow through the right nostril. My mother bent down, took a little dust from the mud floor, and smeared my forehead with it. I walked straight ahead as it was inauspicious to look back. If by mistake I had left something behind I would not have returned; another person would be sent to fetch it for me.

My luggage consisted of a small bedding roll and a steel trunk containing my books and clothes. My father came with me up to Cuttack, and a man from the Harijan settlement carried my luggage to the railway station. It was unlucky to travel in threes and so the Harijan went ahead of us. Friends and relatives came as far as the river to say goodbye.

There were no direct trains to Bombay either from the local station or from Cuttack. I had to change at Calcutta which was an overnight journey. I travelled third class. The train left Cuttack at nine in the evening and reached Calcutta at six in the morning. I felt alone and vulnerable when I left my father at Cuttack. I prayed to all my gods to look after me.

The Bombay Mail left from Calcutta at six in the evening and there was a wait of twelve hours. I went to the third class waiting room which had washing facilities. The attendant guessed I was from Orissa and spoke to me in Oriya. He was from Orissa himself and seemed very pleased to see me. He bought some snacks for me and persuaded me to eat. He told me that I reminded him of his eldest son who was attending school in his village. He had been working in Calcutta for twenty years, and his family lived in the village. He sent them money regularly and was only able to see them twice a year. He was curious to know all about myself. When I told him it was my first visit to Calcutta he volunteered to help. He looked after the passengers' luggage when they wanted to go out and received a few coins for his services. While giving me instructions on how to get to the city centre, he warned me, 'Be careful of the pickpockets.'

Outside Howrah Station stood the iron bridge over the River Hooghly, a branch of the Ganges. It was the gateway to the city. Trams, buses blowing horns, bullock carts, and rickshaws streamed across the bridge along with thousands of pedestrians. The noise and the crowds were overwhelming, and I was worried I might get lost. The air was filled with smoke, and the sky was hazy. I realized why my relatives in the village did not want to come to Calcutta for work.

I took my first tram ride to the centre of the city. I got down at the Maidan and walked around. The Victoria Memorial Hall, the churches, and the imposing government buildings stood as reminders of the British Raj. The streets were full of shops overflowing onto the pavement. I knew the Ganges was a holy river whose water had the power to purify, but I had no idea it could be so filthy. I saw hundreds of people bathing there. A priest came up to me and started speaking in Bengali. In the village I had taught myself to read and write Bengali so that I could read the literature. But this was my first opportunity to speak and I was pleased with myself.

The attendant had asked me to return to the station in good time as I did not have a reserved seat on the train. The trains were always full and passengers had to reserve their seats a long time in advance. The attendant made arrangements with a coolie to find me a sleeping place in an unreserved third class compartment. He bargained with him on my behalf, and a reasonable price was fixed. He asked me to note the number of the coolie. There were so many of them that it was difficult for me to distinguish one from another. They all wore red shirts with numbers engraved on metal armlets.

We went to the platform an hour before departure. It was already overcrowded. As soon as the coolies saw the train approaching the platform they rushed into the compartments to grab places for their clients. My coolie managed to get an upper berth for me. It was really meant for the luggage, but I was able to spread my bed roll out and that became my home for the next two nights.

The compartment was full of men, women, and children travelling long distances. At night many slept on the floor. The train stopped only at the important stations. The platforms were full of life and excitement. Vendors sold snacks, fruits, newspapers, and magazines. Young boys sold glasses of tea. They shouted 'Cha, garam cha' as they walked from one end of the platform to the other. There was a dining car but the caterers also came to serve food inside the compartment. Sweepers came from time to time to clean the floors.

The compartment soon became a family. We talked to each other in a mixture of languages: English, Hindi, and Bengali. None of the other passengers could speak Oriya. We played cards and shared our food. Time passed quickly.

At Bombay's Victoria Terminus I was met by a distant relative who was working in the city. He took me to a hotel near the station. The proprietor was from Orissa, and the Oriyas who visited Bombay usually stayed there. I shared a room with three other guests and food was included in the price. But I could only afford to stay there for one night. The next day I enrolled at the school and moved to the students' hostel.

The School of Architecture was part of the School of Art, established during the British Raj. It was in the centre of the city. The buildings had a western look. They were built of stone in the Gothic style with cornices and conical tiled roofs. When I joined the school, the English teachers had left but most of my Indian teachers had been educated in London.

The medium of instruction was English, and the textbooks were written by English architects and historians. Even the history of Indian architecture was written by an Englishman. The teacher who taught us the history of Western architecture was a Christian from Goa and had a Portuguese name. He had never visited the

West but was always immaculately dressed in Western style, with suit and tie.

My classmates were from all parts of India, speaking many different regional languages. The only language we had in common was English. It was a compulsory subject in high school and the medium of instruction for higher education. As we were not able to understand each other's language, we were forced to speak in English. I found it difficult as I thought in Oriya and translated my expressions into English. Fluency meant speaking quickly. We were Hindus, Muslims, Christians, and Parsees, but we never discussed caste or religion. My principal was a Yahudi.

For the first time I met people from the West. Two of the girls in the first year had pale skins, fair hair, and blue eyes. They came in chauffeur-driven cars, and I thought they were English. But when they told me they were from Scandinavia I was disappointed. They were married to diplomats and left the school after a few months when their husbands were transferred.

The classes were from ten in the morning till four in the afternoon, with lectures and studio work. Bombay was the centre of the Indian film industry and one day a classmate announced excitedly that a film crew had arrived in a nearby street with a famous heroine. We all abandoned our studio work and rushed out to watch. The next day we were warned by the teacher not to do it again. The teachers were like our fathers and we respected them.

My hostel was run by the state government and my school had a number of rooms reserved there. It was ten miles away in the suburbs and I had to travel by bus and train. There were ticket concessions for the students. The hostel was a converted army barracks made up of very simple buildings with verandahs and asbestos roofs. There were outside lavatories and bathrooms. We had a canteen which served vegetarian food and eggs. Sunday lunch was a big event; fresh fruit salad and custard was a favourite sweet of the students.

Architecture was a five-year course and the training was strenuous. We had to prepare a large number of drawings and often stayed up late into the night trying to complete our schemes. I learned to express myself through lines. There was very little time for words, except for writing to my mother. I missed my parents and the village, and when I went there during the vacations, I usually stayed longer than the time permitted. In the school I was taught to design Western-style buildings, blocks of flats, offices, and hotels. But when I went home I sat cross-legged on the mud floor and ate with my fingers. It was difficult for me to explain to my relatives in the village what I was studying in Bombay.

At that time there was not a single magazine on art or architecture published in India. Everything came from England, America, or Italy. The drawing and painting materials were imported from England; handmade Whatman paper was popular but expensive. I had to save up to buy it in order to present my drawings in an attractive way. Two stationery shops opposite the school catered for the students.

My design teacher was a well-known practising architect. 'Open your eyes. Look at buildings and forms', he told us. I went round Bombay with my sketch pad looking at buildings, observing life, and sketching in water-colours. But the paper and paint dried quickly, so I carried a bottle of water in my bag and soaked the paper before applying the colours.

My school was participating in an all-India youth festival to be held in Bombay. The students' union decided to present a dance item and asked for volunteers. A well-known dancer and his wife had agreed to do the choreography. I had always been interested in dance as a means of expression and put my name forward. To select the performers an audition was arranged in the common room. We were asked to move to music, one by one. As I watched the others and saw the expressions on my friends' faces I felt nervous. But when my turn came I forgot everybody and danced naturally. The choreographer selected me and said I ought to take proper lessons. So for the next year, I went to the dance school he and his wife ran in their house. I learned the principles and techniques of Indian classical dancing—pure dance, abhinaya (expression), and mudras (the language of hand movements).

Wherever I looked I saw dance: in people's movements, gestures, and the way they formed groups. Dancing helped me use my hands freely when drawing. Curvilinear forms came naturally to me and my teachers encouraged me to use them in my architectural designs.

The sea formed an important part of life in Bombay. It was visible from wherever I went. Hotels and blocks of flats were named 'Sea Palace', 'Sea Green', 'Sea Belle', and 'Sea View'.

A glimpse of the sea made a building fashionable. My hostel stood on a mound of rocks by the sea, surrounded by palm trees. At high tide the waves dashed against the rocks and submerged them in water. But at low tide the rocks were exposed and provided secluded meeting places for Bombay's lovers. They lived in crowded homes and it was impossible for them to meet in private. In the mornings washermen washed clothes and spread them on the rocks to dry. The colours of the saris transformed the rocks into modern sculptures. A little way away there was a charming little fishing village with a bay where the fishermen kept their boats. Fisherwomen in bright coloured saris walked gracefully, swaying their hips and balancing baskets of fish on their heads.

Bombay seemed much cleaner than Calcutta, but it was very different from my village. There were proper roads with wide pavements, large Victorian buildings, modern apartment blocks, old bungalows, and air-conditioned cinema halls displaying huge posters.

On my way to the school I saw mosques, churches, and fire temples. There was an enclosed park where the Parsees left their dead on the Towers of Silence.

During the day the city centre became crowded with shoppers and workers who poured in from the suburbs by train and bus. In the mornings the trains were overcrowded, and I had to squeeze into the compartment, trying to protect my drawings which I carried in a roll. In the monsoon it rained heavily and continued for weeks. The wind was so strong that it drove the rain horizontally with great force. Gradually the sky became clear and the sea calmed down. A new life began in the city.

At the Gateway of India, small boats carried tourists on sight-seeing tours to the rock-cut temples at Elephanta. Ships waited along the horizon to anchor in the docks. In the evening the promenades came to life with visitors strolling along, gossiping. Vendors sold savoury Bombay 'chat' and a silent crowd gathered outside the luxury Taj Mahal hotel, staring at the guests arriving in taxis and limousines. Excitement grew when a film star arrived.

At night, Marine Drive, a curved bay with expensive hotels and flats, glittered with lights and looked like a jewelled necklace. I walked up and down the pavement with my friends, eating peanuts and enjoying the scene. A little way away at Chowpatty

Beach, performers buried their heads in the sand, spreading pieces of cloth with a few coins to attract the sympathizers.

I enjoyed looking at the shops selling saris of many different colours and design. There were shopping streets specializing in particular items: clothes, jewellery, bedding, china. In some shops bargaining was expected, while others sold at the fixed price. At Crawford Market stalls sold fruits, vegetables, and exotic flowers, which filled the air with their sweet smell. A man sat on a raised platform making garlands and I saw young women buying them to decorate their hair.

Life in Bombay was both modern and traditional. Some women wore saris and some were in frocks. The men wore Western clothes and the traditional dress of dhoti and kurta. As I walked from one area to the other I heard the sound of temple bells and Muslim prayers. Groups of people gathered in front of the churches to attend services. I heard Hindi, Marathi, Gujarati, and South Indian languages being spoken. The whole of India seemed to be represented.

I used to see a European sitting alone on a bench by the sea outside my hostel. He wore a long white robe and there was a serene expression on his face, like a Hindu holy man. I wondered who he was. Then one day he spoke to me in English. He was from Italy, a Catholic priest attached to a convent nearby. From him I learned about Christianity. It seemed very similar to Hinduism, and I visualized Christ as Krishna. When he told me about the birth of Jesus at Christmas, I thought of the stories my mother had told me about baby Krishna.

We love festivals in India and celebrate all of them—Hindu, Muslim, and Christian. Any excuse for a holiday and a feast is welcomed. Bombay had a large population of Christians and Christmas played an important part in Bombay's commercial and social life. The streets in Christian areas were decorated with lights and paper flowers. The cake and coffee shops near my hostel had special Christmas decorations, stars, and snow made out of cotton wool. They were different from the typical Hindu eating places. The Christians were easily identified. They had Western names and the girls wore frocks. They were believed to be more liberated than the Hindu girls.

My school closed for the Christmas holidays but it was not long enough to go home. I sent Christmas and New Year cards to my friends, and on Christmas Day we had a feast in the hostel canteen.

During one of my summer vacations, I stayed in Bombay to work in an architect's office to earn some money. I fell ill with an infection and was bedridden with a high temperature. The hostel was officially closed and only two other people beside me were staying there. The hostel canteen was also closed. A girl secretary working in the office came every day with food and reading materials for me. She was a Christian and very gentle. She made all the necessary arrangements for my medical treatment and I got better. When the college reopened I was kept busy with my projects. After a few weeks I went back to the architect's office to thank her personally. But she had left. About a week later I received a letter from her telling me she had become a nun.

On Sunday mornings jam sessions were held in certain restaurants in central Bombay. Boys and girls met around eleven and danced to live music. There were no alcoholic drinks, only coca-cola, which was considered very Western. My mother was visiting me and I took her to a jam session to see how she would react to this Western phenomenon. To my surprise she did not seem to mind the young boys and girls dancing together. But she expressed strong disapproval when a middle-aged man started dancing with a young girl. In the afternoon I took her to see an English film although she did not understand English. In the film a young girl fell in love with an older man. When they started dancing together my mother cried out loudly in Oriya, 'Look! It's that couple again!'

There were a number of cinemas in central Bombay which showed films in the English language. I was not able to distinguish between American English and British English. Neither could I tell the difference between an Englishman, a European, or an American. They all looked the same. I rarely saw them walking in the streets. They went about in their cars and I did not have an opportunity to meet them socially. During the cool season I watched groups of Western tourists going in and out of luxury hotels, guarded by 'darwans' wearing impressive uniforms and turbans. I did not have the courage to go inside. In Bombay the Western people looked unreal, but I could relate them to the films, most of which came from Hollywood. MGM had their own cinema called the Metro. When I saw the lion roaring at the start of a picture I thought it was the British lion and the films were all English.

After four years in Bombay I got an opportunity to meet an Englishman socially. It was Boxing Day and the Parsee women had produced 'Cinderella' in the open air. A friend had invited me to see it. One of his other guests was an Englishman who worked for a British company in Bombay. He was a little older than me and I felt nervous about talking to him. I was worried he might not be able to follow my English. But we had no difficulty in understanding each other and later that evening I went back to my hostel feeling triumphant. I had been able to talk in English to a real Englishman.

After that we met several times and became friends. He was interested in Indian culture but had no Hindu friends. He said he was never invited to Hindu homes and most of his friends in Bombay were British, Anglo-Indian, Muslim, or Parsee. He had lived in Bombay for nearly three years and still felt an outsider.

I understood from my own experience how he felt. I, too, considered myself an outsider. I was rarely asked by my Marathi and Gujarati classmates to their homes. Even at school they usually formed groups and spoke in their own languages. My close friends at school were from other parts of India.

My English friend's name was Tom and he wanted to know about the Hindu way of life. I invited him to my village. To my surprise he accepted and came with me during the summer vacation. He wanted to experience everything the Indian way, including travelling third class on the train. The other passengers thought he was very poor and told me, in Hindi, how difficult it must be for him to travel third class in the heat. They bought cold drinks for him and he was impressed by their hospitality. But I was amused. I thought of his air-conditioned flat in Bombay and the two servants who looked after him.

His arrival in the village was a big event. People from surrounding villages came to see him. Children followed him wherever he went, scrutinizing his every movement. One evening when we were drinking tea in the courtyard of our house he said, 'Prafulla, how can you design modern architecture from a mud hut? You should go outside India to broaden your vision. When you come to England you can stay with my family.'

Tom enjoyed his visit to the village. It was a real change for him. But when he returned to Bombay he decided to leave India. He realized his future was in the West where he belonged. He got a job in London and left, but we wrote to each other regularly.

From my hostel I watched the ships sail across the horizon and wondered where they were going. A few months after qualifying as an architect I found myself on one of them, on the way to England to continue my studies.

I thought of England as a land of daffodils, crocuses, passing showers, and floating clouds. Men wore bowler hats and carried umbrellas which they seldom opened. There was no poverty and people were honest and fair, like my friend Tom.

I left Bombay in the monsoon. The sea was rough and I was violently sick. I went to the doctor for help but he seemed drunk and pushed me out of his cabin. 'Go and buy some seasickness tablets from the shop', he said. I took his advice and soon felt better.

The boat was like a small floating England. The passengers were mainly British, with a few Australians and Indians. Most of the Indians were students or scholars on their way to English universities. A British family was returning home after spending several years in India and were full of apprehension about their future. They had lived in a luxury bungalow with cooks, servants, and chauffeur-driven cars. They had a wonderful time in India and were not looking forward to life in England. But their only daughter, about sixteen, was full of excitement. She felt isolated in India. She had nothing in common with the memsahibs.

An Australian sheep farmer was visiting England for the first time. I found it difficult to follow his accent. Farmers in my part of India were always poor and illiterate, so I could not understand why people fussed around him. I was amazed when a fellow-passenger told me he was the richest man on board.

Tea was brought to me every morning by the steward. Then, still in my pyjamas and dressing-gown which I had bought specially for the journey, I went to the upper deck for my morning walk. I passed other passengers taking their walks and soon learned the English habit of nodding and saying 'Good morning'.

Because I did not eat beef or pork I was given a table to myself in the dining room. In the beginning I felt self-conscious. I sat watching the other passengers eating huge amounts of meat. The food was mostly cooked in an English way but the waiters were Indian, from Goa. There were always eggs for breakfast—fried, boiled, scrambled, omelettes. I usually had spiced omelettes because I found the other preparations too insipid.

Dinner was formal. Many put on evening dress for the occasion. I had bought a new brown suit in Bombay and wore it with a tie. One night I was invited to dine at the captain's table and I was surprised to see chicken curry, no beef or pork. I was touched by his understanding.

The decks contained every facility for the passengers, even a small swimming pool. Bridge parties took place in the lounge every afternoon and we played for money. I usually won. The others were surprised and often asked me where I learned to play bridge. When I said, 'In my village', there was an expression of disbelief on their faces. I had played bridge with my friends in the village, but never for money. In the Mahabharata there is a vivid description of the Pandava brothers gambling with dice and losing all their possessions, including their wife, Draupadi.

I sat on the upper deck with my sketch pad painting in water-colours. I had no formal training in art. My introduction to drawing and painting was in my childhood in the village, where I decorated the mud houses for festivals and ceremonies. While studying architecture I had to draw perspectives of buildings in water-colours. I enjoyed painting and on Sundays I went out with friends to paint landscapes. But from the boat I saw only sea. Wherever I looked there was water and the sky above.

The monotony was broken when the ship sailed through the Suez Canal. As it floated along the embankment with green fields and palm trees on either side I felt as if we were sailing across the land.

We reached Port Said in the evening and anchored a little way from shore. Groups of tiny boats surrounded us, tempting us to buy souvenirs. Their dim oil lamps reflected on the water, creating a mysterious atmosphere. I went ashore for a few hours with some fellow-passengers. The sights, sounds, and smells reminded me of Bombay. I did not know then it would be my last experience of the East for some time.

The Mediterranean was deep blue. The water was so clear I could see right to the bottom. The air became cool and fresh. Suddenly I realized I was not sweating any more. We passed little islands and had a glimpse of the Rock of Gibraltar.

One morning there was excitement on the deck. 'Look, England!' It was Torquay. I was surprised to see palm trees and white villas. People were playing cricket on the green. We sailed along the coast for a while and I saw the white cliffs of Dover. We were told the ship would arrive in Tilbury in the morning.

CHAPTER 2

First Impressions

I sat by the window watching the lingering twilight. I was not prepared for it and found it difficult to go to bed. It gave me a totally different sense of time. When Tom and his mother said goodnight I wondered how it could be night when there was still daylight outside. In India the sun sets around six in the evening all the year round and there is a clear division between day and night.

I was used to sleeping on hard beds made of wood with a thin cotton mattress and in the village I often slept on a straw mat on the mud floor. But the bed Tom had supplied for me was too soft and I felt uncomfortable. So I sat cross-legged on the bed and meditated. My mind and body gradually relaxed and I was able to sleep.

The next morning the birds sang and woke me up. I looked through the window and saw the sun shining again. The grass in the garden looked like a green carpet. I saw the squirrels jumping from branch to branch.

Around eleven I went out on my own to do some shopping. The streets were quiet with very little traffic. I seemed to be the only person from India. Many prams were parked outside the shops. I had never seen such big fat babies with round, pink cheeks before. When I returned to the flat and told Tom 'I saw some beautiful fat babies in trolleys', he replied, 'They're National Health babies.'

I did not know what he meant but when he took me to his doctor to register he explained the National Health Service to me. Everyone, young and old, received free medical care. I thought of the sick and the starving people in India. Many of my childhood friends had died and I am lucky to have survived. My aunt had told me that when I was a baby I had a terrible cough. One day I stopped breathing and my mother put me in the courtyard so that I could get some fresh air. Everybody thought I was dead but after a while I started breathing again. A few days earlier a woman from another settlement had come to see my mother. She did not have a child of her own and held me in her arms. My aunt thought she had cast her envious eyes on me and that was the cause of my illness. Mothers put black spots on their children's foreheads to protect them from 'nazr' eyes, 'the envious look'. That day my mother had forgotten to put the mark on me.

My eldest brother had died of diphtheria when he was two. My mother was heartbroken. His name was Suka and my mother pined for him. My grandmother had a pet parrot which had been taught to sing the names of God. One day it flew away and my grandmother was sad. A few days later the bird returned unexpectedly and sat on its cage. The Oriya word for parrot is 'suka'. As soon as my grandmother saw the parrot she cried out with excitement, 'Suka is back, Suka is back!' My mother was cooking. She left everything and came running, thinking it was her son. When she realized her mistake she burst into tears.

Tom's mother told me how happy she was to have her son back in England. She never visited him in India because she did not think she could endure the heat or face the beggars. She liked her cottage in the country, its garden, the apple trees, and the roses. To her Surbiton was a lifeless suburb and she came there only to see her son.

I thought Surbiton was a good example of suburbia. I had read about London suburbs during my course in architecture. These were the places where people lived and travelled to London every day to work. There were a few blocks of flats, but most people lived in detached or semi-detached houses with front and back gardens. In the mornings I saw men with brief-cases hurrying to the station to catch their trains. They returned between five and seven. In the afternoons the streets were deserted and I wandered around admiring the flowers in the carefully laid out gardens.

Near the station there was a small shopping street with a cinema hall and several pubs. The shops were always well-kept with an attractive display of goods. I liked Waltons. The fruit was clean and polished, graded to size, and kept neatly in boxes. I was surprised to see pineapples, bananas, and oranges as I knew they grew only in tropical countries. The flowers in the florists were so beautiful that I examined them to find out if they were real. I smelt them but they did not have any scent. The shop assistant had been watching me. 'Can I help you?' she asked. I had gone into the shop to admire the flowers but had not wanted to buy any. I was embarrassed and asked her to select a small bunch of flowers with a nice smell. I gave them to Tom's mother. She smelt them and said, 'What lovely freesias.'

The prices in the shops were clearly marked and I noticed there was no bargaining. It made shopping easy but dull. Shopping was an exciting expedition in India. We selected the fruits and vegetables, watched them being weighed, and bargained about the prices. But in Surbiton the shopkeeper was annoyed when I picked up a pear to see if it was ripe. I looked out for bazaars and open-air markets, but there were none. Newspapers were left unattended on the pavement, with a box containing coins. I saw a man stop, take a paper, and put some money in the box. In an Indian city everything would have disappeared in seconds.

The local shops and the milkman delivered groceries and milk in proper milk bottles. The laundryman brought the clothes. They put them outside the door and every week collected the money which was left in envelopes. The door was rarely locked. I thought English people were very honest and wrote to my parents about it.

Tom laughed when I asked him if the milk was pure. 'It is not only pure, but you can get as much as you like', he replied. In India, milk was in short supply and was rarely pure except from a few dairy farms. But their milk was not enough to meet the huge demand in the cities. Water was added to the milk and sold at different prices according to the degree of dilution.

In my village the milkman was requested to bring pure milk for the babies. Sometimes to assure the customers that the milk was pure, he brought the cow to the door and milked her in front of them.

This happened even in cities. A friend of mine lived on the third floor of a block of flats in Calcutta. He approached a milkman who said he would bring his cow and milk her for him. For the first few days my friend went down to the street to watch the cow being milked. Then he trusted the milkman and did not bother to go down any more. One day a neighbour came to him and said, 'I don't think you are getting cow's milk.' The next day he went down to the street to see the milkman. Instead of a cow he found an ox.

Adulteration is widespread in India; small pieces of stone are mixed with the rice to make it weigh more, sand is mixed with sugar, sawdust with flour. It was a great relief not to worry about the quality of food in England. But I never bought any tinned food. I was suspicious of it because of an unpleasant experience in my childhood. My brother served in the Air Force in the Second World War. During one of his leaves he brought a few tins of sardines for us. My sister and I opened one to make fish curry. But there was no fish, only maggots.

It was a common practice in my village to bathe twice a day in the river, in the morning and in the evening. Before taking the morning bath, mustard oil was rubbed into the body to protect the skin. No soap was used. I started using soap in Bombay where I took two showers a day. I had provided spaces for tubs while designing bathrooms but had never used one myself. In Surbiton there was no shower and it was a strange experience for me to lie in the bath. The water became dirty and I did not feel clean. So I filled the tub again with water and rinsed myself. When Tom's mother noticed that I was having two baths a day she remarked, 'You'll wash yourself away.'

When she had time to herself she sat in the living-room knitting. The windows were always tightly closed and I felt suffocated. I opened one to let some fresh air in and Tom's mother complained, 'There's a draught.'

'What is a 'draught'?' I asked.

'When you get to my age you'll know what a draught is.' She got up and closed the window.

I noticed later that wherever I went the windows were closed. In Bombay and in my village the shutters were kept open for ventilation and there was no draught, only cool breeze.

I sneezed. Tom's mother said, 'Bless you.' What a lovely expression, I thought. When somebody sneezed in the village the old people said, 'May you live for ever.'

Tom had taken a day off to show me around London. We went from Surbiton to Waterloo by train and then to Piccadilly Circus by Underground. It was a terrifying experience and I felt shut in and unable to breathe. I kept worrying what would happen if the doors did not open or the tunnel collapsed. When we reached Piccadilly Circus I ran up the stairs as quickly as possible, but the noise of the traffic in the streets was overpowering and I found it impossible to talk to Tom while walking on the pavement. There were so many people that I thought I might get separated from Tom and be lost in the crowd. I caught hold of his hand but he drew it away. 'It's not done in England', he said. In India it is common to see men of all ages walking together holding hands. It is regarded as a natural expression of friendship.

I did not know how I was going to live and work in London's noise and fumes. I was used to clean air, both in my village and in Bombay. In my village people practically live on clean air and sunshine. During my childhood in the village there was little noise apart from the barking of a dog or the howling of a jackal at night. The only other noise was produced by the rhythmic pounding of rice, which worried me when I was preparing for my matriculation exams. I told my mother and the pounding stopped in my part of the village so that I could concentrate on my studies.

In London there was noise everywhere and nobody seemed able to control it. In restaurants I had to listen to music whether I liked it or not. At Waterloo station piped music was played during the rush hour to help the commuters march faster on their way to work. They looked like army soldiers in grey suits. Occasionally some women in bright dresses brought colour into the crowd.

I was disappointed by Buckingham Palace. I was expecting something spectacular. The kings, queens, and emperors of ancient India lived in magnificent palaces and I could not imagine how the Queen of the British Empire could live in such an insignificant building. But I enjoyed the Royal Parks. At Speakers' Corner in Hyde Park a man stood on a box, addressing a friendly crowd. I sat on a bench by the lake in St. James's Park and watched the ducks glide on the water like boats. Suddenly my meditation was broken by the loud music of a military band. The traffic moved so fast round Trafalgar Square that it was difficult to cross to the fountains. But when I made it I was pleased. It was lovely to see the pigeons accepting the visitors as their friends. We briefly went inside the National Gallery and I saw the paintings glitter like jewels. I wanted to spend a longer time but Tom said I could come back on my own.

We heard Big Ben chime. I enjoyed looking at the Houses of Parliament from the other side of the river; their flat elevation with a series of towers was just like the picture postcards I had seen. We stopped on Westminster Bridge and I admired the river view with St Paul's Cathedral dominating the skyline. From the pier boats took tourists on river trips and we went up to the Tower of London. The guide gave a running commentary and pointed out the important buildings: County Hall, the site of the Globe Theatre, the Royal Festival Hall. At the end of the journey he went round with a plate and I saw tourists putting coins on it. Automatically I did the same.

Everybody expected to be tipped—the taxi drivers, the waiters in the restaurants, and the hairdressers. At the cloakroom the attendant had placed a saucer on the counter with some money in it. I immediately thought of the beggars in holy places in India. They sat on the way to the temples, putting small pieces of cloth with money before them. It was a religious act to give alms to the beggars but we did not tip anybody.

I had studied the architecture of Westminster Abbey and St Paul's Cathedral during my course but nobody had told me that people were buried there. Visiting St Paul's Cathedral gave me the first opportunity of experiencing a church from the inside. I felt no sense of worship and the atmosphere was severe. Hindu temples are full of music, colour, and movement and are always crowded. When I visited other churches I was distressed to see the figure of Christ nailed to a cross. I was told it represented suffering but for me God is life and love.

I was preparing to leave my shoes outside St Paul's Cathedral but Tom said it was not necessary. Shoes or any leather articles are not allowed into temples as a mark of respect to the deity. Leather is considered impure and even leather belts and watch straps must be removed. Indian homes are like temples and shoes are not allowed inside. When I saw Tom and his mother entering the kitchen with their shoes on I thought it was unhygienic.

Later I saw dogs sleeping in kitchens. In my village the kitchen is the most sacred place in the home; it is where the ancestors live. Nobody is allowed to enter it without having a bath and putting clean clothes on. Dogs are not kept as pets and when a stray dog came into our kitchen my mother said all the food, including the clay pots, was polluted and had to be thrown away.

We visited some expensive department stores. The customers were well-fed and well-dressed. There seemed so much wealth in London but so much poverty in India. How could the British get so rich, I wondered. They stayed in India for two hundred and fifty years but did nothing to develop India.

Tom said, 'The British gave India the railways. They were the rulers. They went to India to build their empire, not to develop India.'

When we returned to the flat Tom's mother was busy preparing food in the kitchen. While we were eating she asked me what I thought of Buckingham Palace and whether the Queen was there. I sensed her adoration of the Royal Family in her voice.

In India the Government had just taken power away from the independent Rajas, Maharajas, and Nawabs. Before Independence Orissa had many princely states and my father worked in one of them. When I was very small I visited him in the forest. The Raja and Rani came on shikar and stayed in the dak bungalow. A reception was arranged by the local villagers to welcome them. As the son of the forester I was chosen to present the garlands. I was taken to the Raja and his wife but they looked quite different from the descriptions of kings and queens my grandmother had given me in her stories. I was disappointed they had no crowns on their heads. They seemed so tall that I stood in front of them not knowing what to do. They bent down and I put the garlands around their necks.

After supper Tom gave me an A–Z map of London. 'You can look after yourself now', he said.

The sunshine did not last. There were sudden downpours and changes in temperature. I realized the weather was unpredictable. So it was necessary for me to dress properly. Tom's mother said, 'You must be careful, dear, otherwise you'll get horrible arthritis.' She warned me to air my clothes, especially underwear. I did not take her advice seriously; I did not know what arthritis was.

I went to Kingston to buy suitable clothes and travelled by trolley-bus. It was comfortable and the fare was cheap. I sat on the upper deck, enjoying the view of the River Thames and the houses. I was advised to go to Hepworths and told how to get there. It was a small shop and the manager treated me as a special customer. He reminded me of the tailors in Bombay who treated every customer as special. I bought myself a suit, a raincoat with a lining, and a pair of woollen trousers. I had to make my Indian shoes waterproof by sticking rubber soles on them.

I started feeling tired and exhausted and wondered why. I realized it was due to the extra layers of clothes over my body

—underwear, shirt, pullover, jacket, raincoat. I was carrying several pounds of extra weight. Tom's mother advised me to wear a hat to protect myself from the rain and the cold. She gave me a scarf and a trilby hat. I looked at myself in the mirror. I liked my new image of a 'brown sahib' but only for a while. I soon realized it was not really me and started wearing my Indian-style clothes.

To gain experience in architecture it was necessary for me to get a job, my first in England. I wrote to an architect in London. I knew his name because one of his books was prescribed for my course in Bombay. My teachers had told me he was famous.

I drafted a letter and showed it to Tom. He smiled and without saying anything he changed it completely. 'My respected Sir' became 'Dear Sir' and my opening sentence, 'I most humbly beg to submit', was crossed out. 'Yours faithfully' replaced 'I have the honour to remain, Sir, your most obedient servant'. He ended the letter with 'Looking forward to hearing from you'. After a few days I received a reply calling me for an interview. The letter was addressed to 'P. Mohanti Esq.'. I asked Tom what 'Esq.' meant. It was a polite substitute for 'Sir' or 'Mr' he said.

The architect's office was situated in a small Georgian terrace near Tottenham Court Road tube station. My A–Z map helped me to locate it. Tom had emphasized that I should be punctual and I got there in time for my interview at eleven.

I reported to the receptionist, who asked me to wait. After a while a man came up to me and introduced himself as the architect's partner. He helped me to carry my drawings upstairs to his room. I thought how considerate he was as this would never happen in India where the employers feel superior and use their employees like servants.

The partner was in his mid-forties, dressed in a conservative style. His room was old-fashioned with antique furniture. I was taken aback, first by the building and then by the decor, as the firm was famous for designing modern buildings.

I showed him my drawings. He examined them with great interest and said, 'I like your drawings. We like Indian architects; they're good and conscientious. But you haven't got any experience in this country.'

'If all the architects I go to say they can't offer me a job because I have no experience in this country, how do you think I'll gain experience?'

He smiled. From the expression on his face I knew he was not expecting that reply from me.

'All right. I'll give you the job.'

He showed me round the office and explained the type of work they were doing. It ranged from small housing projects to large scale office development. He introduced me to Tony, the architect I was going to work with.

His secretary brought us coffee. While drinking it he said, 'We have employed Indian architects before, but never black architects. We don't want to offend our South African clients.' Later on, when I moved around London, I saw notices in estate agents' windows: 'No blacks, no Irish, no children, no dogs'.

I was amazed that educated professional people could have such views and express them openly. The architect was honoured by the Government for his contribution to religious architecture.

There were very few Indians in London. They were usually scholars, students, or the sons of the rich. When I saw an Indian in the street I felt happy. We stopped and talked to each other. The students and scholars lived in hostels around Fitzroy Square. A few Indian restaurants and grocery shops had opened to cater for their needs. The Government of India managed a hostel for Indian students, mostly doctors. They worked hard to get their qualifications as soon as possible in order to return to India. Some were married and had left their families behind.

I started my job a week later. I was worried I might not be able to recognize the architect who interviewed me. English faces looked similar to me then and I had difficulty in distinguishing one from another. But as soon as I saw him I knew it was him. That gave me confidence.

The office hours were from 9 to 5.30. I got up early in the morning and travelled by train and underground. They were always full and I had to stand all the way. The journey took nearly one hour and when I arrived wearing all my new clothes I felt so exhausted that I had to sit down quietly for half an hour to recover.

But it was safer than commuting in Bombay where the trains were so overcrowded during the rush hour that some passengers precariously hung on to the carriages from the outside. There were many fatal accidents.

I always thought it was a waste of time and energy to commute long distances to work. But I soon discovered that several of my colleagues in the office spent a much longer time in travelling than I did. Some said they could only find time to read on the train.

Tony was an associate architect in charge of several projects. Apart from me there were three young assistants in his section. They all found difficulty in pronouncing my name correctly and Tony suggested I should be called 'Paul'. I did not like the idea and they asked me if there was a shorter version for 'Prafulla'. I said there was none but my parents called me 'Kuna'. They found that easy but I felt strange at first as 'Kuna' means 'the little one'.

Tony was friendly and kept us all amused. To my dismay my first job was to design a lavatory. Plumbing was not my favourite subject but I was being paid for my work and I could not refuse. I referred to books and magazines on sanitation, designed the lavatory, and produced a set of working drawings. I was relieved when they were not only accepted by Tony but also by the partner—an expert on plumbing, Tony told me later. I was immediately given another lavatory to design. I thought I would be spending the rest of my life designing lavatories.

I visited several architects' offices nearby to find out what they were doing but was disappointed by what I saw. I met a couple of young Indian architects doing work similar to mine. Like my office, instead of designing they were simply assembling, providing space to accommodate prefabricated fittings. The manufacturers were telephoned and their representatives came round to show us their literature. They also brought samples. Materials were selected to suit the design and the price. Most of the work was done on the telephone. I often wondered what would happen if the telephone system broke down.

Tony said he could not understand my English because I spoke too quickly. In India to be fluent meant speaking quickly and nobody had complained about my English before, not even Tom's mother. I felt embarrassed but I knew he wanted to help me. Nobody had ever taught me how to speak. He was like a teacher. He made me stop and repeat what I had said and pronounce certain words again and again. A few years later when I was in India I gave a talk to postgraduate students in English literature. They complained they found it difficult to follow my pronunciation and asked me why I spoke so slowly.

Tony and I became friends. He invited me to dinner to meet his wife and children. They lived in an old Victorian house in Richmond and had two beautiful daughters, one about ten and the other six. They had been waiting up to see me. It is an Indian custom to take sweets for the children and I gave them a box of chocolates.

I thought Tony's wife looked older than him and later that evening she told me that she was ten years older. 'Women live longer than men here. I wanted to marry a younger man so that there won't be a long separation in case my husband dies before me.' In an arranged marriage system the brides are always younger in India. Parents would never choose older girls for their sons. The younger men consider older women as aunts and sisters.

Tony had asked me beforehand if there was any food I did not eat. 'No beef or pork', I said. Tony's wife worked part-time and had cooked the meal herself. She fed the children first and put them to bed. I was surprised there were no older relatives staying with them to look after the children. Tony's widowed mother lived alone somewhere in the South and her mother was living alone in Birmingham. They wanted to lead their independent lives, I was told. Parents in India always live with their children and help to bring up the grandchildren.

After dinner we played an Indian record, Bismillah Khan's sahnai, which I had brought with me. The younger girl came running into the room, screaming. She looked frightened and wanted to know what the strange noise was. She said she could not sleep, so we stopped the music. I was sad it was not appreciated.

In spite of Britain's long association with India I found that Indian culture was largely unknown. Very few Indian dancers and musicians came to London to give concerts. Their performances were organized by the Asian Music Circle, run by the enthusiastic Mr Angadi. He was from South India, married to an English-woman, and settled in London. From his house he ran classes in yoga and Indian music. Mr Angadi was a tall thin man and looked elegant in his Indian clothes. He devoted all his time to promoting Indian art and culture in England and Europe. He ran the organization with the support of a small group of members, mainly Indians but a few British. In London the concerts were usually arranged at St Pancras Town Hall.

Indian dancing was considered exotic and attracted larger audiences than music recitals. A few well-known dancers had already helped to introduce Indian dance to the West but to most English people the sound of Indian music was strange. Mr Angadi tried hard to promote Ravi Shankar's sitar music and I helped him on one occasion. We had to plead with people to buy tickets, but were able to persuade only a handful.

But Hindi films were popular. On Sunday afternoons long queues waited outside a theatre near Piccadilly Circus to buy tickets. It was a family occasion. Women arrived in their colourful saris and it was a meeting place for friends. I saw very few English people at concerts and film shows but Indian restaurants were always full of them.

Veeraswamy's, a restaurant off Regent Street, was famous for its Indian food. One day an Englishman I had met in Bombay invited me there for lunch. A tall Indian wearing a turban stood at the door. The interior was Oriental with embossed wallpaper and ornate brass vases, depicting a stereotyped image of India. There seemed nothing authentic about the food. I thought it was specially prepared for the British palate. My host explained that the restaurant catered for people like him who felt nostalgic about India from time to time.

He had every reason to feel nostalgic. He had been the manager of a British bank and had lived in a large bungalow in a fashionable district of Bombay attended by many servants. He and his wife had travelled everywhere in chauffeur-driven cars and rarely mixed with Indians. Once I had been to see him in his office. It was air-conditioned and tastefully decorated in Western style. He retired when he was sixty-five and returned to England. But his wife died soon after their arrival. He lived in a service apartment near the House of Commons and had a cottage in the country. After lunch he invited me to his flat for tea. The first thing I noticed was that he was doing everything for himself.

When I told Tom he was amused. He said some Indian friends from Bombay had written to him saying, 'Poor man, his wife is dead and he hasn't even got one servant to look after him.'

Tom had warned me before I came to England that he had no servants. Only the very rich could afford to have them in

England. But a woman came to clean the flat twice a week. We all referred to her as the charlady but her name was Mrs Davies. Otherwise we managed everything ourselves. Tom's mother taught me how to make my bed and use the vacuum cleaner. The night before Mrs Davies came I cleaned my room thoroughly in case she gossipped about my untidiness to the neighbours. In India only the women do the housework and I found it difficult to adjust. Occasionally if I happened to be there Mrs Davies made a cup of tea for me. Sometimes she prepared a light lunch for all of us and we sat down together to eat. She dressed and spoke differently from Tom's mother and lived in a small terraced house in Surbiton. Her husband had been killed in the war and she had to work to bring up her son.

Tom's mother stayed for about two weeks at a time and then returned to her cottage. Sometimes Tom and I accompanied her. That gave me an opportunity to experience the English country-side. Everything looked so green in the summer. I wrote to a friend in Bombay, 'Here, wherever you look you see green; green, green everywhere.' At first I found it monotonous but gradually I began to appreciate the many shades of green within the overall greenness.

We went on long walks. The countryside was beautiful, with cornfields, hedges, ponds, and streams. I put my raincoat on the grass and lay down. I saw the blackbirds hopping and rabbits running from field to field. I stopped at hedges and picked blackberries. Wild flowers bloomed along the path and at a distance the church tower gave the undulating countryside a distinct character. I thought how beautiful England was and wanted to capture its spirit in my sketches. But the electric pylons, cars, and aeroplanes disturbed my unity with nature. I wished they could be removed to leave the countryside unspoilt.

Tom's mother sat in her chair knitting and telling me about herself. Her father had owned a grocer's shop in a village near Brighton and her mother had helped to run it. She had no brothers, only a younger sister. Her mother died when she was fourteen, so she gave up her studies and helped her father in the shop. She met a young man who worked in the Town Hall and married him. They went to live in her present cottage where Tom was born. But her husband died a couple of years later. 'People used to die so young in those days,' she told me sadly.

Her youngest sister married and went with her husband to Australia. Her father married again and she lost touch with him. Although she met several men who wanted to marry her, she did not want to do so because of Tom. She poured all her love and affection on him. She brought out two photographs of her husband and Tom from her handbag and showed them to me. She carried them wherever she went.

Tom's mother lived in a small village surrounded by green fields. It had a church, a pub, and a shop. The houses were grouped around the village green which had a pond with ducks swimming on it. Willow trees drooped over its bank. Her cottage was small, like a doll's house, with everything neatly arranged. When I saw the farm workers going to the fields and cows grazing, I felt as if I was in my village. A bus ran to Brighton every hour and Tom's mother told me I must take it and see the sights.

I walked along the promenade admiring the sea but did not see any sand or large waves. I thought of the vast sandy beaches in India. In Bombay going to the beach at Santa Cruz was an occasion. I went there with my friends to swim and drink green coconut water. In Brighton the piers were full of fun. I bought fish and chips and ate them sitting on a bench. The Pavilion looked oriental, like an Indian mosque. I thought it was a delightful folly and made the surrounding architecture dull by comparison. Sadly I had to return to London to work.

I never saw the famous architect. He was guarded by his secretary who was in her fifties and unmarried. She was extremely bossy and ordered everybody about. 'That's the trouble with old spinsters', Tony used to say. Indian women were always kind and affectionate, particularly to men and those younger than themselves. I resented her off-hand manner. But when Tony told me about her life, my resentment turned into compassion. There were several rumours as to why she did not marry. One was that her fiancé was killed in the war when many young men died.

My degree from Bombay was not recognized by the Royal Institute of British Architects. If I wanted to be a member of the Institute I would have to take all the exams, I was told. I thought it was unnecessary and did not want to suffer exams again for another qualification in architecture. So I decided to study town planning instead. My Bombay degree was recognized by the Town Planning Institute and it was not necessary to be a member of the RIBA to work in an architect's office. I was unlikely to have my own practice here, and in any case, most architects' offices required experience, not qualifications. So I concentrated on gaining practical experience. Anyone capable of preparing working drawings was able to get a suitable job. At that time there was a building boom, with more vacancies than trained people available.

I knew that my experience would be limited if I stayed in my present job. I wanted to supervise a building contract from the beginning to the end. I looked through advertisements in the *Architects' Journal* and found one in London which seemed suitable. I applied. The architect was young and had a large practice. When I told him where I worked he was impressed and gave me the job. So my six months of drawing and designing lavatories came to an end.

My new job was a challenge. I had to design an office block in Sheffield and supervise its construction. The architect had good contacts and was able to get large commissions. He employed young architects to carry out the jobs for him. I do not think he ever designed a single building himself but he was elected a Fellow of the Royal Institute of British Architects. This office was also managed by a middle-aged spinster who was bossy. I thought all the architects' offices in London had secretaries who were bossy spinsters.

The project involved a contract of half-a-million pounds. Handling it alone was very demanding. I had to work long hours often taking drawings home to be completed. After four months I asked for a rise in my salary and was told I would have to wait for a year. I felt I was being exploited and resigned.

During the months that followed I changed jobs several times. I enjoyed some for a while, but then found them boring. I knew I was being paid less than English architects doing the same work. Other Indian architects working in London told me of their experiences, which were similar to mine. The first architect I worked for thought he was so famous that it was a privilege for anyone to work for him. He paid much less than the others.

I found myself drawing straight lines all the time, using T-squares and set-squares. Every line I drew had a meaning and cost money. My freedom of expression became restricted. While studying architecture in Bombay I was interested in conceptual design. I was given projects in which I was able to use my imagination and play with ideas—space, forms, and colour, mainly in free hand. In London I had a need for spontaneous expression and found painting in water-colours satisfying. I spent many evenings experimenting, letting the colours flow on wet paper in an organic manner.

There was not much entertainment in Surbiton in the evenings. People returned home from their offices and watched television. Occasionally I went to a local pub. The English pub was the poor man's club, I had been told. I found it full of smoke and noise. When I admired the old beams and the log fire I was told they were imitations and the fire was artificial. The barmen seemed to know the customers by name and the atmosphere was friendly. But I found the English beer too bitter for me.

Before I came to England I had never drunk any alcohol. In my village drinking alcohol is not respectable and thought of as a vice of the lower castes who drink toddy, palm and date wine. In village theatre an alcoholic is always shown as a figure of fun. He enters the stage swaying and staggering, waving a bottle of red water. But hashish leaves are made into a paste and drunk as sherbet on social occasions. Tea is the common drink offered to guests.

On Friday evenings I usually stayed in London and went either to the theatre or to concerts at the Royal Festival Hall. My response to Bach was immediate. The spiritual content of his music touched my inner self. I was not used to the proscenium which separated the actors from the audience, and performances starting and closing at a particular time. There was no audience participation either. In my village performances took place in the open air and lasted all night. The audience clapped and expressed their appreciation openly; some came on to the stage between the scenes to give money and silver medals to the actors they liked.

The autumn came. The countryside looked glorious with various shades of brown and yellow. But the leaves started falling and the air became colder. One Saturday afternoon I was returning home from shopping in Kingston. Suddenly the sky became black with a huge cloud hanging over me. I thought the world was coming to an end. During the night there was a storm. It was just like an Indian cyclone. In the morning I heard on the radio that several people had been killed by falling trees. I looked out of the window. The sun was shining and the sky was clear, but most of the trees in the garden were bare. The leaves had all fallen. I had enjoyed them in the summer and watched them turn from green to reddish brown, but the storm during the night had done all the damage.

The winter was depressing. It became dark by three in the afternoon and the sky was constantly grey. There were thick fogs in the mornings which regularly disrupted the train service to Waterloo. I was marooned in the compartment for hours with my fellow-passengers. I longed for the Indian sun.

One morning I woke up feeling different. The air inside the room felt fresh. I opened the curtains. The garden had turned white and the snowflakes were falling like raindrops. It was my first sight of snow. A little bird sat under a tree trying to keep warm. Everything seemed changed. The trees had taken new shapes and the buildings surrealistic architectural forms. Children played in the streets, throwing snowballs at each other. Londoners in their boots, overcoats, scarves, hats, and gloves moved like creatures from another planet. I enjoyed the new experience for a while, but when the snow turned to dirty slush I grew tired of it.

I had read about snow in India but had never seen it. 'Himalayas' means 'abode of snow'. I knew what ice was because every year we had violent hailstorms in the village. As children we used to eat the hailstones. But I had not tasted icecream until I went to Bombay. In my mind I visualised snow to be a mixture of icecream and hailstones.

In the evenings I sat by the electric fire with Tom and his mother watching television. I liked 'Dixon of Dock Green' which gave a friendly image of the British policeman. He looked like the policemen I had met in the streets of London who went out of their way to help. In India we were always frightened of the police, who enforced law and order by violent means.

Television was a new experience for me but my enthusiasm did not last long. There were very few programmes on art or music but many on sport. I thought watching television was anti-social and a waste of time. When I went to people's houses I found that the television set was kept constantly on. It controlled their lives, without any sense of participation. In my village we entertained each other—singing, dancing, playing music. Groups of villagers sat together singing devotional songs. This helped to develop any local talent.

I looked forward to my first Christmas in England with great anticipation. Around November the atmosphere changed and the shops started displaying special Christmas goods and decorations. The main shopping streets were illuminated at night.

Tom and his mother brought out their address books and prepared lists of friends and relatives. 'Christmas is the time to remember friends and relatives and send them cards', they told me. They bought their cards but I drew mine. I thought it was more personal and my list was short.

In India there is a religious festival practically every month. My village school closed for several days at Christmas. We called it 'Xmas holiday' but did not know what it meant. For the autumn festival of Dassera my father came on a long holiday with presents for me. There was a great sense of participation in the village and my mother prepared many kinds of cakes which we ate and distributed among our friends.

I was disappointed when I was told that my office would close for only two days, but I noticed my colleagues taking time off to do their Christmas shopping. A secretary told me she had been buying her presents since the previous Christmas and had even kept some which were given to her. I noticed that the closeness of the relationship was measured by the price of the presents. There seemed little religious significance, but the shopkeepers were happy.

Christmas also meant party time. I did not like parties in England. Guests stood in little groups clutching their wine glasses, gossipping with their friends, and ignoring the others. But the office Christmas party seemed different. We all joined in, there was plenty to drink, and everybody was friendly. I was also invited to other office parties. In the week before Christmas there were two or three every night. It was a time to be nice to everybody, but after Christmas the smiling faces became gloomy again.

I liked the habit of giving presents; it was very Indian. I bought several small packets of the best Darjeeling tea available in London to give to my friends. I gave a packet to a colleague in the office. She was very pleased and said it would go with the

Christmas cake. After Christmas she came up to me and said, 'Prafulla, we enjoyed your tea very much, but it blocked up my sink.' I had forgotten to warn her that the tea had large leaves.

On Christmas Day I woke up in the morning to find a stocking on my bed, full of little presents. Tom's mother said Father Christmas must have left them.

We had spent many hours the previous day decorating the flat. In one corner of the living room we placed the Christmas tree with all its ornaments—light bulbs, stars, and an angel. Attractively wrapped parcels were piled round its base. We hung Christmas cards on strings and put them round the room. Tom's relatives started arriving at eleven, one by one, carrying presents in their arms. The flat vibrated with greetings: 'Happy Christmas'; 'Happy New Year.'

The table was laid with the best china and the family silver. Tom was very particular about the drinks and had bought champagne, sherry, wine, whisky, gin, brandy, port, and liqueurs. We started with champagne for the Christmas toast. Although I drank very little alcohol I was persuaded to take a sip.

Tom's relatives looked at me with curiosity. 'You are the Indian friend we have been hearing so much about.' I smiled but felt like an exhibit. Tom had explained to me that he had invited his five cousins because they lived on their own.

Tom's mother had spent the whole of Christmas Eve preparing the meal. I knew the menu but was shocked by the sight. I was not expecting to see a huge roasted bird filled with stuffing. Tom was the carver. When he sharpened the knife, started cutting large slices of turkey, and scooped out the stuffing with a spoon, I wanted to get up and run away. In India we never serve whole animals or birds; they are cut into small pieces and hidden by the curry sauce. But I forced myself to stay at the table and gradually settled down to enjoy the food. Roast potatoes and sprouts were served with the turkey, care being taken to give everyone equal portions of white and dark meat.

The Christmas pudding arrived. The lights were put out and the curtains drawn. Tom poured brandy over the pudding and lit it. Everyone applauded as blue flames flickered. What a waste of good brandy, I thought. It was used as medicine in my village.

We slowly ate our way through the vast quantities of food as though we had never eaten before, pausing briefly to hear the

Queen's speech. Tom's mother produced a box of crackers. We pulled them, put on the paper hats, and read out the mottoes. Then the ceremony of the presents began. Everybody behaved like little children, opening parcels and reading the messages. Tom read out a letter from his aunt in Australia sending greetings to the family.

I was touched by the present from Tom's mother. It was a pull-over and a pair of gloves she had knitted herself. I had seen her knitting but had not realized she was doing it for me. 'It's not the present but the thought that counts', Tom's mother said.

In the early evening we went out for a walk. The streets were deserted, the houses had their curtains drawn but I could see lights filtering through. In some windows decorated Christmas trees were clearly visible. For one day the family had come together and the outside world was forgotten. When we returned to the flat we found tea and Christmas cake on the table, prepared by Tom's mother. I had presented her with a tin of Indian tea, which she served with great pride. But I heard some of the relatives complaining it was not strong enough for them. I knew tea drinking was a ritual in England but very few seemed to bother about the quality. Their taste was affected by drinking too much 'English tea' and they were unable to appreciate the taste of pure Indian tea.

When the relatives left in the evening I heard one say to Tom's mother, 'Hope to see you next Christmas, if not before.'

Do they only meet at Christmas, I wondered.

Soon after Christmas Tom became ill with bronchitis and had to spend six weeks in a sanatorium. When he returned home he was very weak and the family doctor advised him to eat steak. 'It will give you strength', he said.

'But I have given up eating beef', Tom replied. I knew it was because of me that Tom and his mother had stopped eating beef. Even lard was not used.

The idea of eating beef is repulsive to a Hindu. In India all cattle are sacred. From my childhood I was brought up to respect the cow as 'Mother' because the children drink her milk. Cows are valuable possessions and treated as members of the family. In Hindu mythology there are many references to cows and bulls. The Hindu god Krishna was a cowherd and Shiva, the God of Creation, had a bull, Nandi, as his companion. When I was a boy

I was told that Muslims ate beef; so a villager would never know-ingly sell a cow to a Muslim.

When I was a student in Bombay I once ate beef by mistake. One lunchtime, on my way to the school I decided to eat at a restaurant. I went in, read the menu, and ordered meat curry and rice. I assumed 'meat' meant 'mutton'. When the waiter put the food on the table I thought the portion of curry was unusually large and there were no bones in it. I put a piece in my mouth and quickly spat it out. It did not taste like mutton. I called the waiter but before I could say anything he removed the plate hur-riedly. That made me more suspicious. I called the manager. He admitted it was beef and was most apologetic. I was shocked and felt polluted. I was not able to sleep for weeks. I imagined the meat entering into my bloodstream, making me unclean. I won-dered how long it would take to purify.

In my mind I tried to justify eating beef in England so that Tom could also eat and get his strength back. I convinced myself that beef in England came from English cattle, which were not holy like Indian cattle. Since I was not a strict vegetarian and ate lamb, I could eat beef.

I told Tom's mother I would prepare the meal that evening. I wanted to surprise them by serving beef. I went to the local butcher. I had never been inside the shop because I disliked the display in the window of whole carcasses and rabbits with their fur on. I asked the butcher to select some best pieces of beef for me. I had no idea it was so expensive. When I asked him how to cook it he said, 'Don't curry it—grill or fry, but don't overcook.'

I returned to the flat and fried a small piece as an experiment. I knew Tom and his mother would not eat beef unless I joined them. I put the meat on a plate and looked at it. Suddenly I thought about reincarnation. I had been trying to convince myself that it was all right to eat English cattle, but there were doubts in my mind. Who knows, the English animal might have been Indian in a previous life. To eat or not to eat. This conflict went on in my head for a while. Then I cut a small piece, closed my eyes, and put it in my mouth. I liked the taste.

When I served the steak to Tom and his mother they were con-cerned. 'You shouldn't have done that', Tom's mother said. 'What would your mother say?' I knew that my mother would be upset. But I reassured myself that I could always go through a purification ceremony when I returned to India. Some of my grandfather's colleagues were Muslims and when my grandmother found out he had eaten with them she made him drink a paste made of cow dung to purify him. Drinking the water from the River Ganges and having a bath in it could also purify a Hindu.

Eating beef made life simpler for me. Whenever I was invited for a meal I said I ate everything. Invariably the reaction was, 'We thought Hindus were vegetarians.'

'There are many fish-and mutton-eating Hindus and I am one of them', I replied.

The staple food in my village is rice. The poor eat it with spinach and the better-off with dal, vegetables, and fish caught in the local rivers and ponds. Only goat meat is eaten but it is considered a luxury. No fish or meat is allowed into the house on Thursdays, the day of the Goddess Lakshmi, the Goddess of Wealth. There are many festive occasions when only vegetarian food is eaten by the villagers. My mother observed strict religious fasts and ate fish about twice a week. In Bombay I ate mainly vegetarian food, but in England I found myself eating meat every day, and I soon started putting on weight.

I thought if I practised my Indian dancing it would help me to reduce it. I tried out a few basic exercises one morning in my bedroom. A few minutes later I heard loud thumps coming through the floor. I realised I was disturbing the neighbours and stopped. But I did not know who I was disturbing.

It was a strange experience to live in a block of flats and not know the neighbours. I had heard the Christian saying 'Love thy neighbour' but it did not seem to apply here. Sometimes I met people in the lift and wished them 'Good morning' or 'Good evening', but that was all. Tom told me it was the English custom to respect another person's privacy. In my village, life was intimate and everybody knew each other. The doors were never closed. Neighbours came in and out without warning and were always welcomed.

One evening I had invited some friends to dinner. I was cooking Indian food when there was a knock on the door. A man was standing there and introduced himself as a neighbour.

'What are you cooking? It smells lovely, but I'm afraid my children don't like it.'

'Why don't you come and try it?' I said impulsively.

To my amazement he accepted and brought his wife and four small children. They ate everything.

A few days later I met his wife in the corridor. 'Prafulla, I tried to cook your curry from the recipe you gave me but my children complained it was not like yours.' Like her husband she spoke with a lovely musical accent. We became friends. They were interested in art and liked my paintings. She used to say, 'Prafulla, you're an artist. You belong to the universe.' I later discovered they were Catholics from Southern Ireland. The husband told me there was no future for his children in England. Suddenly I remembered the notices in the estate agents' windows, 'No Irish'. He told me about the tension between the Catholics and the Protestants. I had no idea there were so many divisions in Christianity; I thought they were all Christians in England. But I later found out there were Methodists, Baptists, Anglicans, even Christian Scientists.

My Irish friend was a schoolteacher and it was difficult for him to support the family on his own income. So his wife did part-time teaching but found it extremely tiring as she had to look after the house and the four young children. A few weeks later they went back to Ireland.

A telegram arrived one day from an architect friend in Delhi saying he was coming to London. I met him at the air terminal and took him to the Indian Students' Hostel where he had made arrangements to stay. He told me he had come to work and study. If he had not arrived then, he would have needed a job voucher to work in England. An Act of Parliament had been passed restricting immigration from the Commonwealth, to take effect shortly. This was the first time I learned there was a Commonwealth Immigration Act.

When I returned to my room I sat by the window, thinking. Although I had stayed in England for over a year it was difficult for me to understand the British mind. Travelling to the office every day by train I watched people hiding their faces behind newspapers. They rarely talked to each other, occasionally lifting their eyebrows to survey their fellow-passengers. But when I started a conversation under the pretext of the weather I found many had a natural gift for gossip. They would go on telling me all about themselves and their families. Sometimes I was even given their telephone numbers and asked to look them up. At first I took their invitations at face value, but when I rang and heard the surprised tone, 'Who?', I felt embarrassed and pretended I had got the wrong number.

I was not used to talking on the phone and had to repeat myself again and again to make myself understood. When speaking to the operator I always had to spell out the names I wanted. As I could never remember the conventional word associations for letters, I said 'M' for 'mango' and 'D' for 'Delhi'. This created further confusion.

I had to learn to say 'please', 'sorry', 'thank you', whether I felt it or not. Once, while buying a ticket at Waterloo, I forgot to say 'please'. The man at the counter was offended and would not give me the ticket until I had said 'please'. When he handed me the ticket he said, 'Say "thank you." ' As I was getting into the train an Englishwoman pushed me with her shoulders, said 'sorry', and hurried inside to occupy the only vacant seat.

On the way to the office one morning a man collapsed in my compartment. At Waterloo everybody left, but I stayed with him until the ambulance arrived and was an hour late getting to the office. I was told it was not my job to look after strangers.

I found that many did not even look after their own parents who were old and helpless. In India it is the duty of the children to look after their parents and old relatives. While serving a meal my mother always gave food to the old relatives and children first and ate whatever was left over. The old never felt isolated. They lived with their families and contributed to the happiness of the house.

At Surbiton station newsvendors cried out '*Star, News, Standard*'. I read about the Great Train Robbery, children being murdered, and stories of divorce. I was brought up to respect education but in England more importance was given to money. The footballers earned more than the teachers. Church services were thinly attended; football grounds were full.

I stood at the top of the escalator watching the stream of passengers entering the underground. I felt frightened at the beginning but once I joined it I became part of the crowd. Going to the office became a habit: catching the train, being at the right platform in the underground, getting out at a certain exit, turning left at a particular road. It became so automatic that I found myself on the train going to the office when I had intended to go somewhere quite different. I had become a machine.

I was made to feel inferior. Indian qualifications were not considered good enough in England, yet schools and colleges in India were established by the British with British teachers. Everywhere I went I met people who had been in India and seemed to know more about my country than I did.

I had come to England to study modern architecture but I had found nothing but apathy. People were more interested in antiquities and old buildings. Architects lacked vision and new ideas and the public showed little interest in their environment. Developers insisted on value for money and ugly buildings went up everywhere.

The thought of another English winter depressed me. I had applied to Leeds to study town planning, but even if I was accepted I did not think I could spend two more years in England. I decided to go back to India. I applied to the Government of Orissa for a job as an architect so that I could be near my parents. When I told Tom I wanted to go back to India he did not seem surprised.

Before returning to India I wanted to visit Europe. A friend of mine working in the Indian Embassy in Rome invited me to stay with him and suggested I caught a plane from there. So I decided to go to Rome by train, stopping first in Holland and then at different places on the way.

The day of my departure came and once again I found myself at Liverpool Street station. Instead of saying 'Welcome to London', Tom had come to say 'Farewell'.

When the train left I felt sad.

CHAPTER 3

Europe

The boat started to move. Gradually England receded into the distance and disappeared from sight. I stood on the deck staring at the cold calm sea. Gentle waves danced on the surface of the water. The idea of exploring the unknown made me feel nervous.

My knowledge of Europe and its languages was limited. I had read about the French Revolution in my history books and Greek and Roman architecture were part of my course in Bombay. I knew of Germany because the Germans were building a large steel plant in Orissa. On British television hardly a week passed by without a war film depicting the Germans as villains.

My first stop was Amsterdam. Mr Angadi, the director of the Asian Music Circle, had given me a letter of introduction to a Mr van Hoboken who was interested in Indian culture. With an Indian passport it was necessary to get a visa. No visa was required for Germany; at that time the German and Indian Governments had a friendly arrangement. When I telephoned other European embassies I was told I could get visas on the way.

At the Hook of Holland the immigration officer stamped my passport and said in English, 'Have a good holiday.'

When I arrived at Amsterdam railway station that evening and saw trains going all over Europe I felt free. There was a sense of vastness. In England I was aware of being on an island with the burden of British imperialism pressing upon me.

There was a tourist information centre in front of the station. The man behind the counter spoke perfect English and after a couple of telephone calls found me a small inexpensive hotel in the centre of the city. He marked it on a map and gave me instructions how to get there.

I was pleased to see trams again. I had missed them in London. In Bombay I went on long tram rides from one end of the city to the other, enjoying the street scenes. Trams were gradually phased out but in Calcutta they still remain the cheapest and most efficient form of travel. In Amsterdam, as in Bombay, there was a fixed price for a journey. One ticket was valid for one hour irrespective of the number of journeys made and a book of tickets was cheaper than buying single tickets. I thought of London Transport and wondered why similar schemes were not introduced on buses and tube trains.

I had no difficulty in finding the hotel, which was situated in a quiet street by a canal. The receptionist also spoke good English and took me to a single room on the third floor, along a narrow staircase. There was no lift. The price included breakfast and was reasonably cheap as the rate of exchange at that time was about eleven guilders to the pound.

I had dinner in the hotel. At the next table there was an English family on holiday touring by car. When I asked them what they thought of Amsterdam the man grumbled. 'Why do they have to drive on the wrong side of the road? It's dangerous.' We had something in common. I had found it alarming to cross the busy roads in Amsterdam with the traffic moving on the right. In India we drive on the left and I had no difficulty in getting used to the traffic in England.

After dinner I telephoned Mr van Hoboken and made an appointment to see him the next day. I went for a short walk along the canal and watched the reflections on the water. England seemed a long way away.

Amsterdam was totally different from London. It was small and clean, with trees and tall terraced houses in red brick lining its many canals, which gave another dimension to the city. Without large buildings and skyscrapers the city centre had a sense of unity. People, trees, buildings, and the canals were a united whole. I was pleased to see so many cyclists riding freely on the roads. In certain areas there were special paths for them. I have always thought it was a most civilized way to travel. It does not produce any noise or fumes and provides exercise for the body.

In villages and towns in India the cycle is the best way of travel for men. Women seldom use it because cycling is not considered feminine. My father taught me to ride a bike when I was twelve. He had brought the first cycle to my village in 1926. Now almost every family has got one.

Amsterdam was a cultural centre and attracted visitors from many parts of the world. Everybody spoke English and I had no difficulty in making myself understood. The museums were always full and the opera was well-attended. The coffee bar next to the Opera House was the favourite meeting place for the visitors. There I met Mr van Hoboken.

He was in his seventies, tall, slim, with a head of long white hair. There was an expression of contentment on his face. He lived with his wife and children in a small town near Amsterdam. After retirement from a government job he worked part-time for Dutch radio, doing broadcasts to India and the East. In his youth he was influenced by the poet Rabindrinath Tagore and had spent several years studying Indian art and culture in Santini-ketan, the university founded by the poet. His knowledge of India was extensive. He knew practically everybody interested in Indian culture, not only in Holland but also in India.

Mr van Hoboken was full of energy and walked everywhere. He took me to an Indonesian restaurant nearly a mile away for lunch. Without an Indian restaurant in the city he had difficulty in entertaining his Indian visitors who did not like sausages and cheese. The Indonesian restaurants were the substitute. The food was more Chinese than Indian and the atmosphere was Far Eastern, with lacquered trays and bowls.

After lunch he took me to the Tropical Museum to show me the collection from Indonesia. Through its colonies, Holland had long connections with the East and I was told many immigrants had come to settle there. The museum also had an Indian depart-ment displaying mainly ethnological objects.

Mr van Hoboken introduced me to a young Dutch musician who had spent several years learning the sitar in India. He was the only child of wealthy parents and they had made comfortable arrangements for him to live and study in India. He had become a vegetarian. 'To be a good sitarist you have to be a vegetarian', he said. He had already started teaching the sitar and giving recitals. It was so different from London, I thought, where even famous sitar players from India had to search for an audience.

Through Mr van Hoboken I met several people deeply involved in Indian art and culture. Among them was a woman in her fifties. She was a distant relative of a famous painter and lived with her husband and daughter in a large house in a nearby suburb. The house was full of Indian crafts which she had bought from shops in London. The shelves were full of books on Indian art and music, mostly in German. She had never visited India but knew a lot about the country by reading about it.

From Amsterdam it was easy to reach cities like Rotterdam and The Hague by train. Everywhere I saw canals. There were little houses, well laid-out gardens, and small allotments where the city dwellers spent their leisure. From the train I could see the landscape expanding like an ocean—no hills or mountains. There was an air of melancholy about it all. The light was clear and patches of cloud floated like foam in the blue sky. When I looked at the paintings in the museums I could see how the environment had inspired the painters.

Breakfast at the hotel in Amsterdam was an occasion. A tray containing an assortment of meat, fish, cheese, and eggs was placed before me. It was impossible to eat them all. I made sandwiches, and when I thought nobody was looking, put them in my bag for my lunch.

One morning at the table next to me I saw a man with a young boy. He smiled and said 'Good morning'. I wished him 'Good morning' and smiled back. It was a refreshing change from England where I seldom saw people smiling. When I looked at somebody in England and smiled I usually received a frown back.

That afternoon I was in the Rijksmuseum looking at the Rembrandts when I saw the man and the young boy from the hotel enter the room. He came up to me and asked if I needed any help. He spoke English fluently but with an accent. He told me he was a doctor from Germany on a short holiday with his son. I looked at him and wondered if he was a Nazi. But his face was kind and sensitive. He invited me to have dinner with him that evening but as I was seeing Mr van Hoboken we arranged to meet for breakfast.

The next morning I sat at his table. He wanted to know all about myself and what I was doing in Holland. I was the first Indian he had seen in Amsterdam. When I told him my story and that I was visiting Europe for the first time, he said spontaneously, 'Why not come to Germany with us? We're leaving by car this morning.' It was so unexpected that I did not know what to say. Unfortunately I had arranged with Mr van Hoboken to record a radio broadcast about my visit to Holland the next day.

'Why not come when you are free?' Before I had time to think he took a train timetable from his pocket and fixed a date and a train for me. 'I will meet you at Essen.'

After they left I sat at the table wondering. Had he really

meant to invite me? I thought of my experiences in England where people often said things they did not mean. When I told Mr van Hoboken about the invitation he encouraged me to go. It was on the way to Rome, he said.

As the day of my departure came nearer, doubts appeared in my mind. What would I do if he did not come to the railway station? Could I telephone and say I had been invited? Would I be able to recognize him? I thought about it again and again. Then I realized he would have no difficulty in recognizing me because I would be the only Indian on the platform.

When I got off the train at Essen I saw the doctor and a little girl waiting for me. I felt they were really happy to see me. She took my hand and bent her knee in curtsy.

The doctor lived in a small town called Gladbeck, about ten miles from Essen and we went there in his car. The area around the station had been destroyed during the war and was being rebuilt. The sky was grey and everywhere I looked I saw factory chimneys belching out clouds of smoke.

When we arrived at the house his wife welcomed me with a smile and greeted me in German, which I did not understand. She could not speak any English but her expressive face conveyed her feelings. She was tall and thin with green eyes. From her behaviour I could sense she was motherly. In my village I was used to the women expressing themselves in silence. Words were not necessary to demonstrate their affection and care. She had been busy preparing the lunch. After eating cheap hotel food for two weeks it was like a feast.

As soon as we had finished lunch several of their friends arrived to see me. Some were able to speak English but none of them had ever been to India. I do not think any of them had seen an Indian before. All they wanted to know from me was my opinion of the Berlin Wall. When I said I did not believe in the division of Germany into two parts they were delighted.

I had never liked the division of India, which caused immense suffering. I was brought up to believe in the joint family system where there is a sense of participation and sharing. When brothers quarrelled in the village and divided the family property it was regarded as a disaster.

The house had three floors with five bedrooms and a large garden. The rooms were decorated with old oriental carpets and antique furniture. There were many original paintings on the walls, including a portrait of a pope. The shelves were filled with family photographs, old china, and wooden carvings. I had brought a few Indian wooden figures with me to give as presents. When I gave the doctor's wife a small wooden elephant she seemed very pleased. 'Sehr schön' she said and put it carefully on a shelf. On the road outside, the traffic—trams, buses, and cars —produced a constant noise, but the garden at the back was quiet. The apple trees were full of fruit and the little girl played happily on a swing. Her mother sat nearby, carrying on an animated conversation with me in German. I could only guess the meaning of a few words and replied in English. We were able to understand each other.

The doctor had three sons; two were doing their military service and the youngest son was at school. His second language at school was English. He was able to read and write well and wanted to practise his English on me. The little girl wanted to teach me German. I soon discovered that the Germans liked England and the English language. I did not hear any adverse comment about England. I could not understand why there was a kind of campaign against Germany in England.

The doctor worked very hard, starting at eight o'clock in the morning and returning home at seven. He was the head of the town hospital. I asked him why he worked so hard. 'To get money for my family, so that they can buy things which will make them happy', he replied. His command of English was perfect. I found that everybody worked hard. The shops opened at eight o'clock in the morning and kept open until six.

Gladbeck was a small town. Parts of it were destroyed in the war and the new town centre looked attractive, with well-designed shops. It was culturally active, with a museum and a small theatre where exhibitions and concerts were held regularly. The events were given full coverage in the daily local newspaper.

Wherever I went people stared at me. A little girl walking with her parents offered me a small bunch of flowers. I wanted to talk to her but she hid her face behind her mother's coat. People were always helpful. I was standing on the pavement waiting to cross the main road when a car stopped and offered me a lift. The driver was going to Hamburg. When I told my doctor friend he said the motorist probably thought I was a hitch-hiker.

Gladbeck is in the Ruhr district where Krupps, the former armaments manufacturer, still had huge steel works. Krupps was responsible for building the steel town in Orissa. It was called 'Rourkela'—'Rour' for 'Ruhr' and 'kela' in Hindi meaning 'fort'. The doctor made arrangements for me to visit the factory. When the manager knew I was from Orissa he treated me as an honoured guest and showed me round. The heat from the molten steel and the noise of the factory were unbearable. When I saw the strong German workers struggling to cope with the conditions I thought of the undernourished Indian workers in Rourkela.

My doctor friend was determined I should not be bored and made plans for me to visit factories, offices, and galleries. As soon as one visit was over another one was announced. That evening he said he had made an appointment for me to visit a coal mine where one of his patients worked as a senior officer. He left me at the imposing entrance gates to the mine where I was met by two large security guards who escorted me to the administrator. He first showed me the modern recreational facilities for the miners, which included games rooms, clubs, and even an art gallery and a theatre. I was then taken to the changing rooms where we had to put on protective clothing and helmets. The mine was three thousand metres deep. To get to the coalface we had to go part of the way in an air-conditioned lift, walk along tunnels, and finally crawl on our hands and knees. I watched layers of coal being carved out. When we reached the surface we were covered in coal dust and my companion was so out of breath I thought he was going to collapse.

As a guest of the management I received special treatment, which included a steam bath and a massage. Standing under the shower I was horrified to see the amount of coal dust being washed away in spite of the protective clothing. My nostrils and ears were filled with it. I could not imagine how the miners could survive with so much coal dust on their bodies every day.

My throat was also filled with coal dust and felt very dry. I was pleased when we were invited by the manager to have a drink with him in his special cabin. Although he did not come with us down the mine he had his massage and steam bath, which I was told he had every day. A waiter came with beer and schnapps. I asked for a soft drink but they insisted I try the German beer.

I watched them drinking small glasses of schnapps at one go, followed by a glass of beer. It looked easy and I thought I could manage it. I became adventurous and drank a glass of schnapps imitating my hosts. It warmed my throat and I felt better. So I had another glass. As soon as my glass was empty it was filled again. I do not remember what happened next. We were supposed to have lunch at a restaurant nearby but I found myself waking up in the morning in my friend's house unable to move. My head felt heavy, as if there were several bags of coal inside.

I was ashamed of myself and did not know how to face the family. But not a word was spoken about my experience. I realized why drinking was considered a vice in my village. Yet taking hash is a part of some religious rituals. I have seen holy men smoking hash and being in a constant state of ecstasy. I do not know any adult in India who has not tasted it. In Orissa it is called 'bhanga'. If taken in small quantities the experience is pleasant. My elder brother took it every night as a drink during the summer and one evening his wife gave me a glass to try. It was soon after my matriculation exams and I was worried about the results. After a while I felt free and happy; my mind was extremely clear. As I walked along I thought I was floating. I slept well that night and there were no after-effects. But the schnapps gave me a hangover for three days.

'You can stay here as long as you like', my doctor friend told me. 'This is your home.' He looked after me like a father. He and his wife took me to Düsseldorf, Bonn, and Cologne. I saw the Rhine and people working hard to rebuild Germany. The devastation caused by war was immense but I did not find a single German complaining about Britain. They all talked about England with affection and practised their English on me. I soon learned a few expressions in German which my friend's little daughter taught me. But I found them difficult to learn and pronounce. She was a strict teacher and insisted that I should learn to pronounce the words correctly, showing me the position of the tongue.

It was a happy family and I soon became a part of it. Every evening after supper friends would arrive, always with a present —a bunch of flowers, a piece of cake, or a bottle of wine—attractively wrapped in coloured paper. My friend received them in the living room and offered them a glass of wine. There were many

kinds of fruit on the table—pears, apples, plums. My friend's
wife peeled and sliced them delicately before passing them
around. There were long conversations in German. I noticed an
air of formality mixed with the friendship, which I had not seen
in England.

One evening my friend asked me to fetch a tin of mushrooms
from the basement. When I went down it was like being in a
shop. There were all kinds of tinned food stored on racks. Ham,
bacon, and sausages were hanging from the ceiling. There was
enough food for the family to last a year. I asked my friend, 'Why
so much food in the basement?'

'We're always afraid of another war and not having enough to
eat', he replied. Many people I spoke to were worried. They
expected another war to take place.

I was introduced to a guest, an architect working in Düsseldorf.
He offered me a job and invited me to visit his office where I
found architects working like machines, producing drawing after
drawing for the new buildings coming up everywhere. The
demand was so great that there was very little time to devote to
the designs. It was not the type of work I wanted to do but I
thanked him for his offer. When I said I wanted to move on and
see other parts of Europe he volunteered to introduce me to his
architect friend in Ulm and made arrangements for me to stay
with him.

When I left Gladbeck my friend's wife prepared a food box
containing sandwiches, fruit, and bars of chocolate. It was just
like my mother giving me different kinds of cakes when I left the
village for Bombay. The little girl said 'Auf Wiedersehen'.

The train journey to Ulm was comfortable but took several
hours. We passed through towns, woods, green valleys, and
along the banks of the River Rhine, where I saw castles on top of
the hills. When I arrived in Ulm it was evening and the architect
and his wife were waiting for me.

They lived in a small modern house which he had designed
himself. It was the first time since leaving India I had met an
architect living in a house he had designed. In England the
architects were designing modern houses in which they themselves were not prepared to live. They preferred to live in period
houses.

Ulm was an old town with streets paved in stone and a magnificent cathedral with a tall slender tower. I stayed in Ulm for a week visiting art and architectural colleges, meeting architects, and seeing their work. My Indian qualifications were not questioned. Wherever I went I was accepted as an architect. There was a feeling of an architects' brotherhood which I had not experienced in England. When I told my host I was going to Rome he introduced me to his architect friends in Munich and Florence.

It was arranged that I would be met at Munich station restaurant at four o'clock in the afternoon. The train arrived at one. The restaurant was spotlessly clean with white table cloths and napkins. It was nearly full but I managed to find an empty table. The waiter came to take my order but the menu was in German and I could not understand it. I looked at the next table and saw an elderly woman eating her lunch. As I pointed to the old lady's plate she looked up and saw me. She conveyed through her gesture that it was good, but the waiter was hesitant. 'You not like,' he said.

'If she likes it, why shouldn't I?' The waiter gave up and brought me the dish I had ordered. It turned out to be tripe cooked in wine, with mashed potatoes. I realized why the waiter was reluctant to serve it to me. It tasted most peculiar, but I ate it to please the old lady, who was watching me with great interest.

When the waiter brought my bill the old lady insisted on paying. I knew so little German that I did not know how to refuse her. Then she moved over and sat at my table. We talked to each other in signs and drawings. She opened her handbag and showed me photographs of her family, her sons, daughters, and grandchildren. From time to time the waiter came and joined in the conversation, helping to translate. Her husband had died during the war and she lived alone. I enjoyed talking to her; she reminded me of my mother. When my mother came to see me in Bombay, she made friends with many people although she was unable to talk to them in their own language.

My Munich host arrived. When I saw the disappointed look on the old lady's face I wished he had not come on time. The restaurant, the old lady, and my encounter with her have remained engraved on my memory. Human relationships go beyond the barriers of land and language.

I spent my three days in Munich like a typical tourist, seeing old buildings, galleries, museums, and gardens. Everywhere I looked I saw people drinking beer and singing happily.

I had to pass through Austria on my way to Italy. In Munich I got a visa for Austria but the Italian visa office was on strike. I was advised to get one at Innsbruck, a small quiet city at the foot of the mountains. The clerk at the Italian visa office could not speak English and indicated that it was closed. I had been told in London to speak loudly and clearly when people did not understand English.

'I want my visa', I demanded.

Another man appeared from inside the office to find out what was happening. Fortunately he could speak a little English. When I explained I was an architect and was going to Florence and Rome to study Italian architecture, he looked pleased. He invited me to his room, offered me a glass of wine, and personally arranged the visa for me. When I reached Florence I understood why the officer had given me special attention. In Italy architects were highly respected.

I saw the works of Leonardo da Vinci, Michelangelo, and Raphael, who had brought architecture, painting, and sculpture together in their artistic expression. The many palaces were built around internal courtyards and the effect was like that of an Indian city. I visited old buildings, squares, and churches where, for the first time, I felt a sense of worship. The candles, incense, and music created the atmosphere of temples in India. The priests reminded me of the Italian priest in Bombay.

I stayed in a small pensione which my architect colleagues had arranged for me. They had a small practice in Florence and used to meet me after office hours and take me out to dinner. Sometimes their wives joined us but I was never invited to their homes. There was a grocer opposite the pensione where I bought bread, cheese, and fruit for my lunch. When I was unable to explain to the grocer what I wanted I drew the item on my sketch pad. One day he indicated that he wanted the drawing and I gave it to him. He did not charge me for the groceries I bought that day. This happened several times. When I expressed surprise he took me to his office upstairs and showed me drawings by other artists who had come to his shop.

My week in Florence passed quickly and I took the train to Rome. It was like being in India again. The compartments were crowded with friendly passengers, talking, laughing, gesticulating, and sharing food with each other.

My Indian friend had come to the station to meet me. He worked for the Indian Embassy and lived in an apartment nearby with his wife and three daughters. I had met them on a train journey to Calcutta and we had become friends. After two months of straining to make myself understood, combining words with signs, it was a relief to be able to talk freely again.

My friends were from Calcutta and could not speak Oriya; so we talked to each other in English and Bengali. His children went to the local school and spoke good Italian and he and his wife were learning the language through them. The children immediately brought out their books and wanted to teach me Italian. I soon learned a few useful phrases and I found it came more naturally to me than German.

Going to St Peter's was like visiting the temple of Lord Jagannath at Puri. Both were holy and places of pilgrimage. When my friend and his wife knelt down and prayed I was surprised because I knew they were Brahmins. Later she told me that a couple of months previously her husband had been ill and she had come to St Peter's to light a candle and pray for his recovery. To her St Peter's was the main religious centre of the world and the concept of the Pope as 'papa', 'father', was appealing. The gurus and holy men of India did not seem very different from the monks and priests of Rome.

I noticed a fundamental difference between temples and churches. The inside of a temple is simple, without carvings and paintings. The deity is the sole attraction. The external walls are carved with figures depicting all aspects of life, and crowds of pilgrims go round looking at them after worshipping the deity. By contrast, the interior of St Peter's was like a museum, richly decorated with stone carvings and paintings of religious scenes. In India the pilgrims are all worshippers. In St Peter's the constant stream of sightseers who had not come to worship disturbed the atmosphere of peace.

For the first time since leaving India I found people expressing their curiosity openly. I was going on my own to see a modern building when I noticed office workers waving at me from the balconies. I waved back and soon the balconies were full. When I told my friend about the incident he said, 'Italians think it is lucky to see an Indian; it is such a rare sight for them.' In England people hid their curiosity. It was not considered polite to ask questions, I was told.

I went around admiring art, architecture, and the landscape. There was a natural blend of the old and the new, with historical monuments and fine examples of modern architecture. The use of water was fascinating, with fountains everywhere. At the Fountain of Trevi visitors gathered in the evenings and threw coins into the water to ensure their return to Rome. I did the same. While travelling by train I saw the Roman aqueducts standing like sculptures, towns built into the rocks and becoming part of the hills, the olive groves and vineyards, the farmers working in the fields. Time seemed eternal as in India.

When I arrived in Venice and walked into St Mark's Square I wanted to dance. For the first time an architectural space took me out of my body and gave me a sense of freedom.

The tourist office had booked me into a small hotel. I had asked for a room overlooking the canal in the expectation that I could watch the gondolas and enjoy the reflections of the buildings on the water in peace and quiet. Early in the morning I was woken up by the continuous noise of the motor boats delivering supplies to the hotels. I changed my room to the other side, overlooking a small street, and was kept awake till the early hours by the passing pedestrians. I heard English voices.

While looking at museums and churches I saw many English tourists. They looked clumsy beside the graceful Italians. I felt a kind of bond, like meeting old friends again. I went out of my way to talk to them about life in England.

When I returned to Rome there was a letter from Tom waiting for me. It contained unexpected news. He had left for Australia to join his cousin in their family business and his mother had decided to go with him.

There were two enclosures. One was from the Government of Orissa with the offer of a job as an architect at two hundred rupees a month; the other was from the Leeds School of Town Planning offering me a place in their next course.

I realized the difficulties I would face if I returned to India without Bilati qualifications. Coming from a village and with no influential relatives to help me, my future in India was uncertain. I made up my mind to return to England and go to Leeds to study town planning.

CHAPTER 4
Leeds

'Are you black?'

'No, I'm brown.'

'Light or dark?'

'Is the colour of my skin important?'

'I'm sorry, the room is gone.' She put the telephone down.

I was shocked. I had never been asked about the colour of my skin before. Without thinking, I said 'brown'. But I had always thought of myself as 'fair'.

While coming to Leeds from London by train a man asked me, 'Where are you from?'

'Have a guess.'

'Spain?'

'No. I'm from India.'

'You must have some white blood in you; you are so fair.'

'My mother would be terribly upset if she heard you.'

'Don't be offended. I meant it as a compliment.'

In India people with fair skin are considered beautiful and I was always described as fair. The colour of the skin is discussed openly. When a child is born everybody wants to know the sex and colour of the skin—boy or girl, dark or fair. Parents are delighted if it is a boy. But if it is a girl, she should be blessed with a fair skin, otherwise it could be difficult for her to marry. In an arranged marriage system the colour of the skin becomes important. The first question the parents ask when looking for a bride or bridegroom is whether the skin is fair.

But in Leeds while looking for a room I found discussing the colour of my skin humiliating. This was my first experience of searching for lodgings. In the village I stayed at home; in Bombay I stayed in the hostel; in London I stayed with Tom; and in Europe I stayed in the occasional hotel but mostly in private homes. Now I was alone in a strange city facing racial prejudice. I felt vulnerable.

Eventually, it was a taxi driver who helped me. When I told him I had nowhere to stay he took me to the YMCA. It seemed a long way from the town centre. As we drove through the streets the buildings looked dark and dull. Tall chimneys were belching out fumes. The sky, filled with dust, hung over the city like a grey carpet. I wanted to go back to Italy, but a voice inside me said, 'No, you must be strong.'

Like the taxi driver the warden at the YMCA was helpful. 'We don't have any single rooms, but we can put you up in a dormitory for three days.'

It was a great relief. I left my luggage and went to the school to enrol. When I paid the taxi driver I offered him an extra tip because he had waited such a long time. But he would not accept. 'You'll need it', he said.

The school was in an old Victorian building in the centre of the city. As I entered the room where the students were waiting to enrol I was surprised to see a number of my classmates from Bombay. They had all come to Leeds to study town planning. I was delighted to see familiar faces and hoped they would help me in my search for accommodation. But they all said it had been difficult for them to find rooms. We talked about Bombay and what had happened to us over the last few years.

I was called to see the assistant to the head of the department. He was from Poland and had lived in Leeds for several years. His colleague was also Polish and they were both well-known town planners and teachers. During my interview he asked me where I was staying. When I said 'At the YMCA', he suggested getting in touch with the accommodation officer as soon as possible.

I spent the night in the YMCA dormitory. It was a funny feeling to share a room with nine strangers. I was a stranger myself, in a strange city. I wondered if I had done the right thing in coming to Leeds. I kept worrying about finding a place to live and how to spend the next two years. I found it difficult to sleep and the man in the next bed started snoring; so I sat up and prayed to my gods to help me. Then I realised I was in a Christian hostel and I prayed to Christ as well.

A bell rang early in the morning to wake everybody up. We had to get ready, have our breakfast, and leave the room by nine.

I went to the school and met my Indian friends. They took me to see their rooms. I was appalled. The houses smelt and the rooms were dark, damp, and dingy. How strange, I thought. We are architects studying to be town planners, concerned to improve the environment, yet forced to live in such unhealthy conditions.

In India, students are looked after by the colleges and universities. Great care is taken to provide them with hostel accommodation. They are considered to be the future of the country and enjoy special privileges like travel concessions on buses and trains. There was a tremendous housing problem in Bombay but the state government provided hostels for students attending its own schools and colleges. My school did not have a hostel of its own, but since it was managed by the government it had several rooms reserved for its students in a government hostel. As soon as I had enrolled for the course I was provided with a room. My hostel was by the sea with beautiful views and sea breezes blowing all the time.

In Leeds the School of Town Planning, a part of the College of Art, was run by the local authority. Yet no hostel accommodation was provided by them. Students from outside the area had to find their own accommodation and the overseas students faced immense difficulties.

I went to see the accommodation officer, who had a well-furnished spacious room to herself. She was in her fifties, neatly dressed in a green floral-patterned frock and a green hat. She wore heavy make-up and her lips were red. I produced a letter she had written to me referring to emergency accommodation.

'But we don't have emergency accommodation' she replied.

I realized there was no point in arguing and requested her to find me a room.

She searched through her files, telephoned somebody, and arranged a room for me. She wrote the name and address on a piece of paper. It was already four in the afternoon, my lecture started at six, and I decided to go the next day.

I had great difficulty in finding the place. It was in the suburbs and there was no direct bus. I had to ask several people how to get there. The house was situated in a well-kept terrace with a front garden. I climbed up the steps and rang the doorbell. A young woman opened the door and looked surprised to see me.

'The accommodation officer has sent me. You have a room for me.'

'Oh no, no', she replied. 'The room is gone.'

Before I could say anything she closed the door in my face.

I felt like an Untouchable. I remembered how the Harijans in my village were not allowed to enter the houses of the high caste

Hindus. Even the doors of the temples were closed to them. In Bombay I was told that before Independence there were exclusive clubs for the British displaying notices, 'Dogs and Indians not allowed'. Even after Independence the Breach Candy swimming pool in Bombay excluded Indians, claiming it was a private club. When an Indian was able to swim the English Channel he was invited to use the pool. That created a precedent and gave the swimming club an excuse to allow Indians to join as members.

I returned to the college by bus, disappointed. The woman conductor gave me my ticket, smiled, and said, 'Thank you, luv.'

My three days at the YMCA were at an end and I had to leave. It was the weekend and the Education offices were closed. After great difficulty I found a small hotel to stay in for a few days.

On Monday I went to see the accommodation officer again. This time she was all in blue, with a blue hat.

'Why didn't you tell her I was from India? She shut the door in my face.'

'You are imagining things.'

'I am staying in a hotel. It's expensive and I can't afford it. You must find me a room.'

'You can't say "I *must* find you".' She seemed to find fault with everything I said. I left.

I wandered around Leeds. Wherever I looked I could see only grey—grey buildings, grey churches, and grey skies. A thick layer of dirt had collected over the Victorian Town Hall and nobody had bothered to clean it. But when I went to the school and saw friendly faces I felt optimistic. I decided I must somehow overcome the difficulties and complete the course.

That night I kept wondering why the accommodation officer had not been helpful. What did I do to offend her? There was nobody like Tom to advise me. I was translating my Oriya expressions into English. Saying 'please', 'thank you', 'excuse me', and 'sorry' had not yet become a habit. Sometimes I thought I might have said the wrong thing but did not know how to put it right. My Indian friends faced similar difficulties and were so afraid of being misunderstood that they avoided meeting English people.

The hotel was comfortable but too expensive for me. After a few days I moved to a bed-and-breakfast place nearer the college. It was run by an elderly couple. He was an invalid and had lost one of his legs in the war. He had an artificial leg but was very active. He even drove a car. They were kind and wanted me to stay with them permanently but I could not afford it. I started looking for a place on my own. Every day I bought the local newspaper and searched through the advertisements for suitable accommodation. When I telephoned and said I was from India I was usually asked about the colour of my skin. I always got the same reply, 'The room is gone.'

One day I saw an advertisement for a room near the school. I telephoned and a woman's voice answered. I explained to her that I was a student from India and looking for a room.

'I have asked somebody to come at ten. Could you come at nine-thirty?' she said.

When I arrived the landlady was waiting for me. She was small, thin, and her skin was as dark as mine. While showing me the room she told me she was a Jew from Rumania. She lived with her husband in a suburb of Leeds and had a number of houses which they let.

The room was on the ground floor of an old Victorian terrace house. There was a fireplace with a gas fire, a large window overlooking the road, and a partitioned area with a sink and a small gas stove. Lighting was free but there was a meter for gas. The bath and toilet were on the first floor. The room was large and the rent was a little expensive. As I was trying to make up my mind the doorbell rang.

'Do you want the room?' she asked. 'Otherwise I'll let these people have it.'

Immediately I said, 'Yes, I want the room.'

I moved in the same day. The owner of the boarding house helped me with my luggage.

I felt relieved to have found a room of my own in Leeds. But I became aware of four walls and a ceiling. I felt alone and lonely in a box, suspended in a space where I thought people were hostile to strangers. I missed my village and my parents and their love. For the first time I realized what love really meant. I received so much of it in my village that I had taken it for granted. The expression of love is natural in India

The walls were dark and covered in old wallpaper. So I drew village symbols of the lotus and Lord Jagannath on large pieces of paper and put them on the walls to create a secure environment

for myself. I spent a long time arranging my room. I took my
gods out of the case and put them on the table. I looked at them
carefully. Jagannath, the Lord of the Universe, an incarnation of
Vishnu, has a black face with round black eyes. The realization
that my god was black gave me confidence. His elder brother,
Balabhadra, has a white face and his sister, Subhadra, has a
yellow face. I am sure this was a deliberate attempt to bring the
races together through religion.

Hospitality is natural in my village. Strangers are always
welcome and it is a religious act to look after them. A stranger
should never leave the village displeased. Who knows, he may be
Vishnu in disguise! Stories are told to children to teach them to
show kindness towards travellers and strangers. I remembered a
story my mother told me.

'Once upon a time there was a Brahmin. His name was Krupa
Sindhu. He was married, but had no children. He was kind,
religious, and so generous that he gave all his wealth away to the
poor. A time came when he and his wife had nothing to eat.

'One day his wife said, ''We have no relatives. You must ask a
friend to help, otherwise how can we manage? There's no food in
the house.''

'Krupa Sindhu replied, ''I have a friend who could help us but
he lives in a distant place. If I went to see him he might solve our
problem.''

'It was decided that Krupa Sindhu would visit his friend. His
wife borrowed some rice from a neighbour's house and she made
ten pieces of pithas, rice cakes. She divided them into two equal
portions, one for her husband to eat on his journey and one for
herself.

'Lord Vishnu knew this. To test the Brahmin couple's devotion
he came to their house disguised as an old man. ''I haven't eaten
anything for many days,'' he said in a trembling voice. ''Please
give me something to eat.''

'When the Brahmin couple looked at him their hearts were
filled with compassion. They felt it was their duty to look after
the stranger. They invited him into their house as their guest and
the Brahmin's wife gave her portion of the pithas to the old man
to eat.

'Lord Vishnu knew there were only ten pieces of pithas in

Krupa Sindhu's house and his wife had given him her portion. He wanted to test the hospitality of the Brahmin couple further, so he asked for more.

'The Brahmin's wife gave him Krupa Sindhu's portion and Lord Vishnu ate one more pitha. That left four which the Brahmin's wife kept for her husband's journey, and they both went without food.

'Lord Vishnu was pleased with their devotion but wanted to test them even further. "I'm so weak. I have no strength to walk. Can I spend the night in your house?" he asked.

'Without hesitation they offered the old man shelter for the night and gave him the remaining four pieces of pithas for his supper. They only drank water.

'During the night they discussed the problems of the old man. "He's so old and weak, if we had enough money and food we could keep him in our house and nurse him."

'Lord Vishnu knew what the Brahmin couple were saying and blessed them. In the morning when Krupa Sindhu and his wife got up they were amazed. Their mud house had changed into a palace and the old man had disappeared. They realized what had happened and knelt down to pray to Lord Vishnu for his kindness.'

But the house in Leeds was not a palace. It was neglected, with an empty basement and a deserted back yard filled with broken furniture. The front door was never locked. There was an old table in the hall where letters were left by the postman. The landlady came once a week to collect the rent and empty the meters. She cleaned the staircase and the passage but the bathroom was always dirty. The water ran cold before I had finished my bath and the comforts of Surbiton seemed like a dream. There was no large garden, only a small patch of grass in the front of the house where I often sat in the morning. The other lodgers were nurses, teachers, and social workers and I rarely saw them.

My street ran along the back of the university, connecting a park with the town centre. It was a long sloping street with a gentle curve and containing some departments of the university, a school, offices, and private houses of which many had been converted into bed-sitters. While walking to school I saw mature trees breaking the monotony of red brick and views of industrial

Leeds; rows and rows of houses and factories with chimneys spreading to the horizon.

Leeds seemed dull to me after London and Europe but it was exciting for the local people. It served as the market centre for the area, with facilities for many kinds of entertainment. It had a theatre, a music hall, and a number of cinemas. The pubs were famous for Yorkshire bitter. An old Victorian pub near the Town Hall sold jugged hare and sausages and mash. It was a popular meeting place for the staff from the university and the college of art. The town centre throbbed with life on Friday and Saturday evenings when the crowds flocked in for a night out. After the pubs closed I saw groups of young people staggering along the pavement singing loudly. There were frequent fights between the men, with the girls trying to restrain them. It was a common sight to see men standing against the walls urinating or being sick. By contrast, well-dressed men and women came out of the famous Queen's Hotel or the theatre and got into their chauffeur-driven cars.

Leeds was a city of contrasts. Some lived in great Victorian mansions in Headingly while many were crammed into back-to-back houses with outside lavatories and no proper washing facilities. The Town Hall, with twenty steps, decorated Corinthian columns, and large stone lions, stood proudly as a great monument to the commercial achievements of the city. It was one of the largest civic buildings of its kind and was opened by Queen Victoria with great pomp and ceremony in 1858, the year after the Indian Mutiny. The words around the vestibule—'Europe-Asia-Africa-America'—reminded the people of Leeds that the Queen's rule extended to all corners of the world.

I passed the Town Hall several times a day on my way to the school. If I had been specializing in Victorian architecture, Leeds and its Town Hall would have provided me with sufficient material for study. To me Leeds was a perfect example of a Victorian city with a great sense of unity.

My school specialized in modern town design and my classes started at two in the afternoon and continued until eight in the evening. Out of eight students in the full-time course, five were from India and only three from England. First there were drawing classes for the full-time students. One was an economist and did not know how to draw. We all helped him. Every lunch-time he brought fish and chips from a shop opposite and ate them in the classroom. We objected to the smell but he said it was an English custom. It was also the cheapest lunch available. A meal at the school canteen cost two shillings, but fish and chips cost him one-and-sixpence.

In the evening we had lectures—the history of town planning, landscape design, planning law, sociology, traffic engineering. Our lecturers were part-time and experts in their own fields. Some travelled long distances to teach us.

My first project was to design a housing estate in a Sheffield industrial area. It was my first opportunity to see for myself what industrial areas were like in Britain. During my previous visits to Sheffield City Centre while working in London, Sheffield had looked clean to me. But as I approached the area the smell of sulphur fumes from the nearby steel plant was overpowering. The sun was struggling to shine through the dusty sky. As I walked round I saw terraced houses covered in thick layers of black dust. A woman was washing the steps of her house. I spoke to her.

'I spend my whole life trying to keep this place clean, but it's impossible. In an hour it will be black again.'

When I told her I was a student of town planning and was studying the living conditions in the area, she invited me in. The house was neat and tidy and spotlessly clean. She made me a cup of tea and told me about herself. Her husband worked in the factory; the children were grown-up and had moved away. She was alone during the day and spent her time cleaning.

'It's a full-time job', she said.

She told me the air was so bad that several of her neighbours suffered from bronchitis and TB. There was an outside lavatory and no bathroom. There was no hot water supply and she had to heat the water in a kettle.

I had no idea that people in England lived in such unhealthy conditions. But later on I found many people in Leeds living in back-to-back houses without proper ventilation, sanitation, or washing facilities. In my report I said the area was not suitable for human habitation. My teacher scolded me.

'You are asked to design a housing estate, not write philosophy.'

'I don't think anybody should live there.'

'Why not?'

'The atmosphere is polluted with sulphur fumes. How can you expect people to live there?'

'That's not your look-out.'

'Should I ignore the fumes?'

'But people do live there', he insisted.

'They shouldn't live there.'

'All right, if you are not happy, prepare a report for the town centre of Richmond. I think you will like it.'

I did like Richmond. It was a delightful town set in the Yorkshire dales, with old houses built of stone and a Georgian theatre. The town was clean and surrounded by green fields. Life seemed gentle. What a different world from Sheffield and Leeds, I thought.

My next project was to design a housing estate with a shopping centre, blocks of flats, and a church. High rise flats, called slabs, were considered fashionable, and so I was required to put some into my scheme. I prepared a layout with a park in the middle. Around the park I placed houses, flats, and a shopping centre connected by a network of pedestrian ways. I did not provide a church because I was not told the religious beliefs of the community. So I designed a multi-purpose building which could also be used for worship. To each house I attached a self-contained flat where the grandparents could live.

I discussed the project with my supervisors and prepared models and drawings. Then it had to be assessed by an external examiner. He was an architect from the university. He looked at my scheme and asked me to explain it to him. When I had finished he said, 'What makes you think grandparents want to live with their children?'

'It's good for them', I replied. 'The family can help each other. The old won't feel lonely and the grandchildren can learn a great deal from their grandparents.'

'You have come here to *learn*, not to *teach* us how to live', he said.

'I'm only suggesting.'

'What makes you think your suggestions are right? And you haven't provided a church.'

'What kind of church? Anglican, Catholic?'

'Anglican,' he replied.

'In the project it doesn't mention the denomination; it only says a church. There are so many divisions I didn't know what kind of church to provide. What about the non-Christians, the Jews or Hindus or Muslims who may come to live there?'

'You are not here to change our society. You have been given a brief and you have to accept it. Get your qualification first and then talk about change.'

My interview was the longest. I did not realize that I should not have expressed my views but only listened to his. Afterwards the head of the department said to me, 'You upset the external examiner.'

'I'm sorry. I didn't mean to. I was only trying to explain my project and the ideas behind it. Do you think I should apologise to him?'

'No, forget it', he replied.

But I got poor marks.

My Polish teacher was disappointed. He was my guide and thought mine was one of the best projects. I had tried to bring people and nature together and he thought my scheme had originality.

'People don't like new ideas in England', he said.

My life soon fell into a pattern. I got up early in the morning and listened to the news on the radio Tom's mother had given to me. It opened like a jewel box and was operated by a large battery. My breakfast was a bowl of cereal with milk and several cups of tea. Then I worked on my drawings for the school projects. Around midday I had lunch in my room and walked down to the school. When my classes were over in the evening I returned to my room and painted. The village symbols changed, reflecting my moods. Gradually they became a means of self-expression.

Lord Jagannath and the lotus had influenced my thought from early childhood. During festivals I decorated the mud walls and floors of our houses in the village with rice paste. I made the brushes myself with straw. The lotus was the main symbol. At harvest festival it was used with stylized footprints to welcome Lakshmi, the Goddess of Wealth. Another version of the lotus symbol was used in the autumn festival of Dassera to worship Durga, the Goddess of Energy. Lotus and lilies grew in abundance in the ponds around the village and I watched the buds gradually bloom. The lotus opened with the sunrise and closed with the sunset. It was a symbol of love with the sun. The lilies bloomed at night and had a romantic relationship with the moon. There are many references to these flowers in Oriya and Sanskrit literature. Vishnu's feet where the devotees offered themselves are compared to the lotus. The paintings were not permanent. After each festival the walls were given a coat of mud plaster and painted with different symbols for the next one.

In Bombay while painting in watercolour, the paper dried so quickly that I had to soak it in water before applying the paint. That is how I developed my present technique. I soaked the paper first in water and applied layers of paint, making them flow into one another, while controlling them to produce the effect I wanted. It needed constant practice and experiment and an understanding of the paper, its grains, absorbent quality, and the reaction of the paint to its damp surface. Once a mistake is made it cannot be corrected. But the result is immediate and I find the medium suits my temperament.

The school of town planning was a part of the college of art. I met the teachers and art students and got on well with them. They invited me to visit their classes and see their work. The atmosphere was stimulating and I was inspired by it. I spent many mornings there painting and making pottery.

One day in the pottery studio I was making a piece of sculpture in clay when the students came and watched me. I was surprised. But they told me they were asked by their teacher to see my work. I was using symbols which were new to them. They wanted to see more of my work and I invited some of them to my room. They liked my drawings and paintings and wanted to exchange them with theirs. For the first time I felt appreciated and that gave me encouragement. Until then the colour of my skin and my Indian qualifications were considered inferior and I was beginning to lose confidence in myself. The teachers and students wanted to know more about my village and its culture and I was invited to talk to them.

At the art college young girls and boys were being trained to be painters, sculptors, and commercial artists. My school of architecture in Bombay was part of the college of art. I saw students there sketching from plaster models of Greek and Roman sculptures.

The art school was started by the British and the method of training was Western. In the life classes I saw students sitting around live models, sketching and painting in deep concentration. The students of architecture often joined these classes but they felt superior to the art students. They were going to be professional people whereas the future of the art students was uncertain. Some became teachers and others designed posters and calenders. I had no idea that artists exhibited their work in galleries and sold them. There were no commercial galleries in Bombay but a charitable foundation had started an art centre with galleries where exhibitions were held.

In my village there were no professional artists, only craftsmen. Each craft was the speciality of a particular caste and the skill was handed down from generation to generation. The family provided the training. The potters belonged to one particular caste and their job was to make pots for the villagers. The weavers, goldsmiths, and carpenters all belonged to different castes. The villagers demanded high standards from the craftsmen. A pot is not only functional but also should be aesthetically beautiful. Villagers spend a long time selecting. In my childhood I watched my mother choose saris, bangles, and jewellery and that helped me to develop a sense of appreciation. Practically everything in our house was handmade. In England I found that art was no longer a part of life. The students were being trained in art colleges but their talent was not used to enrich life. Everything in an English home was mass-produced. This helped me to understand the beauty of my village way of life.

As a child I always thought of myself as an artist. The villagers did too, and invited me to advise them on decorating their homes and selecting jewellery and saris for weddings. In Leeds I realized it was possible to become a professional artist.

I met some art teachers who were devoted to their students. From time to time I showed them my work and discussed colour and technique. They were always ready to advise. There was a sculptor who was interested in India. He had a long white beard and looked like a holy man. He invited me to visit his studio. While drinking tea I told him about my experiences in Leeds.

'Prafulla', he said, 'people don't know anything about India. You must teach them. They are like shells and you have to break them open. You may find a pearl.'

There was a social centre at the bottom of the road. The director was sympathetic and introduced me to his friends. They were
all interested in other cultures and through them I began to
understand the social and cultural life of Leeds.

I met a couple who lived in a large house in Headingly. They
were wealthy and patrons of the arts. They often held parties for
artists and writers to which I was invited. I was collected by a
chauffeur-driven car and brought back to my room after the
party. In their house I met the deputy editor of the *Yorkshire Post*
who helped and encouraged me in my work.

I was introduced to the warden of an adult education centre.
He and his wife lived across the road from me in a modern
bungalow. It was designed by a well-known London architect
who was also responsible for new additions to the university. It
seemed to me that people had no confidence in their local talent
and the important jobs in the provinces were carried out by
architects based in London.

The bungalow was hidden behind the old Victorian college. It
had a private courtyard in front and two wings containing
bedrooms and bathrooms. The large living room opened out to a
terrace, with spectacular views of the roofs and chimneys of
industrial Leeds spreading to the horizon. They had appeared
ugly to me before but looking at them from a distance, seated in a
comfortable armchair, they seemed romantic. During my stay in
Leeds I had many opportunities to enjoy the changing character
of the view—in mist, snow, and at night when the lights were on.

The warden also taught at the university. He was a tall man
with a gentle manner. His wife was thin and looked frail but she
was full of energy. They were originally from Scotland and she
had not lost her accent. They had two daughters. The elder was at
London University; the younger daughter was still at school
doing her 'O' levels. She was a rebel. She advocated women's lib
before that concept became fashionable. Once, discussing life,
she told me, 'I wish I didn't have to depend on a man to have a
child.' Now she is happily married with two beautiful sons.

I became a part of the family. The house was always open to
me. Whenever I turned up I was made to feel welcome. They
called me 'Prafulla' but I did not know how to address the
warden and his wife, who were old enough to be my parents. In
India we address our elders as 'brother' or 'sister' and 'uncle' or

'aunt' according to the difference in age. I could not bring myself to call them 'Mr' and 'Mrs'. The warden's wife was like a mother to me and when I heard her children call her 'Mum' I did the same. She smiled happily and said, 'I am your Scottish mum.'

The family became interested in India and wanted to know about life in my village. I showed them colour slides. My village looked beautiful on the screen against the background of the industrial landscape of Yorkshire. If only there could be an end to the unnecessary suffering it would be an ideal place to live in, I thought. We had long discussions about the way to solve its problems.

I wanted to tell people in Yorkshire there was another way of life. The British Council office in Leeds had a list of organizations who wanted a speaker from India. They welcomed my offer. I visited several small towns near Leeds, giving illustrated talks. In return I was entertained to a meal and given my travelling expenses.

In one of my talks I described my village and its problems. When I explained how the British had neglected the villages and the Indian government was doing the same, a member of the audience interrupted.

'It's not true. I was there last year as a guest of the government and was shown several successful development projects.'

'Of course. If you go as the guest of the government everything is laid on for you.'

The audience laughed. I had no idea I was talking to the chairman of the association. I was never invited back.

I soon realized my audiences did not want to get drawn into discussing other countries' problems; they had so many of their own. So I limited my talks to a romantic view of India. I showed coloured slides of temples, weddings, and festivals and everybody seemed happy.

My immediate problem was money. I was not receiving a scholarship and had to pay for my studies. I tried to find part-time work but it was impossible to get a job in architecture. Some students from the college of art worked at night in factories to earn money. They came from respectable families but wanted to stand on their own feet without depending on their parents.

In India the students consider it beneath their dignity to do manual work. As soon as a farmer's son is educated he wants an office job which will provide him with power and comfort. A Harijan in my village worked hard as a labourer and sent his son to school, but he was not able to pass his matriculation. With so many highly-educated young people unemployed he was unable to get a job. A friend of mine arranged for him to work in a club in a nearby town but a part of his work was serving tea and coffee to the guests. He considered that lowered his status and he left. He now sits at home doing nothing, a burden to his father.

When I saw the students in Leeds doing many kinds of manual work to earn money, my own attitude to work changed. I was brought up to give all my time to my studies, and people from my community did not work as labourers. In primary school my class teacher only wanted me to study and did not allow me to take part in the school gardening class.

When I explained my financial problems to a teacher at the art school he suggested I get in touch with the education department about teaching evening classes. I went to see the man in charge. He wanted to help but had no suitable vacancy. Then, out of the blue, he asked, 'Can you teach yoga and meditation?'

Spontaneously I said 'Yes.'

A new sports centre was opening in a few weeks' time and the director was anxious to get publicity. When I was introduced to him he thought it was a brilliant idea and immediately advertised a lunch-time programme: 'Yoga and Meditation for Business-man—to relieve stress and tension.'

To my amazement I found myself among a group of Leeds businessmen wearing dark suits and expecting instant cures. Children in my village meditate and pray in the evening. From my childhood I had meditated and practised yoga exercises but I had no experience of teaching them. I asked the businessmen to have a shower, put on their swimming trunks, and relax. When I saw their misshapen bodies and protruding stomachs I thought of the starving people in India. I showed them how to sit cross-legged on the floor but they found it impossible. So I concentrated on meditation.

'Forget your business worries. Think of something beautiful, a flower or your lover's face.'

It seemed to work. They came regularly and although the session was for an hour they usually stayed longer.

The director was rewarded. When the Sports Minister officially opened the centre an item appeared on the front page of the *Guardian*—'Yoga and meditation at Leeds Athletic Institute'.

One lunch-time, a middle-aged businessman arrived. He looked nervous and worried. He said he had rashes all over his body and his doctor had advised him to see me. I was taken aback at my new role as a healer. He was anxious to get back to his office but I managed to persuade him to wait a few minutes while I finished my class.

We sat down quietly together. 'Do you have any personal problems?' I asked.

He was shy. 'It's my daughter', he said. 'She wants to marry a man I don't think is suitable for her. But my wife supports her.'

'You must try to understand your daughter. Understanding is the best form of love.'

He told me about his difficulties. He ran a small business and managed everything personally because he thought all the others were lazy and unreliable.

As we talked he began to relax. Suddenly he looked at his watch. 'Oh God, I've missed my appointment! This is the first time I have done that.' He paused for a moment. 'I think it will be all right. It will give me an opportunity to find out how reliable my secretary is.'

He drove me back to the college and said he would come to my class the following day.

I did not think he would but when I arrived at the sports centre I found him waiting with the others, ready for his meditation. He continued for several weeks and gradually his tension disappeared and the rashes on his body started to fade. He no longer felt angry with his wife and daughter and was able to smile. His doctor had also advised him to lose weight but he said he loved food.

In India where the majority have not got enough to eat fat people are considered healthy and wealthy. The sign of good health is a body completely covered with flesh. The successful businessmen and politicians have large protruding stomachs, largely due to eating too much and not taking enough exercise. The businessmen worship 'Ganesha', the god with an elephant's head and large stomach, and often look like him. In Bombay and Calcutta I have seen fat businessmen sitting cross-legged on a mattress, resting against cushions and giving orders to their workers who are usually thin and starved. But at school there was a Brahmin boy who was fat and the children thought he looked funny and nicknamed him 'Ganesha'.

In Leeds the fat businessmen did not consider themselves healthy; they wanted to reduce weight, but did not know how to do so. Why did they allow themselves to grow so big in the first place, I wondered.

It made me sad to see how tense and worried many of these businessmen were. They were prosperous but not happy. They were caught up in the system where time meant money and money meant success. I thought of the people in my village. They are happy, in spite of poverty and suffering. I wished the Leeds businessmen in my classes could be content like the villagers.

News of my meditation classes travelled by word of mouth. I was invited by a group of women in a smart suburb of Leeds to form a meditation group. They belonged to professional middle-class families and were conscious of their figures and mental health. The husbands were out all day at the office; their children were either grown-up or at school. So they had a lot of time on their hands.

The weekly meetings were real social occasions, with tea, coffee, sandwiches, and cakes. It was easier for the women to sit cross-legged on the floor than the businessmen. They enjoyed themselves so much they wanted more and longer sessions. I felt I was in danger of turning into a holy man and before they were disillusioned I stopped.

In any case I had to prepare for my first year exams and could not afford the time. As the dates for the exams drew nearer I felt more and more nervous. My meditation did not seem to help me. I became so ill with stomach problems that I did not think I would be able to take them. My Polish teacher persuaded me to try. As soon as I had completed all my papers I recovered. But I was still worried about the result. A saying from the Bhagavad Gita helped: 'Man can act but the result is not in his hands.'

In India the career of a student depends on the result of the exams. Education is the only means for a poor boy to prosper in life and exams are taken very seriously. Students suddenly become more religious and start worshipping gods and goddesses for a successful result.

This was my first exam in England and I was writing my answers in English for English examiners. I was worried that they might not be able to understand me. I was also anxious to do well to show that my training in Bombay was not inferior. I prayed to my gods, including Mahlia Buddha, the deity in the village. When the result was announced I was surprised by the high marks I received in each paper. I thought the examiners were more generous in awarding marks than in Bombay. There the marking was very strict and only about twenty per cent qualified as architects in my year.

I was so happy with the result of my exams that I wanted to dance. From my childhood I was interested in dancing as a form of expression. It was an integral part of village theatre. The temples in Orissa are decorated with dancing figures and dance was an important part of worship in the temple of Jagannath in Puri. Parents offered their daughters to the temple to become devadasis and dance before Jagannath. Like nuns they were married to the deity. But the British Raj felt the devadasis were prostitutes, and dancing became an art of disrepute. Only now, many years afer Independence, has Indian dance been accepted as respectable. In Bombay I learned classical dance from a famous guru. I was his only educated pupil because it was not considered respectable to perform Indian dance in public.

When the students at the college of art discovered that I knew Indian dance some wanted to learn. They were very keen but their limbs were so stiff that I knew it would take them many years to master the art properly. I devised simple steps and helped them improvise. I related movement to painting and they said dancing helped them to paint and draw better. It broke down their inhibitions.

After a few months they understood the rhythm and were confident enough to give a performance at Leeds City Art Gallery. We received tremendous support from their parents and friends and our photographs appeared prominently in the local newspapers. After our Leeds success we were invited to give dance recitals in other Yorkshire towns. We loved decorating our faces and wearing colourful costumes which we made ourselves. We also made simple musical instruments and composed our own

music, though often we used recorded Indian classical music.
The small fee we received was spent on buying materials for more
costumes. I felt as if I was back in my childhood producing plays
in the village.

The warden of the adult education centre and his wife invited
us to arrange an Indian evening with food, wine, and dance. I
helped the bursar to prepare the food. My Indian student friends
came to help and it was like celebrating an Indian feast. The
organizers were disappointed that they had sold so few tickets but
on the night many people turned up. The warden's wife was
worried. As I was helping the dancers with their costumes she
came up to me and said, 'Prafulla, sixty people have already
arrived and we have only cooked for twenty. What shall we do?'

'Don't worry, the Goddess Lakshmi will look after us.'

Instinctively I had prepared more food than was necessary. In
India when arranging a feast we always cook for more guests
than the number invited. It is expected that guests will arrive
with extra friends and relatives who have to be fed and made
welcome. Hospitality is the most important aspect of Indian
social life.

The evening was a success. The food was not only enough but a
lot was left over. The dancers enjoyed themselves and went on
dancing all evening. Some of the guests thought they were Indian
and talked to them very slowly in simple English. When I invited
the audience to dance with us, several volunteered. Seeing their
children and friends dance had helped them to overcome their
inhibitions. A day later a paragraph appeared in the *Yorkshire
Post* with the heading 'Audience tries steps'. It went on to say 'Mr
Mohanti has brought to Leeds a touch of gaiety which is most
welcome.'

A young clergyman in the audience came forward to dance
with us. He said that dancing was the best form of worship and
invited me to dance in his church. Many of his friends came to
watch. As I danced to the music of Bach, to my surprise they all
joined in. Looking back, it seems the young clergyman and his
friends and the students from the college of art were the first
flower people.

Life in Leeds was relatively dull although it was the cultural centre of Yorkshire. Touring companies staged plays, ballet, and opera at the local theatre but the best performers were reluctant to come to the provinces. At the Leeds City Variety Theatre, old-time music hall shows were regularly presented. Music concerts were held in the Town Hall. The interior pulsated with life and movement when a famous musician came to perform. But this was a rare event.

One evening during the interval an elderly woman came up to me. 'How do you like our classical music?'

'Very much.'

She looked surprised. 'But it must be very different from your own music.'

'Just as beautiful.'

When I went on to say I liked Bach, she exclaimed, 'You like Bach! It is even difficult for the Western audience.'

Once Tortellier came to give a cello recital. He was superb and after the concert I went backstage to congratulate him. He seemed pleased and said it was gratifying to be told that his music was appreciated. My praise meant a great deal to him because I came from a different culture. He made me realize that artists have something in common; they need to be appreciated.

On Sundays I took my sketch pad with me and explored the surrounding towns and countryside. They were in easy reach by bus. A favourite place for the visitors was Ilkley Moor. It was on high ground and from the top there were picturesque views of Yorkshire. The air was clean and fresh after the smoke of Leeds and I went on long walks, stopping to sketch.

York was elegant. The Minster and the narrow cobbled streets surrounded by old walls gave the city an ancient look. There were layers of history engrained in the stones. In the spring masses of daffodils bloomed along the grass banks adding colour to the city. Smart shops sold fashionable clothes and exotic fruits and vegetables. The souvenir shops were crowded with visitors. York came to life when Leeds was deserted.

One summer evening while looking round the Minster I noticed a couple sitting on a bench. They seemed deeply involved with each other and unaware of the world outside. Suddenly a man appeared and started shouting at them. The couple got up and left quietly. The man came up to me and said, 'She's my

wife. He's having an affair with her. I want you to be a witness.'
He trembled with anger and ran after them but did not come
back.

The incident puzzled me, but my English friends in Leeds said
he had wanted me as a witness in divorce proceedings; his wife
must have been committing adultery, which was a ground for
divorce. 'Thou shalt not commit adultery' was one of the Ten
Commandments. Until then adultery was an unknown concept
to me. I wondered how anybody could commit adultery sitting
outside a beautiful church and expressing their love for each
other. In Hinduism there is no such thing as adultery. Radha, the
consort of the Hindu god Krishna, was the wife of another man.
They used to meet secretly on the banks of the river Jamuna
under the kadamba tree and there are many devotional songs
describing this union.

There was no divorce in my caste. Men and women in lower
castes often quarrelled and left each other but it was considered
disgraceful by the villagers. I remember in my childhood my
father talking to his friends about divorce among English people.
'The most divorced women in England are the most respected',
he said. His friends laughed but did not ask him to explain. He
must have heard his English officers discussing divorce and
misunderstood. Although divorce is accepted by Indian law most
Indians, whether living in India or the West, do not approve of it.

The contrast between East and West was the favourite subject
of study for an Indian lady I knew in Harrogate. She lived in a
large house with her unmarried daughter and son, both middle-
aged. She had chosen the town because it was famous for its spas
and public gardens. I was introduced to her by a friend in
London. It was difficult to judge her age but she was well-
preserved and tastefully dressed. She often invited me either for
lunch or tea to tell me about her problems—how difficult it was
to get money out of India and how dreadful the Indian government was in not giving her foreign exchange. She spent large
sums every year in maintaining her twelve-bedroomed house
with maids and servants. To pay the death duties when her
husband died she had to sell her two large mansions. She did not
behave like a typical Hindu widow who leads a very austere life.
She went to parties, opened fetes, and gave talks.

Once while showing me over the house she took me to her

bedroom. It was decorated with antique furniture. A door led to a self-contained suite of rooms, a living room, a bedroom, and a bathroom. The bed was made up and men's clothes, shoes, and slippers were laid out like museum exhibits.

'This was my husband's room', she said. 'When you come next you will sleep here.'

I never went back. She complained to my friend that I had deserted her. But I always felt uncomfortable in her house and kept thinking about the poor people in my village.

My Indian friends at school came from all over India but had one thing in common—they disliked the English weather and longed for the sun. The sky seemed to be constantly grey and the winter fogs so thick that while returning to our rooms in the evening it was quite easy to get lost. The character of Leeds went through a transformation in the snow. The grey city turned white and glittered in the light. But our friend, Sathe from Bombay, found the English winter unbearable. He always suffered from colds and coughs. He was a strict vegetarian, very thin, and lived in a house which was damp. One day he went to see the doctor but did not come back to attend his class. We were all worried and called on him. He was in bed. As soon as he saw us he started to cry. The doctor had told him he had TB. Everybody was shocked but we tried to comfort him. The next day he was admitted to hospital and stayed there for several months. We visited him regularly. When he got better an Indian friend said, 'Thank God you got TB in England, where treatment is free. In Bombay it would have cost you a fortune.'

Khare and Kiran were always at the centre of gossip. They were one year senior to me. Khare was a Harijan and Miss Kiran was a Brahmin, the highest caste. They had been my classmates in Bombay and Khare always helped Kiran in her studies.

In Leeds they shared a flat. For an unmarried girl to live with a boy was unthinkable to the Indian students. Khare and Kiran described themselves to the teachers as brother and sister and the Indian students thought that was funny. But Kiran confided in me that she loved Khare. I was often invited to their place and told how cruel the other Indian students had been to them. In Bombay they were not free to express their love for each other. They had chosen Leeds, rather than London where they had found too many Indians from Bombay. But they had not expected that so many of their college friends would be studying town planning in Leeds. They wanted to get married when they returned to India but were expecting hostility from her family.

In India young boys and girls consider each other as brothers and sisters and have a feeling of responsibility towards each other. Everybody is careful not to destroy this harmony. In England the relationship between men and women is always sexual from childhood. The boys have girl friends and the girls have boy friends. My English friends at the school were always in pairs. It seemed to be a convention for boys and girls to go out together. They expected me to have a girl friend and tried to introduce me to suitable girls. That is how I met Catherine, an art student who lived in Harrogate. She joined our group to learn dance and meditation and seemed to enjoy herself.

One evening I invited her to my room for dinner. She accepted but said she must return home by ten; it was her father's strict rule. After the meal she insisted on washing the dishes for me but I could not find a clean cloth. When she left I kissed her on the cheek.

'Kiss me properly', she said. 'I'm not your sister.'

The next day she brought me a present, a parcel containing half-a-dozen tea-cloths. What a lovely gesture, I thought.

We saw each other regularly. Then one day she invited me to have dinner with her at a restaurant in Leeds. During the meal she said, 'I have something very important to tell you. Promise me you won't be offended.'

'What is it?'

'My father doesn't want me to see you.'

'Why not?'

'He says you're Indian and not a part of our culture. He thinks I find you exotic and that's why I'm attracted towards you. But it won't last.'

'What do you think?'

'Would you mind if we don't see each other for a few weeks?'

I was hurt but not surprised. I could understand her father's point of view. I was a stranger from another country. An Indian father would not have allowed his daughter to go out with an English boy. After puberty girls are kept under strict control and there is no free mixing between boys and girls. It is the father's responsibility to find a suitable bridegroom for his daughter; so he has to be careful that his daughter does not become the subject of any scandal.

We had a few African students in Bombay who complained that Indians were not hospitable. But they had no understanding of Indian family life. When an African student was invited to an Indian home he expected to take the young daughter out. That was out of the question and he was never invited back. The word soon went round and Indian parents became cautious.

A few months later I met Catherine unexpectedly outside the railway station. She was with a young Englishman.

'This is my boy friend', she said.

Boys and girls changed partners frequently. It was like changing cups and saucers. But some stayed together like married couples.

Suresh did not approve of Khare and Kiran living together. He was a Brahmin and the idea of a Brahmin girl associating with a Harijan boy was repulsive to him. We had known each other in Bombay. He was three years senior to me. After qualifying as an architect he got married and came to England with his wife. He worked for a few years in Manchester where his first child, a son, was born.

Suresh studied town planning in the evening, and to supplement his income, his wife worked for a while, but found it difficult. He saw no future in Manchester and came to Leeds because he got a better job. He enrolled as a part-time student in my college to complete his town planning studies.

His second child was born and he invited all the Indian students, except Khare and Kiran, to the name-giving ceremony. Suresh was disappointed the baby was a girl but his wife was pleased. 'When she grows up she will help me in the house', she said. They lived in two rooms of a very old building which was converted to bed-sitters. It was a long way from the city centre in a dilapidated suburb. His neighbours in the house were English and he invited them all to the ceremony, but only a few came. They admired the baby and the vegetarian food which his wife had prepared.

The Indian students had contributed towards buying a present for the baby, and after a long discussion, a small gold necklace was selected. We all helped to put it round the baby's neck and called her 'Leela', the name given to her. Its Indian meaning is

'Divine Play' but it was chosen because it sounded like 'Leeds'.

We all enjoyed choosing the baby's necklace from a small jeweller in Leeds. We wanted twenty-four carat gold but could only get eighteen. We asked the jeweller to test it for us to check if it really was eighteen carat, but he refused. He said it was stamped on the necklace. We were sceptical because in India goldsmiths are never trusted. Long arguments usually take place regarding the price and quality of the gold. When we tried to bargain about the price he got really annoyed. 'It's not India', he said. Suddenly we all felt embarrassed and paid the marked price. When we left he thanked us for providing him with a new experience.

Bargaining adds another dimension to shopping in India. The object is to make the purchaser feel happy that he has paid less than the asked price. Only the seller knows what a fair price should be but he often asks more than twice that amount and leaves the purchaser guessing. The negotiations continue until an agreed price is fixed and the transaction takes the form of an entertainment. While selling expensive goods the shopkeeper serves tea and cold drinks. In Leeds the Indian students missed this but there was a colourful covered market where prices were lower than in the shops. On Saturday afternoons the prices of fish, fruit, and vegetables dropped sharply.

I often bought my fruit from a department store near the school. One day I recognized the woman serving behind the counter. She was one of the guests I had met at a party. I bought some apples and pears and while putting them into my bag she added some extra ones. 'Come on luv, they make so much profit here. I would rather you ate them.'

I looked around to see if anybody was watching.

'Don't worry, luv, I'm the manager.'

That evening I was invited to a party by the director of the social centre. As I was talking to some of the women guests the accommodation officer suddenly appeared with a glass of wine in her hand. I had not seen her since leaving her office over a year ago.

'It seems you are enjoying our Leeds, Mr Mohanti.'

'I would have enjoyed it even better if you had found me a room.'

The next day I was summoned by the head of the department.

'There are serious allegations against you. You have insulted the accommodation officer publicly by saying she was inefficient. A date has been fixed for you to appear before the principal.'

I felt disturbed but too embarrassed to tell any of my friends. To relieve my tension I spent long hours painting in my room, thinking about my village and my parents.

The meeting with the principal was like a court hearing. The head of the department accompanied me and an officer from the education department was also present. After reading out the charges against me the principal asked me to explain why I should not be expelled from the school.

I described in detail my initial experiences in Leeds while searching for a room and the prejudices I had faced. I could sense the hostility from the principal and the education officer, and I spontaneously concluded by saying, 'What would happen if I told the story to the press?' There was silence.

I was asked to wait outside. After a while the education officer and the head of the department left and the principal called me back into the room.

'We have decided to forgive you this time. You are new to this country and don't know our customs. Be careful in the future.'

When I went back to the head of the department he looked pleased. 'The trouble with you is that you are a crusader and so naïve.'

The reaction of my Indian friends was different. 'We shouldn't get involved with English people. Let us get our qualifications and go back to India.' But I wanted to be involved with life in England. Exploring the unknown was an exciting experience.

The Labour Women's Club had arranged a tea party in a Leeds hotel and the organizers had asked me to dance for them. There were about thirty people, among them a well-known politician. As I danced, the garment around my waist started to unwind. I was terrified it might fall off completely and so I gradually stopped dancing and went out to rearrange my costume. When I returned one of the women said, 'What a pity. We were hoping to see a striptease!' There was loud laughter.

I was introduced to the politician who invited me to sit with her. She wanted to know all about me and my village. But as soon as the food arrived she lost interest. The sandwiches, cakes, and pastries were not up to her satisfaction. She spent the rest of the afternoon complaining they were not getting value for money.

I was always in need of money and had to do various jobs. Once a week I taught a group of day-release students at the Wakefield School of Art, just outside Leeds. They were all boys, aged sixteen to eighteen, and were being trained to become plumbers, carpenters, and bricklayers. Their employers gave them one day a week off from work to attend classes in drawing, design, and painting. A number of full-time art students also joined my class. I tried to teach them to paint and draw freely, using lines and colours boldly.

The day-release students were noisy, always trying to disrupt the class. They brought coconuts and broke them in the room and went round distributing pieces. I did not know how to deal with them. Whenever I tried to teach they made noises. I felt they were behaving in that way because I was from India. I was determined not to give up. When I told them how difficult things were for students in India they replied, 'We're not in India, sir, we're in England.'

I realized they were jealous of the full-time students who spoke with a different accent and dressed differently. They were of the same age as the full-time students but they had to work to earn a living. They were only making noises to attract my attention. I felt they were like my younger brothers and taught them individually. Gradually I won them over and they became interested in painting and drawing. Whenever there was sunshine outside they felt restless. With the permission of the head of the department I took the whole class out to sketch buildings and landscapes.

I was interested to see how their behaviour changed once they were outside the school. We became friends and they told me about their problems, even their stealing—how they broke open gas meters and telephone boxes. They said it was exciting.

Two hours with them was exhausting for me. When I told the head of the department of my difficulty he replied, 'You're doing well. The previous teacher only lasted one day and he was English.'

From early childhood the students in India are taught to respect their teachers. The teacher–student relationship is based on the old tradition of guru and sishya, teacher and disciple. The guru is responsible not only for teaching the sishya the techniques of the arts—music and archery—but also for helping the sishya to understand moral values in preparing to face the world. The sishya is always obedient to the guru and often touches his feet for blessing.

In India students always stand up while talking to their teachers and call them 'Sir'. It was natural for me to do the same in Leeds. When I saw the English students talking to the teachers while sitting on their chairs and smoking cigarettes, I was shocked. Smoking inside the classroom was unthinkable in India. In the street students put out their cigarettes when they saw their teacher coming towards them. I did not think the English students paid proper respect to their teachers. They even called them by their first names. It was a modern trend, I was told. Being informal with the teachers broke down the barriers. I was not convinced. I thought it destroyed the student–teacher relationship.

My fees for teaching the day-release students were outstanding. I had submitted my claims but the director of the college had been delaying them. When I went to see him he said, 'Your classroom was empty.'

'I had taken the students out to draw and paint.'

'Who asked you to do so?'

'Nobody, but I asked the permission of the head of the department.'

'You can't take them out without my permission.'

'I don't think you realize how difficult it is to teach them.'

'Nobody's forcing you.'

My contract for the next term was not renewed.

I thought if I could sell some of my paintings it would help to pay towards my education. I knew that London was the centre for art galleries and so I went there with a portfolio of my paintings. I walked along Cork Street and Bond Street looking at the galleries from the outside. Then I plucked up my courage and went inside one.

After looking at my paintings the director said, 'This is not the type of work we show in our gallery, but there is another gallery nearby which has shown the work of Indian artists. Why not try there? He gave me the address. He also suggested that I saw an architect and his wife, teaching at the Royal College of Art. They were both artists and designers and would be sympathetic to my work.

First I went to see the gallery director. She looked through my portfolio with great interest and said, 'Do you know any art critic?'

'No.'

'I like your paintings but how can you have an exhibition without an art critic to write about your work in the papers?'

She gave me the name and telephone number of a critic and museum director and asked me to get in touch with him. When I telephoned him he said, 'Why don't you go back to India?' and put the telephone down.

I telephoned the architect. His secretary answered and asked me to see him during the lunch hour. I met him and his wife and showed them my paintings. They said they liked my work and gave me a list of galleries that might be interested. The architect and his wife were in their fifties, quiet and gentle, like my teachers in India. In a few minutes they gave me a feeling of confidence.

I showed my paintings to the galleries. They all said they liked them but made polite excuses: 'We are fully booked for the next five years'; 'We are not taking on new artists'; 'We don't show this kind of work'. Disappointed, I left.

While returning to Leeds by train I was doodling on a piece of paper, reflecting on my experiences. I thought the galleries in London treated works of art like bags of potatoes.

'How much?' a man sitting opposite me asked.

'What do you mean?' I was surprised.

'I want to buy that drawing', he said. 'How much do you want for it?'

I was taken aback. All this time I had been wanting to sell my paintings but now I faced a situation when somebody wanted to buy and I did not know how to cope. It was like giving a piece of myself away.

'Do you really like it?' I asked.

'Yes.'

'Then please take it.'

He brought me luck. After I returned to Leeds I described my experience in London to the wife of the warden.

'Why don't you have an exhibition in the college?' she asked. We discussed it with the warden and a date was fixed for the opening.

Getting the paintings framed by a professional shop was expensive so I framed them myself in the warden's garage. His wife and daughter helped me to hang them.

On the morning of the private view I felt nervous. When I looked at my forty paintings on the walls I could see parts of myself. My village symbols had become personal statements.

It was a beautiful spring evening and I was worried that nobody would turn up to my private view. Why should anyone come and see my paintings? So I stayed in my room praying to my gods to let people come and see my exhibition.

When I arrived at the college, fifteen minutes late, the room was full of visitors. The warden's wife came towards me looking relieved.

'Everybody's asking me, "Where is the artist and where is the price list?" '

I had not prepared one because the idea of inviting people and handing them a price list was too embarrassing.

A visitor came up to me and said, 'I see you have been influenced by Klee.' He pointed to one of my paintings inspired by my god Jagannath.

'Clay?' I asked. My knowledge of European art was limited.

He started to explain. Without saying anything I left the exhibition and went across the road to my room. I brought the miniature figures of Jagannath and his brother and sister and showed them to the man.

'Who has been influenced by whom? Me by Klee, or Klee by these figures, which are at least a thousand years old?'

A professor from the university bought a painting and congratulated me. 'If a man paints so well, why shouldn't he be a painter?'

'Why not?' I said jokingly.

The head of the painting department came and joined us. 'Prafulla must have been going round with a sledge hammer opening the doors of Leeds. I invite so many people to my exhibitions but nobody comes.'

The professor had come with his eight-year-old daughter. When I said, 'Thank you for coming to see my exhibition', she replied, 'Thank you for painting the pictures. There wouldn't be an exhibition without them.'

The exhibition kept open for a month and many people came to see it. A good review appeared in the *Yorkshire Post*. At that time there was an exhibition of Australian artists at the City Art Gallery. The art critic of the *Daily Telegraph* had come to Leeds to review it. I do not know when he came to see my exhibition but he wrote a couple of lines at the end of his review saying how much he enjoyed it and how Indian my paintings were in spirit. Those lines were of immense help. The Wakefield City Art Gallery bought a painting for their collection and invited me to have an exhibition.

A professor from Sussex University was lecturing at the college and came in briefly to see my exhibition. I happened to be present at the time. He said he would like to arrange an exhibition of my paintings in his university. His spontaneous appreciation was encouraging.

The University of Leeds and some professors bought my paintings. I was also invited by a commercial gallery in Leeds to have an exhibition, and the City Art Gallery bought a painting. I found myself accepted as a painter.

But I had come to Leeds to study town planning. I wanted to complete my course and return to India to help my village. Studying town planning made me aware of people and their problems. It opened my eyes to planning problems in India. I used to dream of towns and villages where everybody was happy. I came to the conclusion that India meant villages and Indian culture is village culture. I worked on the idea of village development, taking groups of villages as social, economic, and cultural units and developing them under a broad national plan.

Nanpur, my village, is a part of a group of villages with a central market place at Balichandrapur where the farmers and craftsmen sell their goods. Similar units exist naturally throughout India. I wanted to start my experiment with my own village. I wrote a letter to the Government of India setting out my plans. I did not know who to approach and so I addressed it to the President.

I realized that people in England knew very little about the Indian village way of life. Even those living in the cities in India were out of touch. A typical example was my closest friend Rajinder.

We had spent five years together in Bombay studying architecture and stayed in the same hostel. He spoke Punjabi and Hindi but we spoke to each other in English. His father worked as a civil servant in Delhi.

In Leeds we went to the cinema together and drank tea in cafes.

We had long discussions about India's development. I said India should have villages and he said India should have cities. There was no compromise.

Once by chance I asked him if he had ever been to a village in India.

'No,' he said.

'Haven't you seen paddy fields?'

'No.'

I was surprised and repeated, 'You haven't seen villages and paddy fields?'

'You know I come from Delhi', he said. 'My father never allowed me to go to the rural areas. I had to stay at home and study.'

Suddenly things became clear. I knew why he had been advocating the development of cities in India. The planners were mainly from the cities. No wonder the villages had been neglected.

Rajinder was quiet and soft-spoken. Although he argued with me he rarely talked to the teachers. The other Indian students were also self-conscious. They said the English people did not want to mix with them. But I knew we had to make the effort. People in England lived in their little worlds and were suspicious of outsiders.

My Polish teacher understood our problem and said we could use his house at any time. We arranged parties and cooked curries and pilaus. 'Not too spicy,' he used to say; 'otherwise the neighbours will complain.'

One day Rajinder said he had something important to show me. We went to the school canteen and he handed me a photograph.

'Is that your sister?' I asked.

He laughed. 'No, the bride my father has chosen for me. He wants me to get married as soon as I return to India.'

I looked at the photograph carefully. She looked like a film star. But Indian photographers know all the tricks. For a small fee they can make the ugly beautiful.

'My father says her parents are wealthy and will give a large dowry. She has an arts degree too.'

'Everything is all right then', I said.

'It's not that simple.' He put the photograph back in his

pocket. 'I'll tell you another time.' We had to leave to attend our lecture.

A few days later I went to Rajinder's place to collect some notes. It was about 9.30 in the morning and I had not warned him about my visit. When I knocked on the door Rajinder appeared in his dressing-gown. He looked embarrassed.

'Come in,' he said, smiling nervously. I thought I saw a figure behind a curtain which separated the living area. After a while a young girl came through.

'This is my fiancée', he said. 'She's from Germany. I meant to . tell you before but never had a chance to do so.'

After qualifying, Rajinder went to Germany to work there. I lost touch with him. A few years later, when I was having an exhibition in Delhi, he came to see me at the gallery and invited me to dinner. There were other people around and I did not have a chance to talk to him about the German girl. But when I arrived at his house, he introduced me to his wife. It was the girl whose photograph I had seen in Leeds.

I had gone to Rajinder for his notes on sociology and traffic engineering. We had to study these two subjects in our second year. Both the lecturers were from the university and I found their approach too academic. They dictated notes and wanted us to copy them down word for word. I found the subjects boring and did not take any notes.

The lecturer teaching traffic engineering was an Irishman who had been educated in America. He spoke with an American-Irish accent, which I could not follow.

One day he noticed I was not writing and asked, 'Why aren't you taking notes?'

'It's not necessary', I said.

'In that case I won't mark you present', he warned me.

Both lecturers complained about me to the head of the department and I was called to his office. I told him I was studying to be a town planner, not a sociologist or a traffic engineer. I also had great difficulty in understanding the Irishman's accent.

'But you will be required to take exams in these subjects.'

'I'll read the notes taken by my friends.'

In my final exams I had to take six papers, including sociology and traffic engineering. I thought I had done well but was again summoned by the head of the department.

'The situation is serious', he said. 'You have failed in two papers. A student is only allowed to fail in one paper.'

'Which two?'

'Sociology and traffic engineering.'

'What about the other papers?'

'You have done very well.'

'We had eight papers in the first year and I did well in all of them. Can you tell me why I have done so well in every paper except sociology and traffic engineering? Whose fault is it, mine or the teachers? My thesis is on a sociological subject which has been accepted. If I didn't know anything about sociology, how could I write the thesis? And I'm not going to be a traffic engineer in any case.'

He listened to me silently and made no comment.

When the result was announced I was declared successful but no marks were entered for traffic engineering or sociology. The spaces were left blank.

I came to Leeds to study town planning and in the process became a painter. For the first time I found the opportunity to stand on my own feet. Adjusting to new values and facing prejudices created inner tensions. I took refuge in my paintings to find peace in myself. The industrial landscape of Yorkshire made me understand the importance of colour in life and how beautiful my village was. The longing to return to India was strong. I had got my Bilati qualification but I had no money to pay for my fare. There were no suitable jobs for town planners in Leeds and so I decided to go to London.

CHAPTER 5

East End

I had nowhere to stay in London. With very little money it was difficult to find suitable accommodation. I did not have the courage to look for a room, my Leeds experience having made me lose confidence. I wanted to protect myself from getting hurt again.

A friend in Leeds had suggested I get in touch with the warden of a social centre in the East End and had given me a letter of introduction. I had never been beyond the Tower of London but when I got out at Aldgate East tube station I felt at home. I saw several Indian shops selling sweets and tropical vegetables. Many people from the Indian sub-continent were walking about in the streets, talking in Hindi and Bengali.

The social centre was like a lotus in a muddy pond. Unlike the surrounding buildings it was clean and had the feeling of an educational institute. A group of English intellectuals lived and worked there.

The warden was sympathetic to my problems and gave me a room in a nearby Victorian building. It had a distinct character, with open staircases and balconies. My room was on the third floor. It was approximately eight feet wide and ten feet long, with a window overlooking a courtyard used for car parking and children's play. There was a sink, a gas fire, and a single gas ring, with coin meters for both electricity and gas. A pane on the window was broken and I covered it with a piece of paper. The warden lent me a bed, a table, and a chair. There was no bathroom, but I had my own outside lavatory on the landing.

The building was occupied by several families with their pets and possessions. When I moved in I met two young women talking in the corridor. I told them I was going to be their neighbour and they volunteered to help.

'Your room has not been used for many months and might be infested with bugs.'

I gave them a key and they cleaned and washed the room for me. One of them asked me if I was able to cook. When I said 'Yes', she replied, 'But you haven't got proper cooking arrangements. You can eat with us for a few days if you like. I won't charge you much.'

'She's a very good cook', her friend said.

I ate with them for a few days. The food was good but monotonous . There were fried chips with every meal. I met her husband, who worked on a building site as a labourer. They lived in two rooms and were trying to get a council flat so that they could have children. But there was a long waiting list.

In India the first thing a couple wants after marriage is a child and particularly a son, essential for the family to continue. Women get worried if they cannot have children within two years of their marriage and start worshipping gods and goddesses. In my village the bride lives with her husband's family and the young married couples do not go through the trouble of searching for a place to live. When the child is born the other members of the family help to bring it up.

An old man lived alone in the next room to me. With white untidy hair and a long beard, he looked like an Indian sage. In the mornings he sat by the door drinking tea and eating slices of plain bread. He was friendly and told me he lived on milk and bread. There were always empty milk bottles outside his door. One day while talking to him I looked into the room. The bed was unmade and there were piles of newspapers and dirty clothes. I wanted to clean the room for him but he objected. When I told the women who had helped to clean my room they said, 'The old man is a loner. He doesn't want anybody to interfere with his life.'

I saw him wandering alone in the streets, talking to himself. But when I was out he kept messages for me from visitors and received parcels. Whenever I cooked I gave him a plate of food and he always ate it with great satisfaction. I thought of him as my grandfather and wanted to look after him. My father's father had died before I was born. The other children in the village had their grandfathers and I was sad I did not have one. My mother's father was also dead. It was a natural instinct for me to look after old people. I wanted to know about his life, but he was reluctant to talk. Gradually he told me that he was not married and had no relatives. There was nobody to look after him. In my village there is a great respect for old age and the villagers go to the old people for advice and blessings. The old are so involved with life and helping others that they remain mentally active. In spite of poverty and suffering I have not seen any mental illness there.

On the opposite side of the road there was a row of shops—a chemist, a hardware store, and a bakery. The bakery was run by a middle-aged woman. She always carried a poodle in her arms and put it on a chair while serving the customers. I used to buy my bread there. One day she said to me, 'Darling, what's the matter with you? A young man like you shouldn't look so lonely. Why don't you come up and see me tonight? I live alone with my poodle.'

A woman standing nearby said, 'Oh, she fancies you.'

'Don't listen to her; she's jealous.'

I felt embarrassed and said, 'I'll try.' But I did not go.

When I went to buy my bread the next morning she did not say anything about her invitation.

Every morning I saw a man standing outside the entrance to the building. He was in his mid-forties, well-built, with a round face. His hair was dark and I thought he looked Greek. He always wished me 'Good morning'. One day he told me that he worked as a window cleaner.

Often when the pubs closed I heard quarrels from the room above me. A woman would scream and a dog would start to bark. There was the noise of furniture being smashed. I felt as if the ceiling was coming down and was worried that somebody was being hurt. Suddenly there was silence.

One night I was preparing to go to bed when there was a knock on my door. I opened it and was surprised to see the window cleaner. I invited him in and offered him a cup of tea, but he refused.

'I need your help', he said. 'There's nobody here I can talk to.' He looked quiet and serious. 'I live upstairs with my wife and stepson. It's my place but they treat me as an outsider; they make me feel I'm not wanted. So every evening I go to the pub to be with my mates. When I return home I'm drunk and we have quarrels and fights. I need love.'

'Please don't get drunk', I said.

Next to the staircase lived a family with a dog. A portion of the balcony was enclosed with a wooden gate and the dog stayed there most of the time without a chain. It would sense me from a distance and start to bark and jump whenever I passed by. I was frightened that the dog would attack me. I complained to the owner. He said the dog had never barked before I came and only barked at me. I reported the matter to the social centre and the dog had to be kept on a chain. But the owner never forgave me. Whenever I passed the dog still barked and he said in a loud voice, 'Poor little dog. He has to be chained for this man.'

When I was about ten years old a friend of mine in the village was bitten by a stray dog. He was the only child of his parents. The dog died after a week and a few days later the boy was ill and started to bark like a dog. His parents worshipped gods and goddesses, but he died. From then on I was frightened of dogs.

Brick Lane was close by. It was full of Jewish shops and Indian and Pakistani grocers. There was no tension; they lived and worked peacefully together. The shops from the Indian sub-continent sold rice and exotic spices, tropical fruits and vegetables, dried fish and papadum. There were a number of Jewish tailors and shops selling cloth. I bought canvases for my paintings from one of them. It was run by two elderly brothers and when I told them I was an artist they sold me their old stock at a reduced price. They often invited me to go inside their storeroom. It was just like an Aladdin's cave, with all kinds of cloth carefully stored on racks. They loved to talk about themselves and their families and were curious to know about me. They had come from Germany before the First World War and had settled in Whitechapel, worked as tailors, and brought up their families. They managed to give a good education to their children, but as soon as they got good jobs they did not want to live in the area any more and moved to Golders Green and Hampstead. But the brothers stayed in Whitechapel where their friends and relatives lived.

It was difficult for me to cook in my tiny room and sometimes I went out to eat. There were two Indian restaurants in Brick Lane. One was better than the other and reasonably cheap. It was a popular meeting place for the Bengalis and I often ate there in the evenings. It was small and clean and the owner was from East Pakistan, now Bangladesh. He was in his thirties, quiet, and sat at the cash desk guarding it carefully.

An Englishwoman in a sari served the customers. I had often spoken to the owner, but never asked who the Englishwoman was; I thought she worked for him. He told me in Bengali that he was married and had left his wife and two children in Sylhet. When he had saved enough money he would bring them here.

Many Bengalis living around Brick Lane had left their families behind. They lived in crowded conditions in houses without washing facilities. The rooms were damp and infested with bugs. Some of them could not speak English properly and stayed together with their friends and relatives. They worked hard to save money to send to their wives and children.

In India it is common for men to leave their families in their villages and go to town to work. On the meagre salaries the workers receive it is impossible for them to maintain their joint families in their places of work. They share rooms with friends and try to save as much as they can in order to send money to their families and educate their children.

One evening I was having my meal when three Englishwomen entered the restaurant. They went up to the woman in the sari and had an argument. Soon it turned into a quarrel.

'I'm not a whore like you. I'm married. I'm respectable', the woman in the sari shouted.

The other women thought it was funny.

'You married? You must be joking', they sneered at her.

The woman in the sari went up to the owner and pleaded: 'Tell them I'm married to you.' But the man sat there silently with a nervous grin on his round face.

They left triumphantly but the woman in the sari sat at a table resting her fragile face in her hands.

I wondered if she knew that her lover had a wife and two children back home. He was a Muslim and was allowed to have four wives in India or Pakistan.

In the evenings I saw shadowy figures lurking on the street corners, women talking to men. I had read about Jack the Ripper who hunted his victims in the streets of Whitechapel and wondered about the fate of the women. But there was never any violence, only a mysterious atmosphere.

If I wanted a change from rice and curry I went to a fish and chip shop in Brick Lane. It was run by two brothers and their wives. They were friendly and while frying and serving they gossiped with the customers. There was a small area for eating, with a few tables and chairs. Once I was having my meal there when a couple entered the shop. They were both in their seventies. The man wore steel-framed spectacles and a Jewish skullcap. They bought fish and chips from the counter and sat at the table opposite me. I stopped eating and looked at them. The old man smiled and went on eating his food. The woman's face was heavily made-up and her white hair was neatly curled. She had no teeth. After they had finished the man asked me, 'Are you Indian or Pakistan?'

'Indian.'

'Good. India is old country, ancient civilization.'

'Have you been to India?'

'No. You like it here?' the man asked me.

'I don't like the weather.'

They both said in one voice, 'We don't like living here, but we have no choice.'

They told me Russia was their home. Because of the war he went to Paris where his cousin had a restaurant. He worked there for a while, but there was no future, and so he came here. They lived nearby in Whitechapel and he worked for a Jewish delicatessen.

When I asked him if he had any children, he laughed.

'We have only been married for ten years, but my wife has a son from her first husband.'

I thought the East End was full of honest and friendly people. Whenever I went to the West End I felt it was a different world. The difference between these two parts of London was like that between my village and Bombay.

I had no idea people lived in such squalor and poverty in England. One day in Trafalgar Square an old man in rags asked me for some money to buy a cup of tea. Instinctively I gave him a few coins. I was brought up to believe that by giving alms to beggars a man achieves piety. God often comes disguised as a beggar. That night I saw in the Strand several people sleeping on the pavement near the ventilation grills to keep themselves warm. But around Aldgate East I saw crowds of people sleeping on the pavement outside the pubs, wrapped in newspaper and cardboard.

As I did not have a bathroom I used the public baths. That did not worry me because I was used to bathing in the river in my village. When I turned up at the public baths I saw many men, women, and children waiting to have their bath. In Leeds there was only one bathtub used by eight occupants of the house. But in the public bath a bathtub was used by hundreds of people. I was worried about cleanliness and carried a bottle of Dettol with me. A few weeks later I developed some skin infection which the doctor said I must have caught in the public baths.

My habit of taking two baths a day was reduced to about three a week in Leeds. Soon it became once a week in London. Every day I sponged myself with warm water and felt like a sick man. In my village when I was recovering from an attack of malaria I felt so weak that I was not able to walk. In the morning my mother would bring a bowl of warm water and a towel. After soaking the towel and wringing it out she wiped my body with it. Then she covered me with a cotton sheet.

I wandered alone, admiring decaying old buildings and observing life. Outside Aldgate tube station I watched people eating jellied eels and shrimps. At Mile End there was a beautiful neglected square which would have been treasured had it been in the West End.

I saw whole streets and squares being pulled down as part of a slum clearance scheme. In their places lifeless modern blocks were soon erected to house the homeless. The local authority architects and planners took pride in them as if they were monuments. There were no parks and it was difficult to get close to the river except near Tower Bridge. I walked along cobbled streets to Wapping. There were two old pubs on the river, 'The Prospect of Whitby' and 'The Town of Ramsgate'. But there was only one spot where it was possible to sit alone and admire the river. The serpentine brick walls, warehouses with cranes and overhanging bridges, and smells of spices gave the place a romantic character.

On Sundays Petticoat Lane came to life with visitors from all over the world. Stalls were erected on the pavement, selling fruits, vegetables, clothes, dresses, and souvenirs. I could hear English spoken in foreign accents. I saw Indians selling cheap handmade goods from Kashmir. The streets became crowded and the stalls overflowed to Brick Lane where there was a large antique market selling old furniture. The market started very early in the morning and buyers and sellers came from all over the South-East. These people would never have come to the East End otherwise. A large queue waited outside the famous Jewish restaurant to buy salt beef and latkas. Whitechapel Art Gallery next door remained empty. After the market closed in the afternoon the streets looked like a deserted battlefield, with litter and rubbish lying everywhere.

I walked from Aldgate East to Earls Court, looking at old squares and new buildings and visiting museums and art galleries. Sometimes I walked part of the way along the embankment enjoying the river view and then took a bus or a tube train. I was surprised to see so many West Indian bus conductors and workers on the underground. London seemed to me like a group of villages and the character of one part was different from the other.

I often stopped at an Indian vegetarian café near Tottenham Court Road tube station. A couple from Gujarat fried puris in front of the customers and served them hot with vegetables. It was a friendly place and many English people came to eat there. One day a man came up to me and said I looked like an artist. He had a small gallery in the West End and invited me to see one of his exhibitions. There I met his wife, who was the headmistress of the primary school next to the social centre where I lived. She asked me to visit the school and have lunch with her and the staff.

The school was a large Victorian building on three floors, surrounded by courtyards where children were playing. As soon as they saw me they gathered round. I asked them to take me to the headmistress. They held my hands and said, 'Sir, have you come to teach us?' I looked at their smiling faces—British, Jewish, Indian, Pakistani, Greek, Turkish. It was a lovely experience. For the first time in England I was made to feel I was wanted. I had always found it difficult to make spontaneous friendships with adults in England who did not know how to demonstrate their affection.

The headmistress showed me around the school and introduced me to her colleagues. They were mostly women and seemed devoted to the children. During the lunch hour they saw that all the children were properly fed. Then we had lunch together. The school had a Jewish kitchen and the food was very good. It was my first visit to an English school and I was very impressed by the care the children received.

In my village primary education is free but not compulsory. Parents have to buy books and writing materials, which are expensive. The children have to be dressed properly, and so the

Harijan parents cannot afford to send their children to school. About twice a week a free bowl of rice pudding is given to the children at midday. When I was a student there was no free food in the school. I carried some pressed rice and molasses and ate them for my lunch. I drew my drinking water from the school well, using a pot tied to a long rope.

The atmosphere in the school in London was exciting and I said impulsively, 'I would love to teach the children to paint and dance.'

The headmistress smiled. 'I was hoping you would say that.'

It was a month before Christmas and the children were producing a play. They wanted to open it with Indian dancing. I selected a group of children and started to train them. They had no inhibitions. As they walked towards me I could see dance in their movement. But when I asked them to repeat what they had done, they did not know what I meant. They had forgotten their natural steps. I explained to them the contrast between pause and dance, noise and silence, and their understanding was perfect. The children from Greece, Cyprus, Turkey, India, and Pakistan were the most graceful. There was not enough time to rehearse properly in the school and I asked them to come to the social centre in the evenings. The parents were happy because they lived in small flats in crowded rooms and wanted the children out of the way for a few hours. Sometimes the children did not want to leave and stayed longer and their worried parents came to find out what had happened to them. There was a mixture of love and neglect in the parents' attitude to their children.

The Christmas show opened with the Indian dance. It was held at a small theatre next to the school, which had proper stage lighting. The children played their own music which they had composed themselves using bells, triangles, and drums. The teachers helped them to make the costumes. They loved their faces being decorated and danced freely on the stage. The parents were thrilled and the evening was a great experience for the children. Those who appeared on the stage did better in their studies, the headmistress told me later. It gave them confidence.

It took six months for me to get a job in London. I had applied to the London County Council to work as a town planner. At that time the Council had an ambitious programme to expand existing towns near London. It was part of a comprehensive plan to

move people and industries from crowded London to the countryside. The towns welcomed the idea because they needed
industries. I wanted to be associated with the projects to help gain
practical experience in understanding and solving planning
problems. After a friendly interview with the establishment
officer and a senior architect, I was offered a job.

The working hours were from 8.45 a.m. to 4.51 p.m. On the
first morning I had to report at eight to attend an introduction
course. During my student days in Leeds I had lost the habit of
getting up early in the morning and I was worried I would over-
sleep. I bought myself an alarm clock from Woolworths and went
to bed early after setting the alarm for six. I could not sleep; the
clock on my table went on ticking—tick, tick, tick. The sound
was disturbing. I got up and put the clock behind some books on
the shelf. I could still hear the sound—tick, tick, tick. I put the
clock inside my suitcase but the sound was still there. Finally I put
the clock outside in the corridor and managed to sleep. To my
surprise I woke up exactly at six. From then on I have never used
an alarm clock.

In my village there were no clocks or watches. The villagers
could tell the time by looking at the sun during the day and the
sky at night. When going to school I guessed the time by looking
at the shadows and I was never late. It was only when I went to
Bombay that I started wearing a watch.

When I reported to the office I found several others who were
joining different departments. We listened to a talk about the
function of the Council and our duty to the public. We were told
that the London County Council (LCC) would become the
Greater London Council (GLC) in a few months time.

I met the planner in charge of my division. He explained the
work, which was to produce development plans for the expanding towns and give planning advice to architects designing
housing projects. My division was part of the architect's department and I was introduced to the people I was going to work
with.

The group leader was a qualified town planner but the others
were architects without any knowledge or training in town
planning. The GLC's (formerly LCC's) architect's department
had a world-wide reputation and architects from all over the
world came to work there to gain experience. They were mostly

young and brought exciting new ideas with them. But the key posts were held by English architects who had worked there for many years.

It was considered more prestigious to work for private architects and planners than for a local authority or government department. Many architects began their careers with the GLC, gained experience, and left to set up their own practices.

The GLC stood majestically on the south bank of the River Thames, looking diagonally across at the House of Commons, with Westminster Bridge in between. Walking along its long corridors it was easy to get lost. The walls were monotonous; at intervals there were notice boards displaying circulars. The whole place lacked colour and life. I wanted to go round with a pot of paint drawing large murals.

The council rooms looked over the river and were comfortably furnished. The senior officers had rooms to themselves, with chairs, tables, carpets, and secretaries, according to their rank. The room in which I worked was next to a busy road. It did not have enough daylight and when we complained an electrician came and replaced the existing bulb with a stronger one.

The GLC nevertheless gave me a sense of belonging. I looked forward to going to the office in the morning and working there. There were ten in my group: two English architects, two architects from Germany, a West Indian architect educated in London, an Argentinian architect, one surveyor, and a sixteen-year-old apprentice. My colleagues lived their own lives outside central London and in the evening I felt lonely. I returned to my tiny room and painted. It became my world where I cooked, painted, and dreamed about life. Around me was a large cosmopolitan city pulsating with activity which I observed as an outsider. Occasionally I went to pubs and cafés with my sketch pad.

When I applied for the job I had little knowledge of grades and salaries. All I wanted was to work for the GLC so as to gain experience and earn some money to pay for my return to India. To my surprise I found that although I was better qualified than the English architects in the division I was employed at the lowest grade.

The GLC had canteens for its employees, one for the general staff and the other for senior officers. In the staff canteen there was self-service, but the officers' dining room was well-furnished, with better food served by waitresses. Once I went there with a colleague of mine pretending to be senior officers. The waitress asked me for my identity card and that gave the secret away. It was unthinkable for an Indian to be working as a senior officer. My English friend had used the dining room several times before but had never been asked his rank. I knew there was something wrong with the system but felt too embarrassed to express my views to anybody.

My first job was to prepare development plans for a small town in Oxfordshire. This gave me an opportunity to travel and make a survey. The town had a population of four thousand, with a small shopping centre, a church, a hotel, several pubs, and a post office. I wanted to get the local inhabitants involved in the planning process. When I talked to them I received tremendous help and support. I was told this was the first time a planner had approached them for their views. The vicar explained the history of the town and its problems. There were no jobs for the young and families were breaking up as people moved out of the area. That gave me an insight into the problems of my own village where family sizes had increased but food production had not kept pace. As a result several people had gone to work in the towns and their families were breaking up.

One of the aims of the department was to get the town authorities and industries interested in our schemes. An exhibition was organized to display the development plans and housing projects with drawings, models, and photographs. The group leader knew I was a painter and asked me to help. The work of our division stood out in the whole exhibition as distinctive. My design teacher in Bombay always insisted on presenting schemes well. 'An attractive presentation will persuade your clients', he used to tell us.

The head of the division came up to me and expressed his appreciation. It was the first time I had had the opportunity to talk to him face to face. From then on we met from time to time and discussed planning and design ideas. When he found out my grade he was surprised and took the matter up with the establishment division. I was called to an interview and upgraded to a more senior position. Immediately afterwards the deputy head of the division said, 'Now you can climb up the bureaucratic ladder and become head of the department.' He was responsible for staff matters and thought I had gone over his head.

When I first joined I had to sign a register in the morning when I arrived and in the evening when I left. The register was taken away at nine and put back at four-thirty. Latecomers had to go to the establishment division and explain why they were not on time. Being late two or three times a month was accepted, but if this was exceeded it went on the official record. This only applied to junior officers. Senior officers were not required to sign the register and sometimes did not arrive until ten. They came and went as they pleased. So when I was promoted to my senior position I was no longer required to sign the register, which I had always found humiliating.

One morning a letter arrived unexpectedly from the President of India replying to my proposals for village development which I had sent him from Leeds. He sympathized with my ideas and had passed my letter to the Planning Commission in New Delhi.

While studying town planning I constantly thought of my village and India's problems. In Leeds I was able to look at India objectively. For me India meant villages where the majority lived, and Indian culture was essentially village culture. I realized there were solutions to poverty, suffering, and malnutrition. In India I had accepted them as an inevitable part of life. I wanted to take my village with the surrounding villages as an experiment to help the villagers to stand on their own feet. If this was successful it could be adopted as a policy for rural development throughout India.

The purpose was to improve the quality of life by providing clean drinking water and proper sanitation; co-operative systems in farming and crafts; small-scale industries such as fertilizers, farming equipment, and foodstuffs; and health and education facilities. Each village unit would have its own centre with an advice bureau, health and family planning clinic, library, community hall, and gallery for arts and crafts.

I selected my own village because I knew I would get the support of the villagers. In another part of India I would have been considered an outsider. The villagers do not readily accept new ideas imposed upon them. My village is part of a group of villages with a central market place. This group has a population of about twenty thousand and was once self-sufficient. Units of this kind exist in India in a natural way. They were never planned. They grew and developed in time as a result of people's needs.

A few weeks later I was called to an interview by the Indian High Commission in London. Two carved elephants decorate the entrance to India House in the Aldwych. An ornate circular staircase leads to the large reception rooms on the first floor. The officials have their rooms on the upper floors.

When I reported to the receptionist on the ground floor a young girl came down and escorted me to a room on the third floor. A man was sitting behind a large desk and was obviously an important official. He pointed to a chair and I sat down. He stared at me without saying anything. I became apprehensive. Then the silence was broken.

'Where are your certificates and references?' he asked.

'I was not asked to bring them.'

'How do I know you have the qualifications? The certificates are important for our records.'

He paused for a while and continued, looking serious.

'Why did you write to the President?'

I had forgotten the Indian practice of submitting certificates as proof of qualifications. When I had applied for jobs in England I had never been asked to produce certificates. Neither the School of Town Planning in Leeds nor the Greater London Council had asked for them. Suddenly I felt that my honesty was under scrutiny. I realized he was upset because I had written to the President direct. I explained why I had done this and gave him a list of people he could write to for references. I also promised to send him copies of my qualifications, but his attitude remained unfriendly.

A month later I received a telephone call from the official's secretary asking me to see him. This time I was greeted with a smile.

'You have got good references.' His opinion of me seemed to have changed. He promised to write to Delhi and I emphasized the importance of my village project.

After a few weeks I was called to see him again. I was told the Planning Commission had offered me a job for six months in their headquarters in Delhi to work as a researcher. During that period I could find a job for myself in India. There was no reference to the work I wanted to do and I refused it. I had already got a good job and if I had to work in a city I thought it was better to work in London than in Delhi, a place I had never visited. It was a long way from my village and at that time I did not know anybody there. Delhi is not a place of pilgrimage. Although it is the capital, very few Indians from the rural areas can afford to visit it. I explained my problems to the officer and he suggested I went to India to discuss my ideas personally with the officials in Delhi and Orissa.

I had been planning to return to India to see my parents whom I had not seen for five years. Every week there was a letter from my mother saying she was longing to see me and waiting anxiously for my return.

Later that year I took three weeks' leave from my office and went to India by plane. After the slums of the East End, New Delhi looked like a garden city, with tree-lined avenues and monumental government buildings. The sun was shining and the sky was blue. I felt happy.

I stayed with a member of parliament for Orissa. My bedroom was huge and the attached bathroom was bigger than my room in London. He lived in a government bungalow set in a large private garden in the centre of the city. All members of parliament are provided by the government with furnished accommodation at a nominal rent. They enjoy every facility—free first class travel in trains all over India, free plane tickets between their constituency and Delhi, and priority on air bookings. Parliament is equipped to cater for their needs, with shops, restaurants, a post office, and a travel bureau.

The Planning Commission was located in a large palatial building with wide verandahs and long corridors. I was taken to meet a senior official. His office consisted of a self-contained suite of rooms luxuriously furnished.

He listened to me attentively.

'But you have no experience in India', he commented.

I remembered my interview with the architect in London when I applied for my first job. 'You have no experience in England', he had said.

I was sent to meet a town planner in a nearby building. Talking to him and his colleagues I became aware of the jealousies among professional people towards those educated abroad. I felt I was being treated as an outsider. During our discussions I was reminded again and again: 'You don't know Indian conditions'; 'Those educated abroad think they can change India overnight, but they have no understanding of our way of life.'

All these remarks were made in the presence of a planner who had been educated in Canada. Later he told me he had come to India because he felt a sense of duty to the mother country. But life had been made difficult and he was planning to go back to Canada. He thought things might have been different had he been related to a powerful politician.

I met several people like him. They all had similar stories to tell me. They were highly-educated in different fields but had little chance because they did not have the right family connections. In India friendship is not enough; you must be related to somebody important or buy your influence with money. I had neither advantage.

The Planning Commission said they could not help me. They told me they had written to the Orissa Government and I should get in touch with them. I knew they were only transferring their responsibility. The MP I was staying with belonged to the opposition party and told me the country was being ruined by politicians and bureaucrats. I had no experience of Indian politics but I found Indian bureaucracy suffocating. Nobody wanted to make decisions.

Bureaucracy has demoralized the Indian mind. The telephone directory is a good example. It lists government departments and officers according to rank, starting from the minister downwards to the lowest officer entitled to a telephone. Both the office and home numbers are given. All government servants are entitled to housing accommodation, the higher the rank the larger and better the quarters. The allocation has no relation to the size of the family. A senior officer with a small family lives in a large house whereas a clerk with a large family lives in two rooms in crowded conditions. Ministers who are elected to serve the poor live in luxury bungalows but Old Delhi, a few miles away, is overcrowded with families sleeping on the pavement.

I took the opportunity to visit Chandigarh, the new capital of the Punjab, designed by Le Corbusier. Even he was forced to accept the Indian bureaucratic system. The town was built on the gridiron pattern, with wide roads. Government offices, the main centre of employment, were placed at one end of the city. Next to them were the large houses of the higher government officials, with spacious gardens. The houses were grouped together according to rank. No consideration was given to family size. The officers who could afford to travel by car lived near their places of work, whereas the peons, office messengers, who could not even afford to buy a bicycle, lived nearly three miles away in two-room tenements. I could not imagine how Corbusier, who professed to be a sociologist, could have agreed to the brief. The Indian architects were sceptical. They felt Corbusier was chosen because he was from the West.

In Delhi I went to eat at a well-known Indian restaurant. When I told the manager I thought the food in their London branch was better, he replied, 'Sir, people come here to eat French and Italian food, not Indian. You should have tried our continental dishes.' For me, he summed up the whole cultural situation. When I visited artists and saw their work I found most of them were imitating the West. Indians who ate continental food wanted Indian Picassos and Matisses for their living rooms as they could not afford to buy the originals. I attended a private view at the only commercial gallery in Delhi and thought it could have taken place anywhere in England.

I left Delhi disappointed and went to my village. As soon as my mother saw me she embraced me and started to cry. In sympathy all the relatives and friends cried with her. My father was recovering from a serious attack of typhoid and he cried. We all cried together. Suddenly my mother stopped crying.

'My son is hungry. He hasn't eaten anything.' She went to the kitchen to get some food for me.

The relatives sat around me in the courtyard asking me about England. They all looked so thin.

'Do you get rice in Bilat?'

'Have you see the Queen's palace?'

'How much do you earn?'

They were curious and wanted to know all about my life. In England nobody had asked me personal questions for five years and I felt uncomfortable.

The children gathered and I distributed the sweets I had brought for them. Most of them had coughs and colds and showed signs of malnutrition.

The word soon went round that I was back. People from the

Harijan settlement came to see me. They stayed outside on
the verandah. When I asked them to come into the house they
refused. My childhood friend, Kailash, was with them. He
looked old, with grey hair. He told me his father had died and he
was unemployed. He was married, with four children, and lived
with his widowed mother and his two brothers and their wives.
There were about twenty in his family and he requested me to
visit them. As we were talking the Brahmin priest arrived to bless
me and the Harijans moved to one side to let him enter the
house. He had a handful of tulashi leaves and gave me one to eat.
Then he went around distributing them to my relatives.

My mother gave him his special mat and he sat cross-legged on
the floor beside me. He said my mother was worried about me
and invited him regularly to worship the gods and say prayers for
me. Then he started talking to us about God.

'God is like a circle, empty. He has no shape, no legs, no arms,
no image. He is infinity. Within this infinity of emptiness there is
light, like the light of a glow-worm. That light is in everybody, in
me, in you, in him.'

The next day I went to the Harijan settlement. Kailash and his
family lived in two tiny rooms built of mud walls and a thatched
roof. Naked children played outside. Kailash offered me a stool
to sit on and asked his wife to give me a glass of milk. I refused
because I knew he had small children who needed the milk. But
he insisted. I realised he wanted to see if I would accept food from
him, a Harijan. He had never done this before although I had
visited the family often during my childhood. It was unthinkable
for a Harijan to offer food to someone from a high caste. I drank
the milk and could see that he was pleased.

He talked to me about the frustrations of his married life. He
was being looked after by his younger brothers and resented it.
He was the eldest and felt it was beneath his dignity to be placed
in that position.

I went with him to see his neighbours. They were all poor and
the land on which their mud huts stood belonged to high caste
villagers. Everybody suffered from malnutrition and many were
ill. Although Gandhi had named them 'Harijans' and the
government had promised to help them, they had received
nothing. When I asked Kailash what it felt like to be called
Harijan he said sometimes he wished he had not been born.

He was seven when he first realized the differences between Touchables and Untouchables. When he wanted to go in the temple he was forbidden; Harijans were not allowed to enter. He asked his parents why he could not go into the temple when other children did. It has been like that for a long time, he was told.

I asked my mother to invite Kailash for a meal but she said, 'What will the other villagers say?' I persuaded her but he refused to come inside and ate his food sitting on the verandah.

When the Brahmin priest came to see me again I asked him, 'If you believe there is God in everybody, there is also God in a Harijan.'

'Yes.'

'If there is God in him, how can he be Untouchable?'

'God has made him Untouchable.'

The villagers told me about a new road which was being built. The local politicians had wanted it to pass through a village two miles away, but the engineers preferred Nanpur. It was on the most direct route as the sole purpose of the road was to carry iron ore from the mines to the port of Paradip.

I went to the spot on the river bank where I had enjoyed many beautiful sunsets. I was horrified to see a bridge under construction, obstructing the view of the distant hills. I knew the peace and beauty of the village were in danger. But the villagers had been isolated for so long that the idea of easy travel to the town was exciting for them.

I saw haphazard development taking place in India, but no attempt was made to remove the main causes of suffering by providing irrigation, proper sanitation, and clean drinking water. The craftsmen were facing competition from industry. Nylon, synthetic fabric, stainless steel, and plastic pots had reached the village. The village weavers were not able to compete with the Indian mills and had put their looms in the loft. The only alternative for them to survive was to work as labourers. A few persevered and worked in primitive conditions.

The first competition the Indian craftsmen had faced was from the mills in Lancashire during the British Raj. But since Independence the effect of Indian industries has been ruthless. When a design created by a weaver becomes fashionable it is at once copied by the mill. I visited the stonemasons, carpenters, potters, and weavers and saw tremendous talent. But they received no appreciation or encouragement from the government. I selected a group and worked with them.

I went to Bhubaneswar to meet the Chief Minister and discuss my village development project with him. Bhubaneswar is the capital of Orissa and looks like a small replica of Delhi. It is a new town and built on the same principle as Chandigarh. The high ranking officials live in large bungalows and the peons live in two-roomed houses.

When I reported at the Chief Minister's office he was not there. I made several appointments but whenever I went to see him he had gone somewhere else, either to open a fair or address a meeting. I decided to see the Governor and made an appointment to meet him. He lived in a large palace, looked after by many servants. But he could only spare a few minutes to talk to me. He did not seem interested in my plan for village development and during our conversation he talked intermittently to another visitor.

I returned to my village disillusioned. I knew it would not be possible for me to live and work in Orissa. I could help my village and my parents more from England. My leave was coming to an end and I did not know how to tell my mother of my decision to continue to live in England. I knew she would be upset. I took her to Puri to see Lord Jagannath in his temple, hoping to find an opportunity to tell her of my decision, promising to visit her regularly.

On our way to the temple in a rickshaw she asked me to stop at a bookstall. She got down and bought a small book. She opened it and asked me to read a couple of stanzas. It read, 'There are so many beautiful islands in the world, but India is the most beautiful of them all.' I knew what she meant. If India is so beautiful, why should I live in England? She must have read my mind.

My mother never expressed her views directly; she always gave examples. When I gave her a jar of expensive honey from Fortnum & Mason, she tasted it and left the room without saying a word. A few minutes later she returned with a bottle and gave me a spoonful. It was wild honey which she had collected from the garden. It not only tasted better but had a lovely fragrance.

When the time came for me to leave the village my mother cried again and everybody around her started to cry. My tears made me choke. It started to drizzle and a friend said the sky was weeping. I went to the railway station but when the train arrived at the platform I felt I had to go back to see my mother again. My friends did not seem surprised by my decision, and my mother was delighted. I spent another week with her in the village.

My flight was from Bombay and I had to travel there via Calcutta. There I saw beggars and lepers decaying in the streets. Outside a luxury hotel a small boy stretched out his hand and said, 'Babu, ek paisa.' When I stopped to speak to him people gathered around. He was a professional beggar, I was told.

Bombay looked dirty, with piles of rubbish lying everywhere. The buildings were not maintained properly and there were families sleeping by the roadside. Had Bombay changed, or had England changed me? The slums, the pavement dwellers, and the rubbish had always been there. I had seen them during my college days but had not noticed them before.

I visited my old school. The teachers I knew had left and the gardens looked neglected. My hostel was still there but the site was considered too valuable for students and had been designated for redevelopment.

I left Bombay by British Airways, having arrived by Air-India. Throughout the journey my mother's frail figure kept appearing before me. As soon as I arrived at Heathrow I wanted to go back to my village. But there was a job and a tiny room waiting for me in London.

I sat in my room staring at the sky. There were clouds everywhere. Behind the clouds there were more clouds. I could not see light and my future seemed dark, like the grey sky. I kept seeing my mother's face. So many people suffered in my village and in India and nobody cared; many lived in squalor in the East End of London and very few cared.

I tried to paint to resolve my inner tension. The simple and direct symbols became complex, subdued colours mingled with each other to produce a feeling of melancholy. I desperately searched for hope.

When I visited the school the children gathered around me in excitement. 'Sir, where have you been?' I sensed they had missed me and realized they needed me as much as I needed them. While walking along the streets I heard their voices, 'Sir! Sir!' I looked up and saw them waving at me from the balconies. They were like flowers and gave me a sense of reality.

At the office my colleagues also gathered around me and wanted to know all about my Indian trip. I told them that my mother cried when she saw me and there was a long discussion about expressing emotions. From childhood people in the West are taught to hide their emotions. But is it more natural for a mother to cry after a long separation or to say, 'Did you have a nice journey?' I remembered meeting a principal of a girls' training college in Yorkshire. She had called me to discuss the possibility of teaching Indian dance to her students. When I explained the importance of expressing emotions through dance she showed immediate disapproval. 'Oh no, our girls are taught to control their emotions.' I was not asked to teach.

The children in the school loved to express their emotions through mime and dance, and the headmistress encouraged them. But as soon as they left at the age of eleven and went to another school they became inhibited.

There was a Turkish girl who was a natural dancer. She had a marvellous sense of timing and tremendous grace in her movement. She told me she always danced at home to Turkish music and practised belly dancing. She gave us several demonstrations. Then she left and went to the senior school. A few months later she came to see us. I was sad to see the change in her. She had put on weight and looked grown-up. The spontaneous smile on her face had gone. 'I don't like it there', she complained. 'There's no dancing or painting. They only want me to study and pass my exams. I wish I could come back.'

My work in the office gave me a sense of purpose. Living in the East End helped me understand the problems of the homeless and those living in slums. After my village the East End seemed full of squalor and decay. In spite of suffering and malnutrition the villagers are able to smile. They live in close contact with nature and that gives them a feeling of security. Although there is not enough food there is plenty of fresh air, blue sky, and sunshine and they are all free. In the East End there was an atmosphere of gloom.

My life fell into a routine. I worked during the day and returned to my room in the evening and painted. In my spare time I taught the children to paint and dance. I saw films and plays. But when I had a meal in a restaurant I thought about the villagers who did not have enough to eat. A part of me was in

India suffering with the villagers and the other part was here, struggling to find an identity.

I asked myself questions: Who am I? What am I doing here? I knew I was a part of my own tradition, an artist from a village. In the village I was the son of a Karan family, in Cuttack I was from Nanpur, in Bombay I was from Orissa, and in England I was from India. These labels were put on me from the outside, not by myself. To me, I was myself and I saw myself as an artist and a person with my roots in the village.

I had a need to express myself spontaneously, and water-colour as a medium helped me. The lotus symbol expressed love, life, and understanding. I painted the images of Lord Jagannath and improvised with related forms. In the confused space I could see inter-related spaces of light and colour. Gradually definite forms emerged. They took the shapes of the sunsets and sunrises I had experienced in my childhood and the images of the village deity. Instinctively I chose shades of red, pink, and blue.

There were personal problems which I could not discuss with anybody. In any case people had little time for the problems of others. When my friends in the office asked me, 'How are you?', I thought they were really interested to know about me. But when I started telling them about myself they did not have the time to listen. They made excuses and left.

London was a lonely place and there were times when I wanted to be with friends. I soon realized it was not possible for me to see them immediately. I was expected to discuss convenient times and dates, like seeing my doctor. It was difficult for me to guess the right time to telephone without disturbing their sleep, a meal, or a favourite television programme. I did not have a telephone in my room and the public telephones were invariably out of order; so in the end I telephoned very few friends and lived in a world of my own.

In my village people turn up at any time of the day or night and are always welcomed. Problems are discussed openly with each other and there is always someone to listen and sympathize. This helps to reduce tension and mental anxiety.

The nights frightened me. Alone with myself I was aware of the noise of the traffic. I put cotton wool in my ears but there was a noise in my head and I could not sleep. I got up and painted.

Sometimes after work at the GLC I went to the Royal College

of Art to see the architect and his wife. They were very busy people but always had time for me. They were interested in all aspects of the arts. Like me they did not see them as specialized subjects but inter-related and they encouraged me in my work.

The professor from Sussex I had met at my exhibition in Leeds was a busy man too, but I managed to see him from time to time when he was in London. Although he was a specialist in his field his vision was wide, with a unique knowledge and understanding of art, architecture, and people in their environment.

One day a friend came to see me. Looking through my paintings he said, 'You must exhibit and let others enjoy them.' After a lot of difficulty I found a gallery in the West End which liked my work. To me my paintings are a process of self-realization and I was nervous about showing them in public. But the director of the gallery was enthusiastic and a date for the opening of the exhibition was fixed.

The architect from the Royal College of Art agreed to open the exhibition and the professor wrote an introduction to the catalogue. My friends were impressed.

'How do you know such famous people?' they asked.

Until then I had not thought of them as famous but as friends with whom I could talk freely about life and art.

I invited my friends and colleagues to the private view. They were eager to give me their support. When I took an invitation card to the press officer of the GLC he volunteered to do publicity for me. It was the first time the press office had done anything like that for a member of the staff.

As the day of the opening came nearer I became more and more nervous. I was afraid not many people would turn up. But the gallery was soon crowded. It was reassuring to see familiar faces. The director of Leeds City Art Gallery had come specially to attend the opening. My professor friend from Sussex had also come to give me moral support.

The architect opened the exhibition with a short speech about my work and, raising a glass of wine, invited everybody to drink to its success. Then the guests moved around looking at my paintings.

Some had preconceived ideas about works by Indian artists. They were expecting to see paintings in traditional forms with gods and goddesses with many arms. I overheard a conversation.

'Are they sexual symbols?' I had not thought there was anything sexual in my work but when I returned to my room I could see sexual images everywhere.

There was great curiosity. I was asked what my paintings meant and whether they had any religious significance. I found myself giving lectures about my village culture and its influence on my work. But when I brought the children from the primary school to see the exhibition their response was immediate—'They're lovely!' They did not try to find a meaning.

The exhibition received support from the media. Several art critics wrote favourable reviews. It was my first London exhibition and I was pleased that it was an artistic success.

My doctor friend in Germany arranged an exhibition of my paintings in his local museum in Gladbeck. I went for the private view and stayed a week. Many people came to the opening, including the Mayor and a representative of the Indian Embassy. I was asked to make a speech. People in Germany love making speeches and listening to them. After dinner a guest is frequently asked to make a speech. I had an interpreter, an old German lady who taught English at the grammar school. She had travelled widely and learned her English in London.

The guests listened solemnly to my speech. When I ended with a few words in German they clapped loudly. The publicity was well arranged and reports appeared in the local newspapers. Each district had its own local and regional paper, well-designed and well-produced with extensive coverage of the arts. It was very different from England where there were very few local newspapers at that time and even the national papers devoted very little space to the arts.

My friend said, 'Why don't you stay and work in Germany? Why do you want to live in London?' He introduced me to an architect who offered me a job. But I knew it would be too difficult for me to start all over again with a new language and a new culture. I had decided that if I had to work outside India it would be in London. I made my excuses to my friend but I do not think he really understood why I chose to live in England when I had the opportunity of living there. Coming back to London was like returning home. The language, places, and customs were familiar. My Indian friends had similar feelings when they returned from holidays in Europe.

I wanted to show my paintings to as many people as possible and share my experiences with them. With the help of my professor friend I held an exhibition in Sussex University, which was new and did not have an arts centre. The university was set on the Sussex Downs just outside Brighton. I felt the architect had ignored the beauty of the landscape and designed boxes of exposed brick with little windows giving occasional glimpses of the countryside. Even the interiors of the rooms were in exposed brick. It was trendy, I was told.

My exhibition was arranged in a room adjoining the students' common room. When I suggested a private view to invite the press and people who might be interested in buying my paintings, I was told that artists in the past had always struggled to survive and the exhibition was meant only for the university students and staff. But my professor friend arranged a reception on his own and invited the press and a few local people. The director of the Brighton Art Gallery came and bought a painting for their collection.

At this reception I met a famous journalist and his wife. They were both interested in India and the problem of South-East Asia. Their horizon was not limited by the sea surrounding Britain. He was a thin, frail man and his wife was large and forceful. She liked young people and encouraged them in their work. They lived in London and invited me to see them there. I visited them often. When I told him about my village he said if I ever wrote a book about it he would be the first person to read it. That planted the idea in my head that some day I would like to write a book about my village. Through them I met a number of writers and intellectuals who had similar attitudes to life.

The journalist and his wife did not have any children of their own. When I arranged a dance recital at school she sometimes came to see it. The schools in inner London held dance competitions in which my school took part, giving performances of creative Indian dance. The children won several prizes but never came first, always second or third. They were disappointed because they knew they danced better than the other children. I also told them stories from Indian mythology and helped them to meditate. We enacted a play about meditation:

'Once upon a time there was a young prince called Dhruva. He meditated in the forest under a tree. The gods became anxious;

they thought he was meditating to gain their place. They sent lions, tigers, snakes, and dancing girls to break his meditation, but were not able to succeed.

'Dhruva went on meditating and Ishwara, the supreme god, was pleased. He came to Dhruva and asked him, "What is your wish?"

' "Make me a star," Dhruva replied. "I believe in truth."

'Dhruva reigned as a pious king and after death became the north star.'

The children loved the story. The part of Dhruva was played by a little English boy about five years old. His sister, about seven, was one of the dancers. They always came together to my class and were keen to learn. I explained to the boy the meaning of the story.

He sat on the floor cross-legged, closing his eyes and joining his hands together in prayer. The girls came as tigers, lions, snakes, and dancing girls and danced around him, singing, chanting, making noises, improvizing, trying to entertain and frighten. But the little boy sat quietly, his eyes closed and undisturbed. I thought he had gone into a trance and would not come back to reality. I was relieved when a girl came dressed as Ishwara and broke his meditation.

The children loved meditation and were able to understand the meaning of silence. The school building was usually vibrating with noise, so silence was important for me when I worked with them. After a while they told me, 'Sir, we didn't realize our school was so noisy.'

One Saturday afternoon a fair was organized in Chelsea by a women's association. The school was invited to take part and two teachers accompanied the children. After I had decorated the children's faces the teachers said, 'Mr Mohanti, please decorate our faces.' They had always wanted their faces to be decorated but had felt too embarrassed to ask me at school.

There was a distance between me and the children. They were not mine. I could not hold them in my arms and cuddle them. Often I felt like doing that to express my affection for them. In the village I was always surrounded by children. My brother had six and I helped my sister-in-law to bring them up. The others belonged to my friends and relatives. In a joint family it is difficult to know who the parents are because the children get equal attention from all the relatives. There are no prams and the children are always carried. The children know they are loved because they are constantly hugged, kissed, and cuddled. They run around naked and nobody expects them to behave like adults. When the mothers are busy the children are looked after by relatives. Older children often look after the younger ones.

I missed the pleasure of holding babies in my arms and the opportunity came when an English friend invited me to his house in Surrey. His youngest son was about ten months old with a round face, pink cheeks, blue eyes, and blonde hair. He was the most beautiful baby I had ever seen. When I picked him up I felt as if I was holding the whole of England in my arms. It was a marvellous feeling and it gave me a sense of security. But when I put him back into his pram he started to cry. I picked him up again; he adjusted himself to fit into my arms and stayed there. Gradually I was able to communicate with him. I think he realized that I liked him. Although he was not able to talk he could recognize me and smile. I felt like taking him to India and bringing him up in my village under the blue sky.

I noticed that he was not breast-fed. In my village the mothers like breast-feeding their children and do it quite openly. If some mothers do not have enough milk of their own the other mothers volunteer to help. Babies are given solid food when they are one year old.

He was named Anthony, after the saint. His brother and sisters were also given names of Christian saints and important figures in British history. In my village the name-giving ceremony takes place on the twenty-first day after the child's birth. Names of gods and goddesses are chosen, like Rama, Krishna, Shiva, Hari, Lakshmi, Durga, Radha, to enable people to utter the holy names every day. But now abstract names are being given like Prafulla, happy, and Asha, hope.

Anthony was bathed in a little tin tub filled with warm water. He was massaged with oil and as soon as he was put in the water he would scream and then settle down to enjoy his bath.

The babies in my village are massaged every day with a mixture of turmeric paste and castor oil and bathed in a bowl of water, warmed in the sun. The turmeric paste keeps the skin soft and protects it from heat and infection. Men and women used it regularly but now it is considered old-fashioned. Soap and scented oil have replaced them, but soap destroys the natural oil of the skin and makes it dry.

Anthony's brother and two sisters were all small and accepted me as a part of the family. I visited them regularly at weekends and often stayed overnight. I remember my first morning in the house. When I woke up I saw them opening the door to look in. Then slowly they came one by one to see what I was doing. But I felt the older ones were already inhibited. Once I put my hand on the elder boy's head to express my tenderness. My father always stroked my head to bless me. But the boy said, 'Why are you stroking me?'

'Because I like you.'

'Why do you like me?'

I did not expect that question from him. In India loving and accepting love was natural. Nobody asked questions. Here I found that you have to say, 'I love you' many times to express love and to convince the other person that you really mean it. Love is often misunderstood and people are afraid of it.

Anthony felt he had a monopoly over my attention. When he was about eighteen months old he was not able to talk properly and some relatives made adverse comments. Are words the only means of communication? I was sitting in the living room with his younger sister on my lap when Anthony came in, holding a toy in his hand. He put the toy on the table and pinched his sister's leg. She got up and left. Immediately Anthony climbed on my knee and sat there.

On another occasion he held my hand and led me to a chest of drawers. He started to jump and I knew he wanted to be held up. When I did so he opened the top drawer and took out a toy. He made gestures to be put down on the floor. I did what he wanted. He was happy and went out to play.

Another time we had gone for a walk along a narrow street with terraced houses. In the front garden of one of the houses a little girl was playing. Anthony indicated to me that he wished to be taken to her and I led him through the gate. I thought he wanted to make friends. But instead he started to pull the teddy bear from the girl's arms and she began to scream. I hastily took him away.

I often wonder if these basic emotions could have been expressed through words. They were like mimes and dances and I was fortunate to have experienced them.

One of the words Anthony first learned to speak was 'my'. Some children from the neighbouring houses had come to visit and they were playing in the living room. There were many different kinds of toys around. Anthony ran from one room to the other snatching a toy away from a little boy's hand saying 'My'. Among all the toys he was able to distinguish it as his.

The children did not learn to share. The expression 'This is mine' was used all the time. 'This is my pencil, my chair, my book, my room'. Anthony's parents bought separate toys for the children so that they would not quarrel among themselves.

In India a child learns to share with other children. In joint families, food, clothes, toys and books, and even love and affection are shared by the children.

Anthony's father referred to his wife as 'Mary, my wife', as if she was his possession, like a piece of furniture. One evening he told me triumphantly while holding his wife's hand, 'We have been married for twelve years.'

In my village people do not count how long they have been married as it is considered unlucky. Once they are married their lives are tied together for ever.

Through Anthony's parents I met a number of professional people. One couple I was introduced to did not want any children. Why should people marry and deliberately choose not to have babies, I wondered. The idea was strange to me. Anthony's father worked hard and was always busy. He had no time for himself. The mother led a busy social and cultural life and the children were mainly looked after by an au pair girl.

One day the children were going to Bristol accompanied by the au pair girl, a Scandinavian with very fair hair. I was asked to look after them in London. I met them at Waterloo and took them to Paddington by taxi. As we walked to the train people stopped on the platform to stare at us.

A woman came up to me and said, 'What lovely children. Are they yours?'

'Yes', I replied.

She looked startled and I knew exactly what was going on in her mind. But I felt as if the children were my own. I knew the sound of their voices and could recognize them from a distance. I was sad when the train left and I had to return to my room in the East End.

The building where I lived was scheduled to be pulled down and the social centre helped me to find a flat in Wapping. It was a dream come true. While living in Aldgate I often visited Wapping. I walked along the river as far as Limehouse, stopping on the way at the riverside pubs. I thought Wapping was romantic. It was an isolated community of friendly working people tightly packed into a few blocks of flats surrounded by docks and warehouses. It was like a village; everybody knew everybody.

My building was part of a group of buildings with covered balconies. They looked like stage sets. Old people stood alone on their balconies observing life in the courtyard which was used for parking cars and as a playground for the children.

An old man lived alone in a bed-sitter on my floor. He always stood on the balcony staring at the courtyard. He looked pale and his eyes were sad. One day he invited me into his flat and gave me a cup of tea. He had two sons, who were born in Wapping but moved away when they got married. He lived with his sons for a while but his daughters-in-law did not like him, so he came back to Wapping. His youngest son visited him once a week. 'He's a good lad', the old man used to say.

Underneath lived his friend John. Sometimes they went out together for a drink. John was born and brought up in Wapping. He had no family and his wife was dead. He had worked in the docks and was now retired.

Wapping was so near the centre of London yet so far from it. There was only one bus service connecting it with Aldgate and it ran infrequently. Wapping was also connected by Underground on the Whitechapel to New Cross line, but there were only two trains an hour except for the peak morning and evening periods. The lines ran under the river at Wapping and the platforms were a long way down. The old-fashioned lift was usually out of order and there was a long walk up many flights of steps. I often saw the old and the disabled and even mothers with prams struggling to climb up the stairs.

Wapping in those days had a small shopping centre with a post office, a supermarket, a tobacconist, two butchers, a baker, a fish and chip shop, a greengrocer, and a branch library. There was also a corner shop but it closed down as it could not compete with the supermarket. There seemed to be pubs in every street.

The view of the river from The Prospect of Whitby was spectacular and it was popular with tourists. The local people rarely visited it and looked on it with suspicion. Coachloads of tourists came every evening and during the summer it was impossible to get inside. It had an expensive restaurant overlooking the river, which was famous because Princess Margaret had once visited it. By contrast, The Town of Ramsgate had retained its old charm and had a regular clientele.

The shops in Wapping were more expensive than in Whitechapel. The greengrocer was disabled and was helped by two women. Their stock was limited to potatoes, carrots, and cabbages. The tobacconist only kept the *Mirror* and the *Sun*. If I wanted *The Times*, the *Guardian* or the *Telegraph* I had to order them specially. There was no variety.

I usually walked to Whitechapel to do my shopping. On the way I admired the Hawksmoor church of St George's, reconstructed after the war, giving the surrounding council estate a sense of identity. The traffic moved fast on the highway but the inside of the church was peaceful. Its empty interior provided me with an ideal place for meditation. Bushes grew on the old railway arches, and round the corner in Cable Street a young social worker was converting an old Georgian house. When by chance I met his father, a famous politician, at a garden party and told him I was living in Wapping he said his son was converting an East End slum.

The East End was so near the City of London yet had remained a slum. Children grew up in squalor and had no opportunity to experience the beauties of nature. There were no proper parks or gardens, only neglected plots of land used as rubbish dumps. But Hessel Street was a beautiful slum, with Jewish butchers and Indian and Pakistani grocers. Prices were cheap and there was an atmosphere of joy and celebration, with Indian film music playing in the background.

A Pakistani family moved into the flat opposite. They were Muslims. The husband was working for British Rail but developed tuberculosis. He had an operation and one of his lungs was removed. He had four children—three daughters and a son. They dressed in traditional clothes and he always wore an embroidered white cap. Once he invited me to his flat but I never saw his wife. His children brought me tea and snacks which his wife cooked in the kitchen. Sometimes I met the family in the street and stopped to talk to them. His wife listened and smiled; she would never talk to me. In India it is the usual practice for women not to talk to men in the street. My mother never talked directly to male relatives who came to the house. She always spoke through me.

An old lady sat alone on the ground floor of my building and observed life through her window. As soon as she saw me she hid her tiny sensitive face behind the curtain. I was told she was the oldest person in Wapping and had a large family, with many children, grandchildren, and great-grandchildren. But she lived alone.

Another old lady lived next door to her and often came out into the courtyard not knowing where she was. Her daughter quickly took her inside. Her white hair was neatly plaited and carefully arranged in a bun. When the old lady's husband died her widowed daughter moved in to look after her.

The asphalt courtyard was the meeting place for the residents. I saw people washing their cars as if they were their children. A disabled man spent hours every morning cleaning and maintaining his car. They always talked to me but I was never invited into their homes. When I invited them to my flat they made excuses.

There was no proper playground for the children, who played everywhere, breaking milk bottles and making a terrible noise. It was not safe for them to play in the courtyard. Cars came in and out at a tremendous speed. I remember how safe it was to play on the village paths when I was a child. We were not disturbed by anybody and old relatives sat nearby gossipping and keeping an eye on us. In the evenings we sat around with our grandparents, listening to traditional village tales.

The life of the family revolved round the children, who were made to feel wanted. I felt sorry for the children in Wapping whose parents were not interested in them. In the evenings I tried to teach at the local youth centre, where the windows were always broken and boarded up, but found it impossible. The older children were not interested in art and disturbed the younger children who wanted to paint and dance. There was an age restriction and the young ones were not allowed to enter the premises. They hung around outside and when they found out I was teaching the older children they wanted to learn too. But there was nowhere to take them.

While carrying paintings to my flat the children would stop me to look at them. Soon I had an audience. Sometimes their parents joined them. They all responded to my use of colour and their appreciation was genuine. The environment was so grey that looking at clean, bright colours was an exciting experience for them.

One day there was a knock on my door. When I opened it I found a young boy of about ten standing shyly. I had seen him before and he had asked me if I would help him to paint. His family was Catholic and he had several brothers and sisters. He said he wanted to give his mother a present for her birthday and wanted to buy one of my paintings. He had saved five pounds from his pocket money which he brought out and offered me. It was a touching experience. I invited him into my flat, painted a small watercolour, which he liked, and gave it to him.

When I first went to live in Wapping I felt like an outsider. But I soon got involved in its life. In early November the children stood at street corners calling out 'Penny for the Guy'; at Christmas they came to sing carols at my door. The neighbours were friendly and always ready to gossip and make jokes.

I enjoyed looking at the old buildings and warehouses. The Pierhead was picturesque with its Georgian terrace on the river front. On the opposite side of the road there was a graveyard with mature trees. A brick wall continued along a rectangular path enclosing a small playground for children. Nearby a man worked single-handed in his spare time converting an old church school into a house. A tree had started to grow on the ruined church tower, like a surrealist sculpture.

I went to Limehouse to eat Chinese food. It was like being in Hong Kong. There was a little pub on the river called The Grapes, with an intimate interior. Its tiny wooden balcony gave the visitors an opportunity to catch a glimpse of the river. A few yards away some Georgian shops had been converted into luxury homes for professional people, among them fashionable artists and politicians. On the other side of the road was a large housing estate.

On Sunday afternoons artists came from other parts of London to sketch. There was only one spot on the river open to the public. I often sat there admiring the view, the church at Rotherhithe and the warehouses rising from the river.

I enjoyed living in Wapping. I spent long hours watching the River Thames flow gently towards the sea. I saw its changing moods, not only during the day, due to high and low tides, but also during the seasons. The reflection of the pink sky on summer evenings made the river glow with warmth, and the rising mist in autumn created an air of melancholy. I saw the river in rain and snow and in brilliant sunshine. I watched the raindrops fall on the water and make patterns. I could have spent my whole life just staring at the river.

The Beatles, the pop singers, learned to play the sitar and meditate. Concerts of Indian music became a regular part of London's artistic life. The Maharishi brought instant transcendental meditation to the harassed businessman. The flower people emerged singing about peace and love. Groups of young men and women in saffron robes and saris danced in the streets of London, chanting the Hare Krishna mantra. Cheap colourful Indian dresses and silk scarves became popular. I felt India had come to England.

One day I opened the newspaper and read a report of a speech by a Conservative member of parliament called Enoch Powell. I had never heard his name before but found out later that he had been a Minister of Health in the government and had many supporters.

In the speech he gave two examples. An unnamed man had told him that he would not be satisfied until he had seen all his children settled overseas because, in fifteen or twenty years' time, the black man would have the whip hand over the white man. His second example was a letter from an unnamed woman writing about an old age pensioner in Wolverhampton. Her respectable street was turning into a ghetto for Negroes and she was being harassed and was frightened of prosecution as a racialist. The speech ended with the famous words, 'Like the Roman I seem to see the River Tiber foaming with much blood'.'

There is a vivid description of a river of blood in the Indian epic, the Mahabharata. It frightens the villagers and is often left out from public readings.

Duryodhan, the eldest of the Kaurava brothers, was returning to his camp from the battlefield where he and his brothers fought with the Pandavas, their cousins. In the battle many of his relatives were killed. The sun was setting when he reached a river, which was filled with blood. Corpses came floating and he recognised many of them. When he tried to use them to ferry himself across the river, they sank. He saw a corpse with its face downwards and desperately caught hold of it. When he reached the other side safely he wanted to know whose corpse it was. He turned it over. It was his son.

Enoch Powell's speech was deliberately intended to arouse racial hatred in the minds of the British who were afraid of these strangers, and the dockers marched to the Houses of Parliament to support him. A Jewish lady in Leeds had told me, 'It's very difficult to survive if you are different. If you have blue eyes among those with brown eyes you will be considered as evil.' I could not imagine how a man who was supposed to be a Christian could have made such a speech. What happened to the Christian belief in peace and good will?

One evening I was returning home after teaching at the youth club. Groups of young boys and girls were sitting outside. A boy of about six came running towards me and hit me with his fragile hand, shouting 'Paki'. The youngsters shouted encouragingly, 'Hit him!' The little boy came running towards me again. I stopped and talked to him.

'It is not nice to abuse people.'

But the older boys and girls shouted with one voice, 'Yaah!'

I returned to my room feeling really upset. I was giving up my evenings to help them and in return I received insults and abuse. I went on worrying about what was happening to the English people and could not sleep that night.

The Pakistani who lived opposite me told me how afraid he was to live in Wapping. 'The young boys here make my life miserable. They abuse me and throw stones at me.' His wife and children were afraid to go out. Their little boy was hit by a stone and fell down unconscious. He had reported the matter to the police but they said they could not help.

Groups of young people who had nothing to do stood at street corners near my flat looking for excitement. When they saw me they came and blocked my path. Sometimes they threw stones, shouting 'Pakis! Go back to your own country!'

At India House a group of people met each month to talk about the relationship between India and Britain. The association was called the Britain–India Forum. I was one of the founder

members. The others were artists, writers, teachers, journalists,
and professionals, both British and Indian. Each month a guest
speaker was invited to talk. An added attraction was tea and spicy
snacks provided by the Indian High Commission. English educa-
tionalists came to tell us how Indians should be educated. Now, I
thought, was the time to educate the British about understanding people from other cultures. At that meeting I told them
about my own experiences in the East End. There was no point in
just talking about ideas; it was important to go and work among
people and educate them about India.

'What a marvellous idea!' they said. 'We should all go and
work in the East End with Prafulla.'

But nobody came. I knew they were embarrassed because they
did not want to accept the fact that racial prejudice existed in
England. While discussing the problem of the blacks in America
they used to say it would never happen in England.

In my work I had to visit English country towns like Witham,
Thetford, Sudbury, and Andover, where the GLC was building
housing estates. I was disappointed. No consideration was given
to family requirements and the environment. The countryside
was totally ignored and houses with paved squares were packed
into small spaces. There was no sense of space or of nature.

'What is the point of coming to live in the country if you
cannot feel a part of nature?' I asked the architects again and
again.

'They are lucky to have a comfortable home', I was told.

I prepared a report with interviews with local people to show
how far the schemes had been successful, but I was reprimanded.
It was not my job, I was told. Two, three, four bedroomed houses
were being designed without any understanding of the needs of
the families who were going to live in them. There was no time
and it would be too expensive to incorporate people's views was
the explanation. The houses were treated like commodities—
refrigerators or washing machines. At committee meetings the
planners, architects, and administrators talked about roads,
industry, and shops.

'What about people?'

There was silence. Most of the architects felt superior and had a
'them and us' attitude. They themselves lived in old buildings,
either in West London or the suburbs, but were designing new

houses built of brick and concrete without any character for people with whom they had nothing in common. The GLC estates stood out as stereotyped patterns. The people who lived there had come from the crowded slums of London, without proper toilets and bathrooms, and accepted what was given to them.

Charlie was one of my colleagues in the group. He was born in the West Indies and trained in London. He lived in Brixton with his wife and four children. When my building was scheduled to be pulled down he invited me to stay with him. But I had begun to like the East End and wanted to live there. When I visited him I found most of his neighbours were West Indian. 'As soon as I moved in, my English neighbours moved out', he said.

Charlie used to tell me how prejudiced the GLC was. He was well-qualified and a good designer but had not yet received his promotion, although English architects who joined after him had got theirs. He doubted whether he would ever be put in charge of a group or a division.

He fell ill and was admitted to hospital. I visited him with some fruit and a couple of books. When he saw me he started to cry. 'This is the first time anyone from the GLC has come to see me', he said.

He was never invited by his English colleagues to their homes and whenever he invited them they always made polite excuses. I remembered at a Christmas party an English colleague remarking, 'Don't these West Indians show off? I think they suffer from an inferiority complex.' Charlie had brought his family. The children were neatly dressed, with clean shoes, smart frocks, and colourful hair ribbons. By contrast, the children of my English colleagues looked untidy in their casual clothes.

Another member of the group was from Argentina. He did not like the regime there and arrived in London via France and Germany. He was small, thin, and dark and spoke English with a Spanish accent. He had decided to settle in London and immediately started looking for a house. He wanted me to join him but I did not want to own property in England; I still wanted to go back to India. He was a strict vegetarian and interested in macrobiotics and compost-grown vegetables. He believed that chemicals destroyed the environment. My colleagues used to joke that he looked so pale because he did not eat any meat. At lunchtime he took me to vegetarian restaurants where we ate brown rice, brown bread and various kinds of raw vegetables, yoghurt, and molasses; there was no refined sugar.

I thought how similar the food was to what I ate in my childhood. Crops were grown using natural manures and the rice was hand-pounded. There were no refrigerators and the food was always fresh. Every villager had his patch of land where he grew spinach, chillies, and herbs. On festive occasions fresh bean sprouts, cucumber, bananas, yoghurt, and molasses were offered to the gods and then eaten by the villagers.

Jim was an Englishman, a surveyor. He was attached to our group to help us with survey matters. He was paid less than the architects and planners and realized he did not have a future in our department. Although he was young, unmarried, with no commitments, he was unwilling to leave the security of the GLC. I tried to persuade him to study town planning so that his added qualification would provide him with better opportunities. He was unhappy with his work but disliked the idea of becoming a student again. When I told him I had given up my job to become a student again he said it was different for me because I came from a different culture and was not expected to behave like an Englishman.

'I need money to buy drinks for my friends', he said.

He loved his pint of beer and spent his evenings in pubs. He was reluctant to give that up for a couple of years. But just to please me he applied for a place and was accepted. Although the GLC was giving grants and time off to certain selected members of the staff, for some reason Jim did not qualify. Fortunately his local council gave him a grant and he left. Two years later he came to see me. There was a big smile on his face. He had become a town planner and got a good job in one of the London boroughs.

A few days later he telephoned me at the office and invited me for a drink. We met at a riverside pub where he introduced me to his fiancée. They were going to be married in a week's time and invited me to the wedding.

The wedding took place in a country church in Somerset where her parents lived. She looked transformed in a white flowing dress and little girls, like angels, accompanied her. One of Jim's childhood friends was the best man and the bride's father gave the bride away. The clergyman performed the short ceremony;

the bride and bridegroom exchanged rings and took vows to look after each other till 'death us do part'. They signed the register and we all came outside for photographs.

In my village the ceremony takes many hours and is a big social event. The bride's father gives the bride away. The Brahmin priest joins the hands of the bride and bridegroom together, chanting Sanskrit verses and pouring ghi, clarified butter, on to Agni, the sacred fire, which is the witness to the union. There are no registers to sign.

In India the bridegroom, accompanied by his friends and relatives, comes to the bride's house for the ceremony. The bride and bridegroom fast for the whole day. They wear paper crowns as symbols that for one day they are king and queen. The bride's father has to give a dowry although it is forbidden by law. The bridegroom's family openly demands cash, gold, and sometimes a car, according to the earning capacity of their son. An Indian administrative officer gets the largest dowry in Orissa, followed by an engineer, doctor, or a bank official. Gold jewellery for the bride, a wrist-watch, a gold chain, and a radio for the bridegroom, and some cash for the bridegroom's father, are the minimum. Now that television has come to many parts of India it has been included in the dowry. As soon as a girl is born the parents start saving for her marriage.

After Jim's wedding a reception was held in a nearby hotel. The guests had brought presents. Jim and his wife had asked me for a painting. The others had brought all the things Jim and his wife would require for their new flat.

After the reception Jim and his wife left for their honeymoon and the guests threw paper petals at their car. In India the bride returns to the bridegroom's house where more ceremonies continue. They do not meet alone until the third and sometimes the fourth night after the wedding. The bride becomes part of the bridegroom's family. She is not only a wife but the daughter-in-law of the house and sister-in-law to her husband's brothers and sisters. The older relatives look after them and solve their initial problems. They do not have the trouble of looking for separate accommodation. When the boy is unemployed the family looks after him and his wife.

In England the boys and girls have to search for houses and flats, which are expensive. They are at the beginning of their careers and unable to meet all the expenses of running the household. Repayment of the mortgage is a heavy commitment. They both have to work and when they return home in the evening, tired, they face the problems of looking after the house and themselves. They do not want to be a burden to their parents and they do not like their mothers-in-law. Because many young people are unable to cope with life on their own, their marriages break up.

When I returned to the office everybody wanted to know about the wedding. Ian, the young apprentice, was impressed by my account, but Trevor, the English architect, was cynical.

'The honeymoon will soon be over', he said.

Ian left school at sixteen and joined the GLC. He was an only child. He lived with his parents in a semi-detached house in North London. His mother did everything for him; she even tucked him up in bed. He was shy and found it difficult to mix with the others, who treated him like a junior. He made tea and coffee for us and carried out our orders. He never complained. I tried to get him interested in further studies but he seemed to lack ambition. He said he often talked about me to his mother because I was on my own with nobody to look after me. He wanted her to invite me to their house but somehow it never happened.

Trevor behaved in a very superior way and his accent was different from the others. He lived near Regent's Park and carried out private work in his spare time. He always talked about theatre and opera to me. When he invited me to his house I realized why he felt so superior. He lived in a large house overlooking a private garden and his wife was the daughter of a man with a title; their friends were all highly-placed. I think he invited me because I was an artist and acceptable to his guests. Nobody else in the group was ever invited to his house.

I had an arrangement with the GLC to get one day off a week to devote to my painting. For that I was required to work two hours extra every day. Other architects and assistants were allowed days off to attend courses, which the GLC considered would benefit them. But they did not think my painting came into that category. I volunteered to paint murals for housing projects, using colour as a part of the environment, but the artist for murals had to be selected by the Arts Council. I was asked to see one of their officers but was not accepted because I was an Indian national. My idea of introducing colour in the environment was considered unsuitable by the GLC architects. When I saw empty brick walls on new housing estates I wanted to paint them. Only a few months later they were disfigured with graffiti.

There were only a few Indian architects working for the GLC at that time. They were mainly from Bombay and we used to meet and talk. One young architect had come on a job voucher scheme with his wife and children. They lived in one room above a restaurant in central London and were paying a high rent. It was impossible for him to manage on his salary. He had asked for promotion but was refused because his English was not considered good enough. How strange, I thought. The drawings have lives of their own and can speak; words are not essential to explain them.

The Indian architects felt they did not get promotion because of their nationality. They held meetings to discuss the best way to impress the assessment board. To help them they even invited a senior British architect in private practice who had worked in India for many years. I do not think they realized how the system worked; how the assessment went from one desk to the other, starting with the recommendation of the architect they worked for. But they all agreed that their group leaders never gave them interesting jobs to do. Unless they could prove to the assessment board that they had made a contribution to the GLC their promotion was out of the question. They resented the fact that all the interesting projects were given to the English architects, but did not have the courage to protest.

The non-British staff worked hard but were made to feel like beggars, with no right to expect justice. I found the incidents disturbing because in India it is taken for granted that the British are just, honest, and fair.

One lunchtime I was in the Royal Festival Hall when I met a young Indian I had last seen in Leeds studying engineering. As we exchanged addresses he wrote down his name as 'Peter Martin'. I was surprised.

'Isn't your name Pankaj Mukerjee?'

He laughed. 'I was Pankaj Mukerjee in Leeds, but now I am Peter Martin.'

He explained why he changed his name. He applied for many jobs but was not even called for interview. A friend advised him to use an English name. His first application as 'Peter Martin' got him an interview and the job.

Changing names to get favourable treatment is a well-known practice in India. In Goa people converted to Christianity and adopted Portuguese names. During the British Raj many Hindus changed their religion and their names to get land and jobs. The surname often reveals a person's place of origin and caste. While studying architecture in Bombay a Bengali classmate told me that his family had settled in Bihar and had taken a Bihari name to avoid discrimination.

I often met an architect working in the housing department. He was interested in transcendental meditation and Indian religion. There was a feeling of serenity about him. His wife was a fashionable publicity agent and they lived in Woking. Every evening he waited for her and they drove home together. Sometimes we had lunch or a drink in the evening.

His wife was expecting a baby and he told me the doctor had given a definite date for the child to be born. She was admitted to hospital and he anxiously waited for the telephone call. In my village nobody could tell when a child would be born but I thought English doctors had all the modern equipment to determine the time of birth. A week passed, still there was no sign of the baby, and eventually a son was born twelve days after the predicted date.

But a month later the architect died suddenly while working in the garden. He had a massive heart attack. It was a terrible shock and his wife was heartbroken. I was sad that he died so young and could never have the pleasure of holding his baby son in his arms.

He had told his wife that he wanted to be cremated. I took the afternoon off and went with several colleagues to attend the funeral service, which took place in the chapel of the crematorium. A clergyman friend of the family conducted the service. It was very short. The coffin, covered with wreaths, was placed on a raised platform. At the end of the service I watched it move slowly and disappear. His wife burst into tears but the others stood silently without expressing their emotions. Everything seemed so impersonal.

In my village when a person dies the relatives cry loudly to express their sorrow. The villagers come to see the dead for the last time and pay their respects. Immediately arrangements are made for cremation, which must take place the same day. Hindus are not buried. The body is wrapped in a grass mat and taken on a freshly-made bamboo stretcher to the cremation ground and only the near relatives are allowed to carry it. They chant 'Hare nam satya hai, Ram nam satya hai', 'God is Truth'. The funeral pyre is made with timber which includes a few pieces of sandalwood. The body is placed on the pyre and the son lights it. Everybody stays until the body is completely burned. A few pieces of bone and some ash are collected which are later thrown into a holy river such as the Ganges.

When a woman dies while her husband is alive her body is annointed with turmeric paste and washed. She is decorated like a bride, with a new sari, glass bangles, and a vermilion spot on her forehead. The old bangles are taken by the other women to wear so that they also may die before their husbands. It is considered very lucky. Music is played and flowers and cowrie shells are thrown on the path by the husband, who leads the procession to the cremation ground.

The family and the relatives remain unclean for ten days. They do not use any oil and only eat one vegetarian meal a day before sunset. The men do not shave or cut their nails or hair and no clothes are sent to the washermen. On the tenth day the barber shaves the relatives and the sons have their heads clean shaven. On the eleventh day the Brahmins are invited to a meal called 'Brahmin Bhojan', as it is believed this act enables the soul of the dead to achieve piety. For one year no auspicious ceremonies like weddings take place in the family.

Every year the death anniversaries are observed. The Brahmin priest comes to the house to perform a ceremony and the villagers are invited to a meal. We worship our ancestors, who are symbolically kept in a small mound of earth in the kitchen, the most sacred place in the house. The first cooked food of the day is offered to them before being served to the members of the family. This helps to remember the dead. In England I found they were quickly forgotten although birthday parties and wedding anniversaries are always being celebrated. In the office there seemed to be a party every week. Colleagues would bring cakes to celebrate their birthdays, promotion, or retirement. This created an atmosphere of friendliness and informality.

I was asked to advise a group of architects on the design of a

housing estate for a small town in Bedfordshire. I had prepared
the master plan. So I had to leave my group and join another.
There were only three people—the group leader, his deputy, and
an assistant. While preparing the master plan I had conceived the
idea of bringing people and nature together. I visualized the
countryside flowing into the housing area giving each person a
sense of relationship to nature. But the group leader supported
the design produced by his deputy. It was a conventional scheme
of high density houses linked by paved courtyards. My scheme
had houses surrounded by trees and open spaces containing children's play areas and pedestrian ways. The group leader and his
deputy were critical. 'What do you know about our country?
You're an Indian; you don't know how people live here.'

'The idea is not mine. I'm only using your village green
concept.'

The final layout had to be approved by the head of the division. I realized that if I presented my scheme it would be opposed
by the other two architects. So I made minor changes to it and
asked the assistant architect to submit it as his. The assistant
architect and myself worked well together and we prepared a
model.

The day of the assessment came. The atmosphere was tense.
First the scheme produced by the deputy was presented to the
head of the division. I was asked for my comments. I said that
people who chose to live in the country should be able to experience the countryside from their homes. Why should they leave
London for a high density area where there was no feeling of
living in the country? I was criticized by the other two architects
for being too romantic.

I then presented my scheme to which there was strong opposition. The head of the division had sensed the tension by this time
and did not want to take sides. I then presented the third scheme
prepared by the assistant architect and myself. I explained the
merits of the design and the head of the department approved. I
was amused because it was really my original scheme.

After that the group leader and his deputy became so hostile
that it was not possible for me to work there and I went back to
my old group.

I sat at my desk thinking about the experience. Why had the
other two architects been so antagonistic to me when our

common aim was to serve the community? Then it became clear
that the main reason was promotion. The deputy wanted his
scheme to go through so that he could be promoted to group
leader. The group leader supported him because they were
friends and had worked together for a long time. Unknowingly I
had stood in their way. I found the office politics suffocating—
one group fighting the other for recognition. To get promotion it
was necessary to please your superior officer and convince the
assessment board that you had made a positive contribution to
the GLC. As an artist I found it demoralizing.

I enjoyed my first two years with the GLC. The experience was
new and exciting and I was involved in creative work. Later on I
found that architecture and town planning were reduced to a
formula which was applied to every scheme. I spent a lot of my
time in meetings arguing about the landscape and the needs of
the people. This did not seem to matter to the others. They were
more interested in car parks, access to industry, and attractive
town centres. No consideration was given to the people who were
going to live there and their views on the kind of town they
wanted. I thought there should be public participation. I was
particularly concerned about the children, their play and safety. I
felt that the route from the home to the school should be a
playground for them, and there should be places where the
mothers could meet. But I was told, 'You are not married. What
do you know about our families?'

In my childhood I walked two miles to the village school,
admiring the birds and butterflies. There were flowering trees
and ponds with lilies. I stopped and watched the fish swimming.
When there was time I played with my friends, using a bullock
cart as a seesaw. Sometimes I read a book as I walked along. I
wanted the children in England to have similar experiences. As
I walked through the English countryside I saw that all the
elements were there to be used.

Cars seemed to be more important than people. My colleagues
thought that they should be able to drive straight into their living
rooms; cars were regarded as shopping bags and umbrellas. I
thought that cars not only brought noise and fumes but also
made families more insular. If there were properly designed
groups of garages close to homes it would give an opportunity for
families to meet. But my ideas were considered foreign.

'Prafulla, don't take the job so seriously', my group leader said. 'It's only a means to an end.'

Architects are fortunate because they are involved in drawing and designing. I felt sorry for the clerks who had to keep files and records. There was an Indian clerk in my office who always looked miserable. We used to talk to each other in Bengali. He had a degree from Calcutta University and had come to London to read for the Bar. The exams proved more difficult than he had thought and he was forced to take a clerical job to support himself in London and his wife and children in India. He studied in his spare time in the hope that one day he would qualify and return to India as a barrister.

I became more and more aware that I was in a trap. I had to be in the office from nine to six, whether I was doing any work or not. In return I received a regular monthly salary which I spent on rent, food, and clothes. What was I gaining? Half-an-hour's creative work in a week. I was now thirty, and life was passing by without any feeling of self-fulfilment.

One morning I announced in the office that I was leaving my job and going back to India. My friends were sceptical.

'People come here to work for security. You won't last a month. You'll come back.'

In many ways the GLC was a good employer. It looked after its staff so well that it often seemed like a prison. The employees had a sense of security and many did not want to leave.

A week before I left the GLC, Ian asked me to go with him to the West End to see a film and have a meal at a restaurant. It was his farewell present to me. He had never had an evening out in the West End before as his parents did not like him going anywhere on his own. We saw a James Bond film and ate at Lyons Corner House. When I suggested a visit to Soho he refused.

My colleagues gave me a farewell party and my four years with the GLC came to an end.

I felt a marvellous sense of release. I was now free to devote myself to creative work. I wanted to spend longer periods with my parents in the village and working with the craftsmen. I decided to divide my time between India and England.

I wanted to have an exhibition in Delhi. When I showed my paintings to a gallery the director said they were unique examples of Tantra. At that time there was a revival of Tantra art. Some contemporary Indian artists were turning away from Western influences and rediscovering their roots. In their case it was a conscious effort. But my paintings were a natural expression of my inner self, rooted in my village culture, in reaction to Western values. It had not occurred to me there was anything Tantric about my work.

The gallery had recently published a book on Tantra which had aroused international interest. As I discussed the concept with the director I realised that every aspect of life in my village was Tantric. Many Western experts confused Tantra with sexual symbolism and practices. But sex is only one part of Tantra and there are many other manifestations like meditation and cosmic consciousness.

Orissa was once under the strong influence of Tantra, the mystic religious practice based on the worship of Shiva and Shakti, female energy. It was believed that through the gratification of the senses, self-realization could be reached. In my childhood I had strange notions of the practitioners worshipping the Goddess Kali in the cremation ground. In Orissa there are many temples dedicated to the mother goddesses, Kali, Durga, Mangala, and Chandi. Animal sacrifices are performed to please them, though sometimes vegetables are used instead.

Shakti is the Mother Goddess. She is Kali, the Goddess of Destruction, and Durga, the Goddess of Creation and Protection. The other goddesses are their incarnations. Their worship forms an important part of village life. In the autumn festival of Dassera, images of Durga are made and worshipped. On Tuesdays women worship the Goddess Mangala to protect their husbands and children. They construct the images by digging a small mound of earth on the mud path, washing it with turmeric water and decorating it with vermilion and red hibiscus flowers. The village deity, Mahlia Buddha, is in the shape of a shiva lingam covered with vermilion but the villagers are not aware of its phallic symbolism.

During the rituals symbols are painted; red is the dominant colour. I learned to write by drawing three circles on the mud floor—Brahma, Vishnu, Maheswar; the Hindu Trinity. I drew the figures of Jagannath, Balabhadra, and Subhadra, and the lotus symbol to welcome Lakshmi at the harvest festival. The red bindu, the vermilion spot on my mother's forehead, must have been a striking visual experience as a baby. Later I saw brilliant sunsets and sunrises. All these forms and colours had unconsciously appeared in my paintings, creating a feeling of Tantra.

My exhibition was well-received. In Delhi we have an all-India artists' organization called the Lalit Kala Akademi. It is a democratic body of artists and holds seminars, conferences, and exhibitions. An international exhibition, the Triennale, is held every three years and I was invited to take part. I became a member of the Akademi and my contribution to the development of Indian art was recognized.

A few years earlier the Arts Council in London had arranged an exhibition of Indian artists. The expert in charge had included my paintings, but he went to India, became involved in folk art, and stayed on. Another expert was appointed to complete the exhibition. He rejected my paintings, saying they were not Indian and he could not relate them to the works of other Indian artists.

I could not adjust myself to the Indian art scene. I found that the majority of buyers in Delhi were foreign diplomats or tourists. The works were too expensive for Indians.

Most middle-class Indians decorate their homes with calendars or reproductions of gods and goddesses. When an artist sells his work to a foreign buyer for one thousand rupees he feels appreciated. For the foreign diplomat the amount is insignificant. In their country an original work of that size would cost ten times as much. They can easily spend that amount of money entertaining friends in restaurants. But it gives the Indian artist an inflated opinion of himself and the prices of his works go up. Indians who would like to buy paintings cannot afford them and the artists feel they are not recognized by their own people. The Indian artists are also pampered by foreign diplomats, who invite them to embassy parties. The diplomats want to demonstrate how much they appreciate Indian culture. The atmosphere in Delhi was too artificial for me. I kept thinking of the poverty in my village. I returned there to work with the craftsmen. The little money I got from selling some of my paintings was spent in helping the craftsmen and paying for the studies of a few poor students.

I was immediately involved with the lives and problems of the villagers. They came at all times of the day and night expecting help. They sat patiently for hours waiting to talk to me. Their needs were so great that I could not turn them away. Most of them did not have enough to eat and suffered from chronic illnesses caused by malnutrition and infected drinking water. Some needed immediate medical care. Using my limited resources and helped by a few doctor friends I had to assume the role of a full-time social worker, without any government help. I had no time to paint or think. I longed for the peace and isolation of my life in London where I could reflect on my experiences and express myself through creative work.

The noise of London was overwhelming. The role of silence in life has always been important to me. I wanted to create an atmosphere of peace, taking dance to the level of pure art.

A painter takes a brush and paints with colours on a piece of paper or canvas and expresses directly. But a dancer depends on musicians and costumes, which restrict self-expression. Dancing is also regarded as a series of movements with jumps and leaps accompanied by music. I wanted to give the space a feeling of movement by standing still in silence, like Buddha in meditation.

My hands have fascinated me from childhood. As I paint, write, and draw, I feel they are figures with lives of their own. I use them like dancers, improvizing patterns of movement with a sense of rhythm coming from within myself. I do not use music and aim at dancing as abstract.

I called my experiments of relating my paintings to dancing 'The Dancing Hands' and gave performances in London at the Institute of Contemporary Art and The Place. I hung my paintings on the stage in different positions and arranged coloured lighting which went from soft to bright. The lighting changed as I moved among the paintings with my dancing hands in great concentration. I wanted to create an atmosphere of contemplation and share it with the audience.

The art and dance critics of the national newspapers were invited. Performance art was completely unknown as a contemporary art form and the art critics did not come. But the dance

critics of *The Times* and the *Telegraph* came and described my
performance as original and unique. But I do not think they
understood what I was trying to convey. They still had preconceived ideas about dancing and painting as being separate
disciplines.

One evening after I had finished my dancing the audience sat
quietly in their seats, reluctant to move and afraid of breaking the
silence. I was delighted that my experiment worked. I was able to
give my audience an experience of inner silence.

I received a telegram from the gallery in Delhi saying that
Mataji, a holy woman, was arriving at Heathrow and requesting
me to meet her. It gave the date and the flight number. I was free
that day and went to meet her at the airport but there was no sign
of Mataji. I thought she had been held up by immigration and
telephoned them.

'Why is she coming to England?' I was asked. When I
explained she was on a spiritual tour they said nobody like that
was with them. I left the airport disappointed.

The next day the telephone rang around three in the afternoon. A foreign-sounding voice said that Mataji was in Hammer-
smith and wanted to see me immediately. I knew it was a
command.

An English friend had come to see me and I persuaded him to
take me there in his car. When we arrived we found an old
Victorian house in a quiet tree-lined terrace. A man with a white
beard and long hair, looking like a biblical prophet, opened the
door. He told me he was from Poland and had lived in England
for many years. I could smell incense as I entered the house. The
living room was dark, with old furniture, aspidistras, and Victorian knick-knacks on the walls. It seemed as if time had stood
still. After a few minutes he took me to meet Mataji.

An Indian woman in her forties, wearing saffron robes, was
sitting cross-legged on the floor. On a small table was resting the
statue of the goddess Durga. There were red flowers, incense, and
a burning oil lamp. The room had been transformed into a
temple of an Indian goddess.

I introduced my friend to her and sat cross-legged on the floor.
With great difficulty my English friend also squatted beside me.

Western visits give Indian holy men prestige, and Mataji had
come to England on a spiritual tour, on her way to America and

Canada where meetings had already been arranged for her. As soon as she saw my English friend she devoted all her attention to him.

'Why don't you become my manager?' she said. 'You won't have to worry about anything. I'll look after you.'

I was surprised that she spoke English so well.

My English friend said he was married with a family and politely refused.

Then she looked at me. She had large penetrating eyes and I felt she had the power to see the unseen.

'I've seen your paintings and I like them. They are Tantric. I want you to come to my meetings.'

I gave her my telephone number and we left.

A week later I received a telephone call from an Indian businessman in the East End saying that Mataji wanted to see me urgently. An hour later she arrived in a Rolls Royce accompanied by three businessmen. She had moved to the East End where she was planning to celebrate Dassera and wanted me to paint an image of the goddess Durga with ten arms and riding a lion. It was not my style but I could not refuse her. The businessmen promised to supply me with all the painting materials I might need.

The majority of Mataji's disciples were Indians from East Africa. While Enoch Powell and the National Front cried out that Britain was only for the white British, they had come here to settle; many were expelled from Uganda and held British passports.

In the late nineteenth century several thousand Indians were taken to East Africa by the British Government to build railways. The workers settled there, educated their children, and set up prosperous businesses. Most of them were Gujarati-speaking Hindus, but there were Muslims and Christians among them. They had a distinct culture of their own and did not adjust to the tribal cultures of the African people. In India tribal culture is considered inferior by the educated and the government has a policy to give the tribals modern education.

The Asians who came to settle here were educated and had some financial backing. Their arrival changed the character of Britain. They worked hard and many started shops, keeping them open late. Although they provided a valuable service their shop windows were broken by English youths and their shutters disfigured with National Front symbols and offensive slogans.

Mataji visited the homes of her disciples to give them the moral and spiritual support they needed to adjust to living in a new country. It was the time of Dassera and the Indian community wanted to celebrate the festival to worship Durga, the Goddess of Protection. Mataji was asked to organize it.

As I started working on the painting she came to supervise and discuss her ideas with me. She had seen the image of Durga in her meditation. She told me all about herself. She spent her youth in the Himalayas, wandering around in the forests. After her enlightenment she came to Delhi where she received many disciples, among them several maharajas and highly-placed politicians. She said she liked visiting me; she felt I was a friend with whom she could talk and exchange ideas. Everywhere she went in the East End she was regarded as divine by her Indian disciples.

One day she brought some eggs and gave them to me.

'Boil them for me', she said.

'Aren't you a vegetarian?' I asked.

'They're unfertilized eggs.'

I had read in books that Tantric practitioners drink wine, eat meat, and experiment with sex. But I had not met a true practitioner. While having lunch she looked straight into my eyes and said, 'Why don't you become my disciple? You won't have to do anything, only paint and obey my orders.'

I was silent.

'Think about it', she said. 'I want you to come with me to America and Canada.'

A few days later she telephoned and said, 'Stop painting Durga. It is not going to be for the Indians. She will be for the British. Durga will have four arms, standing on a lotus with a benevolent look in her eyes.'

I did not understand what she meant and so she came to see me. She drew the face of Durga in her own way, with eyes expressing compassion. She said the image would be taken to the Sussex Downs overlooking the sea. Englishwomen would sleep in tents and wear saffron suits she had been designing for them. She would stay with the image of Durga in one tent and in the tent next to her I would stay with an exhibition of my paintings. She would tell her disciples to buy them.

The meditation camp was well-organized. Luckily it did not rain and the sun was shining. Mataji said she had ordered the sky to become Indian for three days. It was a lovely sight to see the English women in saffron robes floating about the Downs and occasionally sitting down cross-legged to meditate. They were all middle-aged and wanted a different kind of weekend away from their families. When I asked one of them how she felt, she replied, 'It is marvellous to be away from my nagging husband.'

Mataji ordered everybody about and I could see her controlling my life. She had power over people. She was really shakti, the female energy. I wanted to retain my freedom as an artist and politely said I would rather stay in England and not go with her to America. She understood but lost all interest in me.

Shortly after Mataji left for America, I heard on the news that the coastal districts of Orissa were severely damaged by a cyclone. My village was in the affected area and I was worried about the safety of my parents. I tried to get definite information but the reports from Reuters were brief and the Indian High Commission did not have any information at all.

I felt helpless and booked a telephone call to a friend who lived in the nearest town to my village. When I told the operator that my parents were affected by the cyclone and I was anxious to find out whether they were safe, she promised to connect me as soon as possible. A few minutes later she rang back to say the lines from Calcutta to Orissa were out of order but she would try the next day.

The next day the lines were still out of order. I was planning to go home as soon as possible and asked the operator to find out from the Calcutta operator if the trains were running between Calcutta and Orissa and if she had any news of the floods. Calcutta is only two hundred and fifty miles from my village and many people from Orissa work there. I thought she might have heard some news.

When the London operator asked for the information she replied, 'Ask the Indian High Commission. I can't give you any news.'

I was listening to their conversation.

'I'm not asking for your defence secrets', the London operator said. 'My client is worried about his parents.'

The Calcutta operator was stubborn. 'I can't give you any news. Ask the Indian High Commission.'

'Now you know how helpful your own people are', the London operator told me.

I telephoned several friends to say I was leaving for India. One of them was a publisher. When I told him about the problems in my village he said, 'If you write a book about your village, I'll publish it.'

'Only if you commission it. Then I'll write it for you', I said jokingly.

To my surprise he said 'Yes'. The contract was signed in a couple of days and he gave me a small advance. That gave me a sense of commitment.

I had met the publisher by chance in a pub in central London. I rarely go to pubs but that evening it was warm and I was feeling thirsty. As I was drinking a glass of beer a man sitting opposite started talking to me. He said he was a publisher and interested in town planning. Later he told me he talked to me because he thought I looked lonely. We discovered we had mutual friends and exchanged addresses. Afterwards, from time to time, we met each other for drinks.

I arrived in the village a few days later and was frightened to see the extent of the damage caused by the cyclone. My parents were safe but many houses had collapsed, huge trees were uprooted, ponds and wells were polluted. The cyclone occurred a month before the harvest and the crops were ruined. People had no food, no money to rebuild their houses, and many were ill.

The magnitude of the problem was so great that I felt completely helpless. I went to see the government official whose duty it was to give aid to the cyclone-affected areas, but I was told there was nothing special about my village. I wrote to my friends in the Indian cities asking for help but they preferred to donate to the refugees from Bangladesh. It was a political issue and fashionable. But a few friends from England sent some money, which was of tremendous value in buying food, clothes, and medicines for immediate relief.

I spent several months in the village collecting material for my book. It was not possible for me to write much there because I was never left alone; so many people came to me for help. They thought that because I lived in England I had plenty of money and influence and could solve their problems instantly.

When I returned to London I shut myself in my flat and started to write. I became the village myself, its people, the trees, and the river. At night I woke up feeling frightened. I wondered how they had all managed to survive when everything was against them.

A publisher friend came to see my paintings. When I told him about the book he looked surprised. A few days later I received a note from him saying, 'I hope you are as good a writer as a painter.'

My medium of expression was through line and colour. I liked painting in water-colour because the medium was fluid and helped me to express my emotions directly and spontaneously. Colours and forms placed together created illusions of space, movement, and music. The arrangements were my own, after many years of experiment. My writing in English was limited to composing letters, reports, essays, and a few articles for art and architectural magazines in London. I had never thought I would be able to write a complete book in English.

In my writing I tried to use words as brush strokes, creating a series of word pictures like my paintings through which I could take the reader to the heart of my village. The words with their associations and definite shades of meaning worried me because English was not my mother tongue.

I used to write a couple of pages, run out of inspiration, and start to paint. I enjoyed painting; it was like talking to myself. Had I been left alone I would have gone on painting but a friend was helping me to type the manuscript and imposed a discipline on me. Every day I had to get the manuscript ready for typing, whether I was in a mood to write or not.

I completed my book and gave it to the publisher personally. It was a Friday. I think he was surprised. He said no author he knew had been able to keep to the deadline. He promised to read it over the weekend and tell me what he thought on Monday. They were two anxious days for me. It was like waiting for an examination result. He telephoned me on Monday and said he liked the book, but with reservations. He had given it to one of the best editors he knew. That worried me. I thought the editor would take a red pencil and cut my book to pieces.

Three weeks later he invited me to lunch. I was anxious to know the editor's report and feeling very nervous. When I arrived at his office there were some friends with him. He introduced me to them and said, 'Prafulla has written a beautiful book for us.' I was amazed. What has happened to this man, I thought. The other day when he telephoned he said that he liked the book but with reservations; now he says it is a beautiful book. I did not dare ask him anything.

He took me to an Italian restaurant, very select and expensive, and insisted that I should start my lunch with an artichoke. The situation was absurd, with me, writing about my Indian village, sitting in an expensive Italian restaurant in London trying to eat an artichoke. As I started, slowly and nervously taking a petal out of the artichoke and dipping it into the sauce, I thought the publisher was going to tell me about the book and what the editor had said. Instead he went on telling me about his life, how difficult it was to get a mortgage, how helpful his bank manager was, and how he enjoyed spending the weekends in the country. After lunch we walked back to his office and at last he showed me the editor's report, which I thought was rather like a school report. I was told the book would be published next year and I felt happy.

As the time for publication came nearer I was apprehensive. The words of my other publisher friend kept ringing in my ears: 'I hope you're as good a writer as a painter.' Why should anyone want to read about my village? I corrected the proofs and a date was fixed for publication.

The success of a book depends on the reputation of the publisher and the author. Nobody knew me as a writer and my publisher's was a small firm, with little scope for publicity and distribution. He did not believe in advertising his books. He said it was the duty of the newspapers and magazines to tell their readers about a good book. 'I have done my duty by discovering a good author and publishing his book. It is up to literary editors to bring it to the notice of the public.'

I learned that hundreds of books are published but very few get reviewed. In the literary pages of the newspapers I usually saw the books written by famous authors from well-known publishers reviewed first. Not starting my career as a writer I had very little knowledge of the publishing world.

My publisher took great care in producing the book. It was well-designed but I noticed a small mistake in the lettering on the jacket. That disturbed my eye. As an architect and painter I was trained to appreciate good design. When I told the publisher he said nobody would notice it. To my amazement nobody has noticed it yet.

The book was sent out to the literary editors for review. The publicity was being handled by an elegant young lady. I went to see her in her office which was the luxury living room of her apartment. It overlooked a garden and was tastefully decorated with comfortable furniture. My meeting with her had a touch of unreality. There I was, with a glass of wine in my hand, trying to tell the world about my poor village through a smart publicity agent.

An Indian village has no news value, she told me. Nor does it relate to people's lives here. It is a distant place and would appeal only to a limited group of people. How strange, I thought, were her reactions. A week before I had invited two women friends of mine to dinner. One was from India, in her thirties. She had been married to an Englishman for about ten years, but he had left her and the children and gone to live with a girl from the West Indies. The other girl was from Israel. She had studied in England but decided to make her life in the new country. After dinner I read them the chapter on women in my book. I had described a real incident in the life of a young widow who became pregnant by a married man in the village. He abandoned her and she had to have an abortion. She felt ashamed and bitter at the way she was treated by the other villagers.

The next day my Indian friend telephoned to thank me for the evening. Then she said that on the way back to their flat they discussed the life of the widow. It was so real that she felt it was about her. But her friend insisted it was about herself. I was amazed how similar the emotions of women were, irrespective of the country where they lived.

The publicity agent was a specialist and was definite about her plans. So I left the book, as my publisher put it, in her capable hands to promote and bring to the notice of the public. I knew as an artist that it was essential to tell people that you exist and go on reminding them about your existence, otherwise they soon forget.

The book was sent out to all the literary editors in Fleet Street. I was told by a journalist friend that most of the books received were discarded and sold at a cheap rate to a local bookshop. 'I haven't seen your book there yet, so it might have been sent out for review.' Slowly reviews appeared, at long intervals.

A book has a life of its own. Once it is written the author has no control over it.

I tried to arrange for the book to be published in India but no Indian publisher was interested. 'The book won't appeal to Indians and won't sell.'

I could understand their apprehension. The bookshops in India are full of Western paperbacks depicting sex, violence, and mystery. Every railway station bookstall displays them prominently. Books by Indian authors are usually kept out of sight and you have to search for them or ask the stallholder. The magazines copy the American format and concentrate on politics, films, gossip, and scandal. One magazine tried to promote literature but had to close down.

Writing the book was an exhausting experience. It was so painful I promised myself never to write again. Gradually I got over the feeling. My painting helped; it acted as a therapy. As I worked with colours and forms on large surfaces I felt free and relaxed.

I do not see the arts as separate but as interrelated. My painting, writing, dancing, and architecture complement each other. Painting and dancing help me to understand colour and movement in writing; architecture gives me a sense of discipline and an understanding of form and structure. Writing for me is like painting with words. But as an art form, painting is purer than writing.

I was returning home after spending a happy evening with friends in Chelsea. I caught the last underground train from South Kensington to Wapping, changing at Whitechapel. When the train arrived at Wapping station, apart from myself, four other passengers got off, two boys and two women. One of the women was middle-aged, but the others were all young, in their teens.

The railway line runs under the River Thames at Wapping. There was an old-fashioned lift, usually out of order, but that night it was working. I got into it together with the other four passengers. One of the boys came up to me and tried to spit in my face.

'Why don't you behave properly?' I said.

He moved away silently and the two women kept staring at me.

I came out of the station and started walking along the deserted streets. It was past midnight and the whole place was silent. The four passengers followed me, taunting, 'Indians and Pakis stink of curries.'

I took no notice of them and continued to walk. As I was about to enter my block of flats the two boys came running towards me. I could not do anything. I just stood there, frozen. The two women were shouting, 'Hit him! Hit him!' I saw a hand coming towards me.

When I woke up it was like coming out of a deep sleep. I opened my eyes and saw the buildings move round and round I wondered why I was lying in the courtyard. I tried to get up but the buildings started moving rapidly and I fell down again.

I heard the noise of a car and saw lights. I thought it was going to run me over but the car disappeared in another direction. My head hurt. I touched it and saw blood on my fingers by the faint light of the lamp-post. I suddenly realized what had happened and panicked. That gave me the strength to stand up.

I saw lights inside the flat on the ground floor and could hear people talking. I knocked on the door again and again but nobody opened it. I gave up.

I do not remember how I got into my flat. I must have done it instinctively, taken the key out of my pocket and opened the door. I wanted to telephone a friend but could not remember the number. I was worried that I had lost my memory. My throat was dry and I went to the kitchen for a glass of water. It was painful to swallow. Somehow I dialled 999 and asked for an ambulance. A few minutes later I telephoned again.

'You just telephoned me', the operator said. I could not remember doing so.

Two men arrived with the ambulance and asked me if I had been unconscious. I was shivering and trembling. They put a blanket over me and I vaguely remember what happened next. I was taken to the local hospital and left lying alone, feeling sorry for myself. There was nobody of my own, no friends or relatives, and I was a long way away from home.

A doctor examined me and asked me questions. I cannot remember what they were or how I replied. I was X-rayed and taken back to the casualty department. I was examined by two doctors and admitted to a ward. During the night at regular intervals the nurse took my blood pressure, temperature, examined my eyes, and tested my legs and hands to see if they were moving properly.

Early in the morning a tea trolley came round. I was offered a cup of tea but could not drink it. My lips and throat were swollen and painful, my head ached, and I was unable to move it.

I was again thoroughly examined by a doctor who said, 'What have they done to you? Your throat is swollen.'

The nurse persuaded me to eat, but it was difficult. She washed my face and asked me to be strong and get up and walk to the bathroom. When I tried to stand up I felt dizzy, but slowly I managed to walk. I looked at myself in the mirror. I felt like crying. My face was like a mask and I looked many years older. I controlled myself and walked back to my bed.

The patient in the next bed was an Englishman. He came and talked to me. He had been in hospital for three days after being beaten up at night by a group of youths. He suggested I telephone the police.

Around four in the afternoon a man appeared at my bedside smelling of drink.

'Why did you telephone the police?', he asked in a stern voice.

I was frightened. I thought he was the father of the boys who had attacked me and had come to take revenge.

I asked him who he was and he said, 'CID'. He took a piece of paper from his pocket and started writing. He asked me many kinds of questions—name, age, where was I born, what did I do, why was I out so late at night, was anything stolen, did I know the boys, did I know their names, had I ever invited them to my flat for drinks. I was interrogated as if I were the culprit.

'To us it's a very minor injury', he said. 'In this area people get killed.'

'So you are only interested if a man is dead?'

'Have you ever been hit before?'

'Never.'

He looked surprised. 'You have had a soft time.'

He said the police would arrest all the boys in the area and line them up so that I might identify my two attackers.

'What about my safety? Would you give me protection?'

'It's not possible', he said.

The way the police officer treated me I knew I could not go through the ordeal of appearing in court as a witness. I thought, why should other children be put into an embarrassing situation because of these two boys?

I lay on the hospital bed thinking about the incident. The youths were encouraged by the two women shouting 'Hit him! Hit him!' This would never happen in India. When men quarrel the women always try to pacify them. I thought of my mother. She was full of love for everybody and looked after the other children in the village as if they were her own.

When my friends living outside the East End heard about my attack they said it would never happen in their areas. A few years earlier when discussing racial violence in America they had said it would never happen in England.

My teeth were so loose I thought I was going to lose them. A nurse took me to the dental department in a wheel chair. She was an Australian and had lived in England for two years. While waiting for the X-ray she said, 'England is such a small island and there are so many Asians here. No wonder there is tension.' She had seen a group of Asian youths run over by a car outside White-chapel tube station. The English driver did it deliberately and the youths were badly hurt. There were many people about who simply watched and did nothing to help.

After two days I was discharged from the hospital. I had developed a fear of the East End and was frightened of living alone in my flat. When I went to see my doctor I could not stop crying. I wanted to control myself but could not. How silly, I thought, a grown-up man crying like a child.

My doctor was very concerned and gave me a prescription. I took it to the chemist but when I saw him preparing the mixture

I became suspicious. Who knows, he might put some poison in it to eliminate one more Indian from England. Then I saw an Indian assistant helping him in the dispensary and felt reassured. When I came back to my flat I took the prescribed dose and immediately became so cheerful I wanted to laugh. A few days later I went to see my doctor again and asked him the name of the medicine he had prescribed, but he said he could not remember.

At night I had dreams of people marching through the streets of London accompanied by hair-raising music. They were carrying banners. A well-known politician led the march, wearing the skulls of Asians round his neck. They stopped in Wapping outside my flat. I was dragged down and presented to the politician.

'You are a threat to our purity', he said. 'You must leave.'

'I love my friends. I want to stay', I pleaded.

He gave an order to a man standing with an axe. I was forced to kneel down and bow my head. Soon it was detached from my body. A spurt of blood became a stream and ran down to the River Thames, gradually turning it red. My parents sat beside the river, crying. In sympathy I started to cry and woke myself up.

Red is my favourite colour and while painting I choose it spontaneously. For me it symbolises life, creation, and energy. But when I painted again the colour red started to flow like blood. I thought of my village in the evening when the reflection of the setting sun made the river glow in crimson. I controlled myself in order to find peace and meditation.

I went to see my dentist. He was a young idealist but said he could not treat me; I needed specialist attention. He gave me a letter to the dental institute of a teaching hospital. I saw the consultant, a young African woman, tall, thin, and elegantly dressed. While examining me she said, 'So many people like you come here beaten up. Always the blacks. I don't know what has happened to this country.' She was anxious to save my teeth and prescribed a special treatment which would start the next day.

When I reported for my treatment I was seen by an English consultant. He examined me and said my teeth were all right and it was not necessary to have any treatment. I asked to see my original consultant but was told she was absent that day. I went to see her assistant, whom I had seen before. He was young and fresh from the dental school. I told him what the consultant had said.

'You must have the prescribed treatment, otherwise you will lose your teeth', he replied.

I went back to the consultant and told him I would prefer to wait for the other consultant. He looked displeased and reluctantly agreed to my treatment.

While treating me, the young dentist said, 'It's a good thing you persevered, otherwise you would definitely have lost your teeth.'

Fortunately the treatment was successful and I felt grateful to the consultant and her assistant for looking after me.

The attack on me was a traumatic experience. I needed the love and security of my parents and left London. On my way to Orissa I spent a few days in Delhi.

One night while I was in bed I felt I was sinking into the bottom of the earth and coming up again. I woke up frightened. I thought my brain was moving inside my head. I went to see a doctor who referred me to a specialist in the ENT department of the All-India Medical Institute. He examined me, took some X-rays, and said my inner ears were damaged. He was horrified to learn that I was kept in hospital only for a couple of days. In India a patient with a head injury was kept in hospital for observation for a minimum period of ten days. He had qualified in England in the sixties and thought the standard of care in London hospitals had deteriorated since then.

In the art gallery where I had exhibited my paintings I met a friend unexpectedly. He invited me to a literary meeting that evening which he had organized to welcome a well-known Indian poet and writer. It was being held in a smart hotel. I arrived a little late and saw my friend anxiously looking out for me. To my surprise he led me to the platform and a young girl put a garland round my neck. I was introduced to the audience as the chairman.

'We are proud to have Mr Mohanti among us. He has just arrived from London where he is respected as a famous artist and writer.'

There were other Indian artists and writers in the audience but I was treated as special. They came up to me, eager to learn about the cultural and social life of England. Some wanted my help for introductions to galleries and publishers.

They had read about the harassment of Indians in the UK and wanted to know my views. I found it easy to give an objective account of the problem but could not bear to tell them about my attack in Wapping.

I met the head of the British Council who invited me to a party at his house to welcome a touring theatre company from Britain. I was introduced as a successful writer living in London. The British High Commissioner and his wife learned I was in Delhi and wanted to meet me. 'We read your beautiful book during our holiday in Scotland', she told me while pouring the tea.

They were all so kind and appreciative that I was unable to tell them my experiences of racial violence in England. Neither could I tell my parents and friends in the village. I did not want to upset them. The love, peace, and beauty of my village helped me. I was soon involved with the life of the villagers again. They came to me with their problems expecting immediate solutions and I had no time to think about myself.

One of the craftsmen I had been working with was seriously ill with stomach ulcers. I took him to the hospital at Cuttack hoping he would be treated immediately. But the surgeon wanted money before he would admit him to the hospital. The National Health Service in England had made me forget the Indian system. In theory the hospital service in India is free. In practice, doctors working in hospitals see patients privately, on a fee-paying basis. Beds and operations are arranged on extra payment. I paid and the craftsman's life was saved.

It was the time of the State elections. Since Independence my state of Orissa had a series of unstable governments. After a few years of Congress rule, various coalition governments precariously controlled the state. Then Congress came to power but collapsed a year later when a group of members defected. President's rule was then imposed, but that year the harvest was good and it was considered the right time to hold an election.

Large images of cows and calves were prepared by the local craftsmen and displayed by the Congress Party as their symbol. Millions of posters and leaflets were distributed or pasted on walls and hoardings. The city of Cuttack was decorated with garlands of leaflets because a famous Congress politician was contesting. So much paper was being wasted, yet children in schools did not have enough to write on. In England I had complained to a friend how much paper was wasted for wrapping, toilet rolls, and napkins when children in my village could not afford to buy paper for their studies. In my childhood writing paper was so expensive that I had to use brown wrapping paper to make my notebooks.

As election day drew nearer the excitement increased. Politicians delivered speeches in the market place and made extravagant promises for the future of the area—new roads, a hospital, an irrigation project, etc. In the surrounding villages attempts were made to gain votes by distributing money and clothes—dhotis, saris, and shawls. My village usually voted for Congress because it was the only party they knew. But now other parties presented new ideas and the villagers were confused.

Election day was like a festival. The voting booth was at the school and the villagers came to vote wearing their best clothes. Since the majority could not read or write the symbols of the parties were important. The cow and calf symbol of the Congress Party was appealing and they won easily.

But the politicians who had made glowing promises were not seen again. The villagers accepted it as normal and life continued as usual. The successful politicians became important people. Those belonging to the ruling party enjoyed many privileges and the ministers were provided with furnished accommodation, staff, and chauffeur-driven cars. Only a few days before the election they were coming to the people. But now, when people tried to approach them, they found an impenetrable barrier of bureaucracts, sycophants, and hangers-on.

I enjoyed many evenings listening to my mother telling me traditional village tales. I had first heard them from my grandmother in my childhood. My mother was a good story-teller. The stories came out of her naturally as if she really believed in them, her voice changing to express different moods. She was told most of the stories by her grandmother and in this way they are passed on from generation to generation.

Story-telling is an art which depends on the story-teller's imagination and narrative power. Although the basic structure remains the same the narrator improvises the stories to make them interesting. Children gather round their grandparents in the evening to listen. They are expected to say 'hun', 'yes', from time to time to show they are appreciating the story and not falling asleep. The stories reveal the imaginative power of the villagers, describing their problems. They also express the cruelty of life and a deep insight into human character, often told through birds and animals. Some have a moral, but others are just entertaining.

The tradition of story-telling is dying out as people become educated and leave their villages to live in towns. When the old die the stories die with them. For me the stories were beautiful and timeless, to be enjoyed both by children and adults. I wanted to share my experience with my friends in England. I wrote to my publishers suggesting a companion volume to *My Village, My Life*. They welcomed the idea. I collected a number of stories in Oriya and returned to London to work on the manuscript.

At Heathrow I was detained by the immigration officer. After many questions he stamped my passport, 'Given leave to enter the UK for an indefinite period.'

When I entered my flat I had a strange feeling. There was something different about it. Net curtains were hanging on the windows and the furniture was rearranged. On the table was an ashtray with cigarette ends. Squatters had been living there in my absence. But the place was clean and my painting materials were tidy. Nothing was stolen. The neighbours had not seen anybody. I hoped the squatters would come back so that I could talk to them. But they did not return and I never found out who my mysterious visitors were. I was pleased they used my flat in my absence.

In England shelter is not a luxury but a basic necessity. A person needs protection from the cold, damp climate, apart from the dignity of having a home. In India's warm climate some people choose to sleep out of doors, but there are millions who have never had the experience of living in a house. They have lived by the roadside for generations, mainly on the pavements of the large cities. I have written a book about these 'pavement people' but so far it has not found a publisher.

I still had frequent spells of dizziness and told my doctor. He referred me to an ENT specialist who examined and confirmed the diagnosis of the specialist in India. My inner ear was fractured, causing dizziness and instability. He advised certain exercises which helped a little. It took me a long time to be able to walk properly. Whenever my dizziness returned the memories of that night in Wapping came back and I felt sad and depressed.

I tried hard to lead a normal life, painting, writing, having exhibitions, and meeting friends. Retelling the village tales in English was a challenge. I wanted to keep them as authentic as possible, preserving the rhythm of the Oriya words and expressions. Some of the stories were a play on words in verse and it needed great care to convey the simple innocent thoughts of the villagers to English readers. I enjoyed recreating the stories and illustrating them with my line drawings. I called the book, *Indian Village Tales*. Meanwhile *My Village, My Life* was translated into Norwegian, Danish, and Japanese. A paperback edition also appeared which was widely distributed in India. A bookseller in Delhi said, 'You have done a great service to India.' The literary success of both my books and the encouragement I received from my friends helped me to come to terms with the racial tension I experienced all around me in England.

I saw Wapping change. The greengrocer sold avocado pears and the newsagent *The Times*, the *Guardian* and the *Telegraph*. Wapping Pierhead was converted into luxury homes and St Katharine's dock, near Tower Bridge, was transformed into a marina, with a hotel, pubs, and shops. But groups of youths still stood menacingly at street corners passing racist remarks and throwing stones at Asians. I was afraid of walking to places in the East End which I had enjoyed before. I could not travel alone at night. I soon discovered that many of my Asian friends had similar experiences and lived in fear.

Jeevan lived in Leytonstone with his wife and two small children. They were harassed so much that they decided to go back to India. His house was in an area mainly inhabited by English families. Fascist literature was put through the letter-box and National Front signs were painted on the door. One evening when they were having dinner, stones were hurled at them. The windows were shattered and pieces of glass fell on the dining table. He telephoned the police but they were not helpful. When his wife went out to work the young boys followed her, making obscene remarks. Once her handbag was snatched away.

Jeevan worked for the Greater London Council as a housing inspector and faced discrimination at work. He did not get the promotion he deserved and while trying to help the residents of the housing estates he was insulted by the English tenants. When he went to visit their homes the usual remark was, 'We will only allow an Englishman to inspect, not a foreigner.'

He and his wife were both graduates from Calcutta University and came from educated families in Bengal, with a wide outlook on life. Although his children were born in London he did not want to bring them up in a racialist atmosphere. The money he and his wife earned was not sufficient for them to buy a house in a respectable suburb. He complained to me that England was becoming more and more racist and it would be difficult for his children to survive even if he moved to a different area. The children were still young and could adjust to India. He was very sad to leave London but felt there was no alternative.

When I came to England I did not know there was a place called the East End. But it helped me to understand life in England and played an important part in my development as an artist and writer. Coming from a poor Indian village I identified myself with the problems and suffering of people in the East End. I wanted to devote my spare time to helping them. I thought the East End was safe, with honest and friendly people. I walked everywhere freely, enjoying the river, the docks, warehouses, and old buildings. The East End provided me with the solitude and isolation essential for my creative work. But the violence around me was so frightening that I could not move out of my flat without feeling apprehensive. I knew my romance with the East End was over.

CHAPTER 6
Pimlico

Every day I had to pass the spot where I was attacked. It was difficult for me to forget the experience and I wanted to move out of Wapping.

There were constant reports in the media about racial violence and several of my friends were victims of it. I looked for places in 'safe' areas, but the rents were too expensive for me. An English friend offered me the top floor of a house in Pimlico where I could live and paint.

I had seen the film 'Passport to Pimlico' but did not know the area. The moment I moved in I liked its cosmopolitan character, with Italian and Indian shops, fish stalls, and open-air markets. Outside the Catholic church on Sunday mornings a man sold newspapers, including a wide selection from Ireland, printed in different colours.

The approach to my studio was up five flights of stairs. There were two large windows, one facing the street and the other overlooking the backyards of the neighbours' houses. A tree outside my window gave me the feeling of being in the country. Birds danced on its branches and filled the air with their songs.

I walked around Pimlico admiring its squares and wide streets. There was a feeling of affluence. The one-way traffic system reduced the noise and made it so quiet that, with the trees and the church spires, the place had the atmosphere of an English village.

The embankment stood as a barrier between the river and Pimlico. The traffic moved so fast that it was dangerous to cross. When I managed to reach the other side there was no place where I could sit quietly and enjoy the river.

Occasionally I walked over Chelsea Bridge to Battersea Park and sat on a bench watching the river. But I was aware of the constant noise of the traffic. Without wharves and warehouses it did not seem to me like the same river I had seen in Wapping. It had a different character which lacked the mystery of the East End. I found it more natural to walk to St James's Park, my favourite park in central London. While working for the GLC

I used to go there at lunchtime and stand on the bridge across the lake, enjoying the towers and domes which created an oriental look along the skyline. Behind me was Buckingham Palace.

There were several ways of getting to the park from my studio. I saw people playing cricket in Vincent Square. At midday Strutton Ground became full of office workers who stood in queues to buy fruit and vegetables, or searched for bargains at the open-air stalls. I liked the architecture of Queen Anne's Gate but the new Home Office building was totally out of scale and looked like a prison. Not far away there was a huge and ugly modern office block. It was built by the Department of the Environment to house its staff, I was told.

I saw many houses in Pimlico being converted into flats. I wanted to rescue old books and tiles which were being thrown away. The workmen ignored me at first but when I offered them a few coins to buy drinks they went out of their way to select objects from the rubble.

Some evenings, after the pubs closed, I saw a woman standing on the pavement, pleading, 'Please open the door.'

'Go away, I don't know you', a man replied from inside. Eventually he opened the door and let her in.

This happened frequently. The man and the woman ran the local off-licence. He was in his fifties and looked as if he loved food and drink. There was an expression of detachment on his face. When there were no customers in the shop he used to read *The Times*.

By contrast, she was tall and thin and her straight hair was combed back in a pony tail.

One afternoon I was painting in my studio when the doorbell rang. I looked out of the window and saw the woman from the shop.

'Have you seen my black hat?'

I thought the wind had blown her hat into the yard. I looked but could not see anything.

'I can't see any hat', I called down.

'Not hat, cat', she shouted.

I looked again but could not see any sign of a cat. A couple of hours later I heard a 'miaow'. I looked through the window and saw a black cat walking slowly and gracefully along the parapet wall. I heard the woman's voice calling, 'Penny, Penny!'

I thought of the little cat I had in my childhood. I had found a
tiny kitten sheltering from the rain under the hedges along the
village path. I took it home and nursed it. She became my companion and friend. I was delighted when she became pregnant
but she died soon after giving birth. I was so upset that I did not
want another pet and gave the kittens away.

Penny made me aware of the cats in Pimlico. I had seen many
kinds of dogs being taken for walks at night and early in the
morning. But now I saw cats everywhere. They walked from
house to house and often crouched under cars, protecting themselves from the weather. A woman a few doors away put food out
for them, but her neighbour, a man living alone, put plastic
netting along his railings to prevent them entering his basement.

An old man kept a small hardware shop. He sold everything
from sheets of glass to tiny screws, but I rarely saw any customers.
An old bicycle was always parked outside to show that the shop
was open. He had used it when he was a young man. During the
summer he sat on a chair on the pavement outside his shop
enjoying the sunshine, listening to the cricket commentary on
the radio. When I locked myself out of the house by mistake I
went to him for help. He consoled me and managed to open the
door. I offered him money but he would not accept.

'Keep it, son', he said.

He told me he lived alone in a flat in Pimlico. He had no other
interest in life apart from the shop, but felt he was getting too old
to manage it. I often saw him walking slowly, wearing baggy
trousers and an old hat, carrying a few bits of shopping. I felt sad
that he had nobody to look after him. One Christmas I invited
him to have lunch with me, but he politely refused. He said he
would rather be on his own and take things quietly.

A few months later I noticed the bicycle had gone and the shop
was empty. An estate agent had taken over the premises. I saw
him shortly afterwards in the street and was anxious to know how
he was. He told me that the shop had been worrying him and he
now felt completely free. But I was sorry that a part of old Pimlico
had gone for ever.

I saw old inhabitants moved out of their unmodernized rented
flats and the houses put up for sale at high prices.

On Saturdays Warwick Way came to life with the local people
coming out in casual clothes to do their shopping. I heard English

being spoken in sophisticated accents and recognized faces of politicians and actors I had seen on the television screen.

An old woman in a floral dress stood on the pavement selling flowers. Her face was lined by age and experience. I watched her graceful movements as she served the customers, smiling and talking to them. Sometimes I bought flowers from her. In the afternoon when she thought she had done enough, she sold the left-overs at cheap prices. I felt sorry for her. But one day I saw her being collected by a middle-aged woman in her car. When I asked her if the old lady was her mother, she replied 'Yes'.

'Aren't you lucky to have such a wonderful mother.'

'All mums are wonderful', she said.

Pimlico is mixed. It is a collection of private houses, flats, council estates, small hotels, and cheap boarding houses. Buckingham Palace is nearby and the Houses of Parliament are within easy reach. Members of the House of Lords, MPs, judges, lawyers, and journalists live side by side with window cleaners and building workers. They buy their drinks from the local off-licence but rarely talk to each other.

One day I was buying a bottle of wine when a middle-aged man asked me if I was from India. When I said 'Yes', he enquired if I knew the Maharani of Bhagalpur. Her son was a close friend of his and he had been to India several times to play polo with him. His family had long associations with India and he had a large collection of Indian miniatures. He invited me to dinner to show them to me.

He lived round the corner but gave me his card. Before his name was written 'Hon.'. I thought he was a judge, because a barrister friend, soon after being made a judge, was called His Honour. But another English friend said 'Hon.' meant 'Honourable' and he must be the son of a peer.

When I arrived at the house there were a number of other guests. His father was also there, an old man in his seventies, sitting in a large armchair in the corner of the room. As soon as I was introduced to him he said, 'It was very mean of the Government of India to take away the privy purses of the maharajas.' He loved India and often visited his friends, who were maharajas and nawabs.

Many of the guests had titles and assumed I was from a princely family. The Indian visitors they had met before in the house were always Indian aristocrats. They went out of their way to be friendly and asked if they could come and stay in my palace when they visited India. I said I was from a village and lived in a mud house, but they thought I was joking.

When I described the incident to a journalist friend planning a visit to India, she said, 'You cannot understand Britain unless you understand the class system.'

'You can only understand India if you understand the caste system', I replied. 'A Hindu is born into a caste and it cannot be changed. Money can buy class, but not caste.'

A person can buy class, if not for himself then for his children and grandchildren, by sending them to famous public schools and selected universities.

When I asked my barrister friend which class he belonged to, he said, 'Upper middle-class professional'. It was an achievement for him. He started from a working class background, never thought about class but was conscious of it all the time. His father, a skilled labourer, was determined to give his son a good education. He went to university where he mixed with the middle and upper class students. There he became aware of his working class background. But he knew he could not belong to the exclusive upper class set which was dictated by birth.

Another friend had also started from a working class background. He was a brilliant student and won a scholarship to Oxford, became a professor, and then a member of the House of Lords. Without money his talents took him from the working class to become a member of the establishment. But a prominent Harijan politician in India who has held many high positions in the government will always remain a Harijan in spite of his wealth and education.

As part of my town planning course in Leeds I studied British forms of government and social history. Leeds represented a good example of the industrial class system. The factory workers lived in back-to-back houses and the managers lived in the suburbs in semi-detached and detached houses. Some lived in cottages in the countryside. The prosperous businessmen lived in mansions but the upper classes lived in large country houses. There were a few professional people—architects, engineers, lawyers, doctors—who associated with different classes in the course of their work, but there was very little social relationship between them.

As I analysed the class system in general I tried to find out how it worked in practice. Society was broadly divided into the Royal Family, the aristocrats and the landed gentry, the middle class, and the working class. The middle class was divided into three groups—upper middle class, professional middle class, and lower middle class. The working class was divided into two groups—skilled labourers and manual workers.

In India when there were kings, the kingdom consisted of the king, the ministers, the priests, and the rest, who were divided into different castes according to their work—warriors, farmers, businessmen, carpenters, etc. The priests were the spiritual advisers and were consulted about everything.

In England I found the church playing that role to a certain extent. The priest in India was superior to the king, whereas in England the king was superior and the head of the Church of England. The tradition continues. That is why the power of the church in England has diminished but the Brahmins in India have remained powerful while the kings have gone.

The Brahmins belong to the highest caste. Although many are poor they consider themselves superior because they are the priests and only they can perform the religious ceremonies required by Hindu religion. People from the other castes accept their place in the community and hope for a better incarnation in their next life.

Inter-caste marriages are not allowed. To Brahmins, all non-Brahmins are Untouchable. If a Brahmin marries a non-Brahmin or a person belonging to a different religion, the children born of the marriage are not accepted by the Brahmins. They form their separate caste. A Christian painter friend told me that his family were converted Brahmins who still believed in the caste system. They were Hindu Brahmins by caste but Catholic by religion. Members of his family did not marry Christians converted from lower castes.

A Brahmin professor in Orissa fell in love with a Kshatriya girl and married her. They were both highly-educated but their daughter was not accepted as a Brahmin. Educated people in India do not observe the caste rules in their daily lives and have friends from other castes. But at the time of marriage, caste becomes important and the Brahmin professor could not find a Brahmin boy willing to marry his daughter.

In India it is natural to discuss a person's caste. When meeting a stranger the first question people ask is, 'Which caste do you belong to?' Nobody is offended. People are proud of their caste because it provides a service to the community. Writers acknowledge their caste in their books. Gandhi described himself as a bania, a businessman, and Nehru accepted his caste as a Brahmin.

A caste operates like a trade union, protecting its members. For religious purification hair has to be cut by a barber and clothes have to be washed by a washerman. At childbirth and death the family is ritually unclean and purification is essential. Although the Brahmins belong to the highest caste they depend on the services of the barber and the washermen for their own purification. This means that castes are inter-dependent. If one caste goes on strike the life of the community breaks down.

A family in my village was ostracized and the barbers and washermen refused to work for them. The family tried to get barbers and washermen from another village but they also refused. They belonged to the communities of the barbers and washermen of my village with caste councils and strict rules of unity. The family had no alternative but to negotiate and find a peaceful solution.

When the villagers go to towns to work they carry their caste with them. Although there are hair-cutting saloons and laundries, for rituals of purification special arrangements have to be made for a barber and a washerman to come to the house. A Brahmin is needed to perform the rituals.

A Brahmin from my village went to work in the steel factory at Rourkela. Brahmins consider it beneath their dignity to do manual work and carry out the orders of others. But for economic reasons they are now found working in many occupations. Although the salary was good, the Brahmin boy felt miserable. He had to work side by side with the lower castes on an equal basis, and he felt he had lost his identity. A colleague needed a Brahmin for religious rituals and invited him to perform the ceremony. Others heard about him and he soon found himself in demand as a priest. That not only brought him extra money but also gave him a special place in the town. The workers on the factory floor respected him as their priest.

The Hindus in Britain also have a need for Brahmins. While

eating in a restaurant in London an Indian came up to me and enquired if I was a Brahmin. He had been searching for a priest to perform his house-warming ceremony.

When I was a student at Leeds we were celebrating puja in honour of Saraswati, the Goddess of Learning, and needed a Brahmin priest. But we could not find anybody. A Brahmin student came to our rescue. We persuaded him to chant a few Sanskrit verses, offer flowers, and sprinkle water. His family was Westernized and he did not know how to worship gods and goddesses. But for us, his presence as a Brahmin was enough.

Hindus believe in the theory of karma and rebirth. They are born into a particular caste because of their deeds in a previous life. Future incarnation depends on their deeds in this life. Any change of caste or form of life takes place during many incarnations until Nirvana is reached.

The British brought the class system to India. They had their exclusive clubs with rigid social divisions—the ICS and the army at the top and the box wallah, trader, at the bottom. In between there were other officials like the police and members of the forestry service.

To maintain bureaucracy the British introduced an education system to produce babus, clerks. English was the language of administration, the courts, and higher education. This divided Indians into those who spoke English and those who could not. The British were the masters and felt superior to the Indians, the servants. But the Brahmins always felt superior to the British, whom they called 'mlechhas', the beef-eating unclean people.

When trains came to India other forms of class separation were introduced—first, second, third, and even inter. Now there are even more divisions—de luxe, air-conditioned, air-conditioned chair car. But the majority of Indians who can afford to travel can only do so in the cheapest class.

Previously the villagers walked everywhere and only the privileged went about riding horses and elephants, often being carried in palanquins like gods. The poor peasant boy was treated for one day in his life like a king. On the wedding day he came in a palanquin to take his bride away.

My friend Raju is a Brahmin and a university professor with a doctorate from a British university. He was in England recently on a research project.

'England has changed so much during the last five years', he told me. 'Everything has become expensive. I also feel the racial tension. I don't know whether it is in my mind or what I have read in the newspapers in India, but I have an unknown fear when I'm walking alone in London. The attitude of the British authorities has also changed. They don't treat us with respect. When British scholars visit our universities we go out of our way to look after them and make them feel at home.'

Raju's father was poor but everybody respected him. Raju felt superior because he was a Brahmin and a good student. At school he had two special friends. One was the son of a carpenter and the other the son of a barber. They were both bright but discontinued their studies, and he could not understand why. Looking back he realizes it was because of their caste. Their families provided them with no incentive to study and they were expected to join their fathers' occupations to supplement the income. But Raju's father encouraged him in his studies.

He joined the university as a lecturer and was awarded a fellowship to come to England for his Ph.D. He stayed for four years. When his supervisor underlined certain English expressions he had used in his writing, he was embarrassed. He was unable to ask him to explain because he was frightened of upsetting him in case he received an adverse report. It was the first time he had been criticized for his use of English and he felt inferior.

In England he felt lonely. When he returned to his room in the evening he did not know how to spend his time. For the first time in his life he felt bored. In India he was always surrounded by people. He thought English people did not want to mix with foreigners. As a result he did not make any English friends. Those he got to know were all outsiders like himself.

Fortunately, after a year Raju was able to bring his wife and two young sons to live with him. They found a modern house in a middle-class neighbourhood. His sons, seven and five, went to the local school where they were the only Indian children. One day Raju got a report from the teacher saying that his elder son was naughty and not behaving like the other children. He was surprised by the teacher's reaction. In India, a teacher would have understood the child's problems and treated him with sympathy.

His sons soon settled down at school although some of the other boys called them 'Blackies' and 'Pakis'. The elder boy was able to make English friends and they visited each other's homes. The English boys did not like curries, so his wife cooked mashed potatoes and baked beans for them. Raju's sons ate English food at school and Indian food at home.

Once he was buying food in the supermarket when his younger son pointed at the minced meat and said, 'It's very good.' He realized his son must have been eating beef at school but decided not to discuss the matter. He did not want him to feel different from the others.

When Raju went to meet his children from school he noticed that they did not participate wholeheartedly in the games in the school playground. But it was different at home. They played football with the neighbours' children and went fishing in the countryside. In this way Raju and his wife got to know several English families. But he thinks it was a superficial relationship. There was no closeness and he always felt a certain distance.

His wife felt lonely when he went to the university and the children went to school. He made arrangements for her to attend an adult education class. Then their third child was conceived. When his wife was in hospital for the delivery of the child Raju told his sons they might have a sister very soon.

'We don't like girls', the boys replied. 'They have juicy bums.'

He was shocked by the expression they had picked up at school. 'What about your mother? She's a girl. Don't you like her?'

'Oh yes, we like her. She's our mother. But we don't like other girls.'

His wife gave birth to another boy and his sons were happy. When the nurse found out the baby was his third son she commented, 'What a shame it's not a girl.' But his relatives and friends in India were delighted. They wrote letters of congratulation saying how lucky he was.

When the time came for the family to return to India the children were reluctant to leave. 'We don't want to go to that dirty place.' They had seen television programmes about the poverty in India and had begun to dislike the country.

When Raju arrived back in India with his British doctorate he felt superior to his colleagues with Indian degrees. His friends started treating him differently. They talked to him in English and served him food on china plates with knives and forks.

But soon he was aware of his economic inferiority. During his four years' absence things had changed. His classmates who had become civil servants had built themselves luxury houses with gardens and lived in style. He wondered where they got the money from because they were receiving the same salary as himself.

He lives in a small house and cannot afford to run a car. He considers education more important and sends his children to a private English-medium school where he has to pay fees. One of the boys in the school is the son of a rich industrialist. Raju's children often talk about him, how he arrives in a large chauffeur-driven car and brings expensive presents for the teachers. 'Then *I* feel inferior. I have education but no money.'

A publisher friend was organizing a book exhibition at a local school and invited me to take part. Several publishers, writers, and teachers from all over London were participating and he wanted me to read some stories from my book *Indian Village Tales*.

I sat in a classroom reading my stories, and groups of boys and girls came to listen. They were English, West Indian, and Asian, between the ages of thirteen and fifteen. Their favourite story was 'Benguli'.

'There once was a Brahmin. He was poor and grew brinjals in his garden to earn his living. Every market day he took a basketful of brinjals to sell in order to buy rice.

'While working in the garden one day he saw a glossy purple brinjal. It was so beautiful he could not bear to pick it. He decided to keep it for seeds.

'The Brahmin's wife was pregnant. She saw the brinjal and had a longing to eat it, but she was too shy to tell her husband.

'One day, when the Brahmin had gone to market, his wife picked the brinjal, baked it, and ate it with rice.

'When the Brahmin returned he found the brinjal had gone. He was very upset. "Who would steal it?" he thought. So he made a curse, "Whoever has stolen my brinjal will give birth to a frog." The Brahmin had no idea his wife had eaten the brinjal.

'Nine months passed. The Brahmin's curse came true and his wife gave birth to a frog. It was a girl. The Brahmin and his wife were distressed. The wife reproached herself. "If only I had told my husband this would not have happened."

'Although the baby was a frog, the Brahmin's wife really loved her. It was her own child and very beautiful to her. She affectionately called her "Benguli"—"Little Frog". She took great care of her baby and massaged her with oil and turmeric paste. The years passed and the frog grew up.

'There was a fair outside the village and all the children were going to it, dressed in their best clothes.

' "Mother, can I go to the fair?" Benguli asked.

'Her mother replied, "You are so small, how can you go to a crowded place? Somebody may tread on you, or a crow might attack you. Please don't go to the fair."

'But Benguli kept on asking, "Please let me go."

'Her mother gave in. She dressed her daughter up and put some money in a purse and tied it around her waist. Benguli went happily to the fair.

'On the way she saw a pond. She looked this way and that way. Nobody was in sight. She turned into a beautiful woman and came out of her frog's skin. She swam in the pond and her beautiful black hair made waves in the water.

'A Brahmin youth on his way to the fair stopped at the pond to wash his feet. When the girl saw him she hurried back into her frog's skin. The Brahmin looked again; the beautiful girl had vanished and there was a frog in her place. He could not believe his eyes. It was like magic. He followed her and asked the passers-by who the frog was. They told him she was the daughter of a Brahmin. He returned home and told his parents that he wanted to marry the frog.

'His parents did not approve, but he was obstinate. He refused to eat or drink. As he was the only son his parents wanted to please him. So his father went to the Brahmin's house with the marriage proposal.

'Benguli's mother was delighted and agreed at once. The wedding took place and Benguli came to her husband's house to live with her parents-in-law.

'The Brahmin youth was happy with his bride and had asked his mother not to be unkind to her. But the mother-in-law was resentful. She knew the villagers were laughing at her. When her son was not at home she scolded Benguli and told her she had brought shame to her household.

'One day, while the Brahmin youth was away, his mother beat Benguli and told her to leave the house. Benguli went into the garden and sulked under a bush.

'When the youth returned home and did not find his wife, he asked his mother where Benguli had gone.

'His mother said, "How do I know where frogs go?"

'He looked everywhere and at last found Benguli in the garden. "What are you doing here?" he asked her. "Please come home."

' "Your mother beat Benguli and drove her away", she replied. "Benguli is not going back to that house."

'He went and told his mother to take her back.

'Unwillingly the mother-in-law came and asked, "Benguli, please come home."

'The frog replied, "You beat Benguli with a broom and drove her out of the house. Benguli is not going back."

'The mother-in-law promised not to beat her again. When the youth pleaded with her to return Benguli said, "If you greet Benguli with a procession of musicians and the village children dance for her, Benguli will go back."

'All this was arranged and Benguli returned home, sitting on a palanquin.

'When there was nobody about in the house, Benguli turned into a beautiful woman and did all the housework. She cleaned the rooms, cooked rice, curry and vegetables, boiled the milk, drank some herself, and before anyone returned, went back into her frog's skin.

'Her parents-in-law could not understand what was happening. People gossiped about it in the village.

'Benguli used to sleep in the same room as her husband. While he slept, she turned into a woman, went out to urinate, and came back to her skin again.

'Her husband saw this happen one night and thought of a plan. Before Benguli came into his room he hid an oil lamp under a pot and pretended to snore. Benguli thought he was asleep, so she came out of her skin and went outside as usual. The youth got up suddenly and set light to the skin. In seconds it was burnt to ashes. When the woman came back and saw what had happened she said, "Why did you do that? My body is burning. How can I live?"

'The Brahmin youth replied, "I will massage you with cream. I married you, we are husband and wife. It is not right that you remain a frog. When I saw you in the pond I loved you and wanted to marry you. Let us live happily together."

'They started to talk and fell asleep in each other's arms. In the morning the mother-in-law knocked on the door to wake her son. They were fast asleep and could not hear. She was worried, so she made a hole in the roof and looked through. She was amazed to see a beautiful woman sleeping beside her son.

'When her son explained, the mother-in-law was delighted, but the whole village was astonished. The news soon spread and people came from long distances to see the woman who was once a frog.'

After the story we had a discussion. All the children agreed that the mother-in-law was cruel and made no attempt to understand her daughter-in-law. A West Indian girl said the mother-in-law did not like the daughter-in-law because she was different. She was only accepted when she became human, like everybody else. 'If it happened today, the daughter-in-law would be on television and become famous', one of the English boys said.

A young Indian teacher joined one of the groups. He told me his name was Sudhir Roy. He worked in a comprehensive school in London and invited me to meet his class. Half the children were of Asian and West Indian origin. When I told them the story I found their reaction was very similar.

I talked to the Asian children separately. Many of them said they did not like living in England. People picked on them because of their colour. A few had English and West Indian friends and said they were happy. They all lived in joint families and liked their brothers and sisters, obeyed their parents, and respected their elders. The girls seemed content for their marriages to be arranged by their parents. All of them wanted good jobs, comfortable homes, and cars.

Afterwards Sudhir told me about himself. He came to England in 1968 with his mother and two younger brothers to join his father who was working in Yorkshire. He had a degree in English Literature and wanted to take his MA at a British university. But his Indian degree was not recognized and he had to start all over again as an undergraduate at one of the new universities.

During his first week at university he was shocked when the medical officer said that every year a large number of women students became pregnant. Some had to have abortions but contraceptives and advice were readily available.

He was the only Indian student studying English Literature and his colleagues wondered if he would be able to understand the language of Dickens, Arnold, and Mill, as they found it difficult. They were surprised to hear that Indian students of English literature were more familiar with Victorian English than themselves.

Friends in India were impressed that he was attending lectures by scholars whose names were well-known to them. But he found that even the most famous did not live up to the image he had formed of them in India.

In his final year he became worried about his future. His English friends got jobs with the BBC, the banks, and other large commercial organizations. When he was interviewed for a trainee course in financial management the interviewing officer explained to him that white workers would not like to work under a coloured officer.

His parents were delighted when he was accepted as a graduate entrant to the civil service in London. They considered it prestigious. He started off doing the basic clerical jobs. 'We don't mean to insult your intelligence', he was told, 'but you will have to prove yourself and go on to better things in due course.' He worked in the true tradition of a hard-working obedient Indian servant.

There were a number of Indian and Pakistani workers in clerical grades. They told him he should consider himself lucky and not aspire to higher positions as they were not for Indians. He did not believe them at first, but as the years went by he saw white officers of his rank, who came after him, promoted to positions of responsibility while he was passed over. When he raised the matter at annual inspection time he was told he did not have the required experience. It became apparent to him that he could not expect justice and fair play in the civil service. There were two nations and he belonged to the wrong one.

He decided to change his job to teaching, in the belief that

education departments were enlightened, without discrimination. During his post-graduate teaching course he visited schools
in south London. When he asked the English children how they
spent their spare time, a twelve-year-old boy told him that he
went around with his mates throwing bottles at Pakis and hurling
stones through their windows. They also tied fireworks to the tails
of cats and dogs and watched the 'fun'.

When he went for interviews headmasters told him Asian children preferred to be taught by English teachers. Finally, after
many applications and very few interviews, he got a job teaching
English in a large comprehensive school at Scale 1. After eight
years he is still on the same scale although English teachers his
junior and less qualified than him have been promoted.

During his first term an English girl said, 'You are an Indian.
Why don't you go back to your own country?' Her West Indian
companion joined in, 'My dad says "How can an Indian teach
English?" ' He explained to them that he had a degree in English
Literature from an English university and they would have to get
used to his accent and his brown face.

A few weeks later the headmaster came to him one morning
and apologized for the slogan on the school wall. He did not
know what the headmaster was talking about but when he went
to see he found, in large black print, the words 'Paki Roy must
die'. He laughed, but a feeling of uneasy fear came over him.

The world of education was not as enlightened as he had
believed it to be. The same subtle practices of discrimination exist
in schools as in the civil service.

I enjoyed going to the Army & Navy department store where
customers were treated with respect. Some afternoons, when it
did not rain and I needed a change from my painting and wanted
to be with people, I walked to St James's Park. On my way back I
stopped at the department store to have a cup of tea and observe
life. I saw many old women sitting alone, drinking their afternoon tea and eating scones and jam. The restaurant had a peaceful atmosphere. I wrote my letters, made notes, and sketched.
The restaurant closed at five. Once I arrived about ten minutes
before closing time and noticed that most of the staff were West
Indian. The counters had already been cleared but a waitress

grudgingly served me. When I asked for a spoon she said, 'If you come late you will have to use your fingers.'

I sat down at a table and an English waitress brought me a spoon. 'What did she say to you?'

'Nothing.'

'She was rude to you, wasn't she? They can get away with anything. If we treated the customers the way they do, we would get the sack. Why don't you complain to the management?'

A few days later I was at the Commission for Racial Equality, not far away from the store. I had gone there to collect some materials for an article I was writing. The librarian made arrangements for the papers to be copied and asked me to go to a particular room. When I got there I found two West Indians talking to each other. I asked them about copying facilities and they said it was in a room two doors down the corridor. I went there but the door was locked, so I came back for help. One of the men was leaving and I met him in the corridor.

'The door is locked', I said.

'It's the other door.'

'I didn't see any other door.'

'Jesus, are you blind?' he shouted.

'Why are you shouting?'

'Fuck off, you Indian nit', he said, and left.

During the summer of 1976 Londoners had no need to go on expensive package holidays for their suntans. There was continuous sunshine for three months. Office workers abandoned their formal suits and appeared in open-neck shirts. The streets looked colourful, with the women in thin cotton dresses and children with ice cream in their hands. I saw people sitting on their balconies sunbathing and drinking chilled wines. The pubs ran out of ice and, sometimes, beer. West End theatres suffered. The few with air conditioning advertised the facility prominently; the play became a secondary attraction. The grass in the London parks turned yellow and withered completely; the ground cracked. The reservoirs became empty and restrictions were imposed on the use of water. The sale of fans went up. Many were imported from India.

The enthusiasm did not last long. The sun was too strong and soon people started complaining. Prayers were offered in the churches for rain. Hindu priests chanted mantras to help their English friends. The mantras had not worked in India where droughts occur practically every year.

Six hundred years before Christ, Orissa was hit by a severe drought. The holy men chanted mantras together, pouring ghi on to a fire to attract the rain, but nothing happened. The king was worried and consulted his ministers. They told him that the king of a neighbouring state had a white elephant which caused the rain to fall. A deputation of priests was sent to the king and the elephant was brought. Still there was no rain.

But as soon as a minister for drought was appointed by the British Government it started to rain in England. The smell of wet earth reminded me of the first rain of the monsoon. The parks soon turned green again. The prolonged sunshine had made people friendly and happy, with smiling faces, exchanging stories of how they coped with the heat. With the change in the weather the streets and parks became deserted. It was cold at night and I had to slide under blankets to keep myself warm. The sky was grey, but I did not see anybody praying for the return of the sun.

In India, people were praying for the State of Emergency to end. The opposition leaders had organized protests against the government all over India under the inspiration of an old and frail socialist leader, Jayaprakash Narayan, and Mrs Gandhi had put them all in jail. The Emergency gave absolute power to Mrs Gandhi and this was exploited by her supporters for their own benefit. There was a strict press censorship and nobody knew what was happening. Rumours circulated: people disappeared, the old politicians were harassed, young men were castrated.

I was on my annual visit to India at the time. When I went to see a friend I was told he had been arrested the previous night. A very old politician, once a Congress minister in Orissa, was put in jail because he no longer supported the state government and was considered a threat to the Chief Minister.

In the cities many lived in fear of being arrested. There was an atmosphere of suspicion and terror. Friends would only talk to me behind closed doors. While going through Cuttack one day I saw a man searching for food in a pile of rotting vegetables and fruit. He had wrapped himself in a cloak made of torn pieces of cloth. As I went to talk to him he looked frightened and moved

away. I felt sorry to disturb him and wondered why he was so
afraid. I went nearer. Again he moved away.

'What's the matter?' I asked him.

'I'm frightened.'

'Why?'

'You are police. You will drive me out of the city.'

When I told him I was not a policeman he relaxed and said,
'I'm very hungry.'

I took him to a tea stall and bought him some bread and
vegetables. While eating he said that he had lived in the city for
many years, under trees, on pavements, on people's verandahs.
In the morning and evening he went out in search of food;
sometimes he begged. He was from a village but had lost everything in the floods.

That evening a friend of mine was going to Calcutta by train
and I went to the station to see him off. On the platform I saw two
policemen guarding a group of people. There were men, women,
and small children. The policemen had lathis in their hands and
were forcing the people to enter a compartment in the train. They
were crying and screaming for help. I was shocked to find the
man I had seen in the morning among them. As the police
pushed the people through one door they tried to escape through
the other. But a policeman stood there with his lathi and drove
them back into the compartment. They had their small bundles
and aluminium pots with them and there were signs of terror on
their faces. Spectators gathered on the platform to watch what
was happening. Some of them laughed, thinking it was funny.
But the poor people who had lived in the city for many years
could not understand why they were being driven out. The road-
sides, the pavements, were their homes.

The train left on time. It was, according to some Indians, a
'plus point' of the Emergency.

I stayed in India for several months. I painted, held exhibitions
of my paintings in Delhi and Calcutta, attended international
seminars on art and literature. But I felt apprehensive wherever I
went. For the first time I was frightened in India.

Although the villagers did not really know what was happening, they disapproved of old politicians, women, and young
people being put in jail. They felt as if their own families were
being ill-treated. News travelled by word of mouth and was more

effective than the printed newspaper; the majority cannot read or write. There is a saying in Orissa, 'The sound of a drum can reach a mile, but the human voice can travel hundreds of miles.'

Thousands of people were sterilized in India, but no attempt was made to provide the villagers with clean drinking water. Many of the illnesses in my village are caused by bad sanitation and polluted drinking water.

Working with the village craftsmen gave me satisfaction but their problems overwhelmed me. A Harijan came to see me with his son, a boy of eight who had suddenly lost his speech. I promised to take him to the hospital at Cuttack, thirty miles away.

The next morning we went there by bus and reported at the out-patients' department. The boy was first seen by a specialist in general medicine who referred him to a psychiatrist. When we got to his clinic I saw a group of young doctors gossipping. Nobody took any notice of us. After some time the consultant arrived and looked displeased. Reluctantly he attended to the boy, asking him questions to which he could not reply. The doctor looked at his colleagues and laughed cynically.

'What is there to laugh about?' I asked.

'If you behave like that I will certify you and you will be kept in hospital', he threatened me.

I realised that any protest against injustice during the Emergency was dangerous. You could end up either in jail or a psychiatric ward. MISA, the Maintenance of Internal Security Act, and the suspension of habeas corpus had completely destroyed the freedom of the individual.

The Emergency looked like continuing for ever, in spite of adverse comments in the international press. Unexpectedly and to everybody's amazement, Mrs Gandhi called an election and all the political prisoners were released in January 1977. Her political moves had always proved right. My Indian friends said, 'Of course she'll win, otherwise why should she call an election? The towns and cities may vote against her but the villages will definitely vote for Congress.'

Mrs Gandhi's victory seemed certain. With only five weeks to prepare for nominations and three weeks to campaign for election, there seemed little hope for the opposition parties. They were divided into several groups quarrelling with each other, but Jayaprakash Narayan miraculously brought them together to form the new Janata Party, People's Party, united in their opposition to Mrs Gandhi.

The timing of the election was perfect. It was soon after a good harvest. The countryside looked fresh and green. The mango trees were full of blossom. The mud walls of the thatched houses were decorated with rice paste to welcome Lakshmi, the Goddess of Wealth. There were posters, banners everywhere, even pasted on the trunks of trees.

I asked an old Harijan, 'Will you vote?'

'Of course, it's my birthright', he replied.

Rights mattered. The rights of the individual became the main issue in the election campaign. The Janata workers, mainly student volunteers, went from home to home explaining to people how Mrs Gandhi had murdered democracy.

'For a stable government vote for Congress', chanted the Congress workers. 'There is no unity among Janata and they won't last long as a party.'

'The Janata Party is right wing and will not look after the minority', shouted the Communists. 'Congress favours the bourgeoisie. Whatever you do, don't sell your votes', they warned the Harijans.

As election day came nearer the atmosphere in the village grew tense. Market days were exciting. Political workers came with banners, posters, leaflets, and loudspeakers. The noise was overwhelming but the villagers went on buying and selling, completely undisturbed.

An eminent politician came to address a Janata Party meeting. After many months of silence during the Emergency this was the first time the villagers had an opportunity to listen to opposition views. People came in large numbers from the surrounding villages. The speaker had a natural skill for communicating with the villagers and was popular.

He accused Mrs Gandhi of dictatorship. 'Those who brought freedom to this country from British rule were put in jail. They were called traitors because they did not agree with Mrs Gandhi. The Congress President said "India is Indira, and Indira is India." India has rivers, lakes, mountains, streams, and paddy fields. Has Mrs Gandhi got all that? If two palm trees fell down, can we say that Mrs Gandhi's two teeth fell out? What would happen in a school if a child is asked to draw a map of India and he draws a figure of Mrs Gandhi? If you don't vote for Janata this will be the last election in Indian history. We'll spend the rest of our lives in jail.'

People listened silently and clapped when they liked what he said.

Only thirty per cent of the villagers could read or write, and so party symbols were important. The Congress symbol of a cow and a calf was familiar, but the Janata symbol was new. It showed a farmer carrying a plough within a wheel. Janata workers took advantage of this and confronted the villagers. 'If you are a man, you'll vote for a man. If you're a beast, you'll vote for a beast.' They went from house to house with dummy ballot papers, explaining to men and women how to vote. 'Have a change, try us for five years', they pleaded. They were local boys and were able to get into the houses.

One week before the election the price of mustard oil, the only oil used for cooking, doubled in price. This gave Janata workers another opportunity to attack Congress. 'You can only afford to use it as medicine', they told the villagers.

It was generally believed that Congress bought votes. The young volunteers who had been collecting money from the villagers sang, 'We say "Give a note, give a vote"; Congress says, "Take a note, give a vote".'

Election Day was sunny with blue skies. The booth was open in the village primary school and the atmosphere was that of a festival. Men and women in bright clothes waited outside to vote. There was a great sense of participation. Several stalls sold snacks, sweets and tea, and toys for the children.

Around three in the afternoon the polling officer came out of the booth to get a breath of fresh air. He looked tired but pleased.

'What do you think of the polling?' I asked.

'It will be a sure victory for democracy', he replied.

But throughout the campaign the villagers had been cautious in saying who they were going to vote for. 'We'll vote wherever our hands move spontaneously, and the lucky one will be elected.' Many were sceptical. 'It doesn't matter who we vote for, Congress will win anyway.'

Yet people danced with joy when the election results were announced. They had voted for a change and the Janata candidate had won with a huge majority.

When I went back to the village a year later nothing had

changed. The politician whose speech had impressed me had
become a minister in the state government. I went to see him in
his comfortable bungalow in Bhubaneswar, the state capital, to
convey the grievances of the villagers. My appointment was at
nine in the morning. When I arrived he was in his living room,
surrounded by people who were throwing requests at him from
all corners—jobs, transfers, action against corrupt officials, etc.
As soon as the minister noticed me he asked me to wait.

At ten-thirty he said, 'You can see how chaotic it is here. Come
to my room at the Secretariat at eleven-thirty.' I got there on time
but the minister had not arrived. I waited until two in the afternoon but still there was no sign of him. His secretary told me he
was due to leave that afternoon on a three-day tour, opening
schools and addressing religious meetings; so I left.

A few weeks later I met him accidentally at a religious gath-
ering. 'Why didn't you come to see me?' he asked.

When I said I waited for three hours he replied. 'You can put
that in your book.'

'Then you won't let me come back to Orissa', I joked.

He paused a little and said, 'A man came to bathe in a river.
He thought the water would be cool and refreshing, but instead
he found an ocean with roaring waves. He was frightened.'

The parable could be interpreted in many different ways.

The villagers said, 'We'll give Janata two years. If they don't
do what they promised, we'll throw them out. We have been able
to remove the mighty Congress; Janata is nothing in comparison.'

During the next two years the Janata leaders quarrelled among
themselves as to who should become prime minister. The party
split into Janata and Lok Dal. The latter formed a minority
government for a short period and called an election. Ironically
the price of mustard oil, kerosene, and onions went up. Congress
exploited this and Mrs Gandhi came back to power.

Indian elections made me feel how dull English elections are.
In England politicians act before television cameras and there is
very little sense of participation from the public. Without television coverage in India, the politicians have to act on a real stage
surrounded by thousands of spectators. But the most interesting
similarity is the importance given to the price of commodities.
When the Labour Party said, 'Inflation will not affect the pound
in your pocket', the Conservatives warned, 'It will determine the

goods in your shopping basket', and won the election. But prices still went up.

During the Janata Government the atmosphere at the Indian High Commission in London changed. The High Commissioner made the members of the Indian community living there welcome.

I went to see him about opening a new exhibition of mine. I had taken two copies of my books. He looked at them with interest and asked if he could buy them from me. 'We spend so much money here unnecessarily. I would rather buy books.' While noting down his instructions his secretary asked, 'Would the author charge extra for signing the books for us?'

His official residence was kept open for the Indian artists. 'You can have exhibitions and invite your friends', he said. But his officials resented his friendliness with the Indian community.

I was asked by the Area Museums Service and South-East Arts to organize a travelling exhibition relating my paintings to the art and culture of my village. The idea was originated by the director of the Towner Art Gallery in Eastbourne, who liked my paintings. After a short preview at India House the exhibition was opened at Eastbourne by the Indian High Commissioner. It was a success.

'Is there so much creative talent in your village?' visitors asked me with amazement. All they knew from the media about India was poverty and ignorance.

The exhibition was scheduled to last a year but proved so popular that, without consulting me, it was extended. When the exhibits were returned a number of items were missing, several were damaged, and some of my paintings had been trimmed to make them fit into the frames. When I pointed this out to the organizers I was told, 'An artist should consider himself lucky to have had such an exhibition.'

A swelling bothered me in India and the doctors said it was caused by filariasis. This disease is caused by germs carried by mosquitoes, with symptoms of fever and swelling of the glands. After my return to London it became painful again. I went to see my doctor and he referred me to a specialist.

He examined me thoroughly but did not think the swelling was due to filaria. He referred me to a consultant surgeon who said he suspected a tumour and wanted to operate on me quickly. He looked so solemn and serious that I was frightened to ask any questions. Suddenly I was faced with a situation where I could not plan anything for the future. I thought of my mother. The day I left she clung to me and said, 'Come close and sit on my lap.'

It was a sunny summer's day. I was near Regent's Park and wanted to see the roses. As I was crossing Tottenham Court Road a young man in a passing lorry spat on my face. His head was clean shaven. He looked back at me, grinning triumphantly. Instead of going to the park I returned to my studio to paint.

I prepared myself for the worst. I became more perceptive and the whole world seemed beautiful. I went back to the East End to look at the places I had enjoyed. In my old street the building had been pulled down and in its place stood a lifeless box. But the bakery was still there. When the woman saw me she said, 'Darling, where have you been? I haven't seen you for ages.' The Indian restaurant had changed. I saw English people eating there and credit card facilities were displayed. Young men sold copies of the *Socialist Worker*. It was a protest against the National Front marches, I was told. Several people living around Brick Lane had been beaten up by English youths and women were frightened of going out. An Indian writer was organizing the Bengalis to fight against racialist attacks. The older people reluctantly agreed with the young—to control violence you need greater violence.

When I arrived in Wapping I saw limousines covered with elaborate wreaths. The old lady who used to sit by the window had died. The man who lived in the flat underneath offered me a cup of tea and asked me how I was.

'All right', I said, without thinking.

'Are you really all right? You don't look it.'

My neighbour had moved to an old people's home and the other old lady next door had died. My flat was occupied by a young couple. Wapping still looked romantic and the river continued to flow.

The morning of the operation came. It was a bright sunny day, one of the nicest days of the summer. A friend had offered to take me to the hospital by car. I packed a few things in a case and left with him.

The car would not start. We looked for a taxi and after some difficulty found one. The traffic was heavy and the driver took us a roundabout way.

Everything was going wrong and my village upbringing made me feel superstitious. I was apprehensive about the outcome of the operation.

At the hospital the nursing staff had been expecting me and a young nurse showed me to my bed. She was an English girl and very cheerful. While taking my temperature and pulse she told me about herself. She was a student nurse and her father was a doctor. In India nursing is not considered a respectable profession and girls from educated families rarely choose to become nurses.

A few minutes later a young doctor came to examine me. Earlier that year he had spent three months working in a hospital in Bombay as part of his training. He liked India and made many friends there. According to him the doctors were very good but did not have proper facilities and enough medicines.

When I woke up after the operation I was confused. I was aware of somebody by the side of my bed. It was one of the nurses and all through the night she kept a watch on me. Whenever I opened my eyes she was always there, enquiring if I was all right. When I fell ill in the village my mother would come and stand beside me, stroking my body and whispering a prayer. That had a healing effect. The nurse was like my mother, concerned about me.

I longed to know the result of the operation but did not have the courage to ask. In the morning the young doctor came to see me. My heart thumped.

'I am happy to say we removed the tumour. It was not malignant.'

In my village a patient has to learn to live with his tumour or die if it turns out to be cancer. The National Health Service gives people a sense of security by providing free medical care for all, from birth to death. Nobody need be afraid of falling seriously ill and dying without being properly looked after.

Doctors and politicians have been debating the future of the National Health Service. The doctors complain that they are overworked and underpaid and some politicians argue it is inefficient and too expensive for the country to afford. The public take it so much for granted that they even complain about the small disadvantages of the Health Service. But the nurses, in spite of being underpaid, are dedicated to serve the sick. They carry out their difficult task with a smile.

I was discharged from hospital but felt so weak that I could not move out of my flat for a month. Friends came to look after me. One of them said she had lit a candle for me. I was touched by her concern and thought how similar it was to the Hindu practice. Lights and special pujas are offered to deities in the temples for a friend's or relative's recovery from illness.

When I felt better she took me to her church. We lit candles and attended a serivce. The church was open to everybody irrespective of religion or colour. But in India non-Hindus are not allowed near the deities or in some places inside the temples. There is a continuous worship from morning till night relating to the activities of the day. In the morning the deities are woken by the priests, washed, dressed, decorated with flowers, and offered food. After lunch the gods rest for a while. In the evening music is played to entertain them and in the old days devadasis danced. When the ceremony of supper is over the gods are put to bed.

Hindus see their gods and goddesses in their own image. There are gods and goddesses of creation as well as destruction. This helps Hindus to recognize these contradictions within themselves. Non-violence is the reaction against the violence in everyone. Hindus also believe that God is half-male and half-female, reflecting the Indian attitude to sex and human relations. Every god has a consort and together they form the divine union.

Apart from the communal deities the villagers keep their personal gods in their homes. They can perform their religious rituals without going to a temple.

I was in the village when an exciting event took place. A new god had arrived. A group of children had placed a piece of oval stone in the back garden of a villager and started worshipping it as their personal god. It was a part of their play. They bathed the stone in turmeric water, decorated it with vermilion and flowers, and offered molasses. The worship continued for a few days but stopped when there was a quarrel among the children. Suddenly, one of the children, a seven-year-old boy, became hysterical and started rolling in the dust of the village street. The villagers thought he was possessed by a spirit and brought healers to cure him. They chanted mantras, but nothing happened. The boy cried out that he was the new god, lying neglected in the back garden and must be worshipped with fruit and flowers. A

Brahmin performed the ceremony and the boy got better.

The church service in London was very orderly. The priest preached 'Christ is light, Christ is the way.' He spoke like a politician and addressed the congregation like an army commander. People marched out like soldiers to conquer the world.

For Hindus there are many ways to reach God. Nobody says 'This is the only way.' This belief makes Hinduism all-embracing and tolerant towards other religions. Without rigid services as in a church, there is a constant flow of worshippers into the temples and priests are always available to attend to them. The sole aim of the devotee is to have 'darshan', a personal meeting with their deity.

After the service I saw the influence of the church everywhere. The theatres and concert halls were designed like churches, the actors performed like priests, and the audiences behaved like the congregation.

A letter arrived from a politician friend in India saying he was coming to London for a few days on his way back from Europe. I went to see him at his hotel and found him sitting in the lounge looking dejected. With him was another Indian politician, wrapped in a shawl. They had travelled together and were feeling tired. There was a confusion over the reservation of their rooms. In India they were used to receiving VIP treatment wherever they went, but in London they felt neglected.

My friend said he would like to stay with me. His companion had a fever. All he wanted to do was go to bed and sleep; so I brought them both to my studio.

My friend was a strict Hindu and had not eaten any food or even drunk a cup of tea as he had not done his morning rituals. Immediately he went to the bathroom, washing himself and chanting Sanskrit verses. He came out with sandalwood paste on his forehead and sat down on the floor to say his prayers.

He was then ready for his breakfast. It was two o'clock in the afternoon. He was a strict vegetarian and I had to take special care to hide any meat or eggs. Their sight and smell would contaminate him.

While eating a bowl of cornflakes and milk he told me about his European visit. He had given speeches relating Hindu philosophy to politics. They were highly praised and wherever he

went people congratulated him. The other politician woke up
after a long sleep and said he felt much better. In the evening
some distant relatives came from south London to take him to
stay with them.

During my friend's stay I acted as his guide and secretary.
Every day there were telephone calls from the Indian High
Commission enquiring about his plans. But he preferred to see
London with me.

Apart from visiting the usual tourist places and being
photographed against the background of the Houses of Parliament, he wanted to know how the Indian community lived in
London. I took him to Southall to meet the community leaders.
The editor of a local Indian newspaper arranged a reception. That
pleased him because it gave him an opportunity to deliver a
lecture.

As we approached Southall by car the atmosphere began to
change, with more and more Indians in the streets. In a small
park two old men in white turbans sat gossipping. A group of
women in saris sat on the grass and small children played around
them.

We were received with garlands of flowers and the meeting
took place in true Indian style with long speeches of introduction.
My friend had carefully prepared his talk in English but the
chairman requested him to speak in Punjabi. He only knew a few
Punjabi phrases, but delighted the audience by speaking in
Hindi.

After the meeting we were invited to a meal in a crowded
Indian restaurant. It was strange not to see a single European
face. In the West End the Indian restaurants are mainly patron-
ized by English people.

We had a guided tour of the area. Every shop was run by
Indians selling Indian goods—silk and nylon saris, different
kinds of tropical fruit, vegetables, and delicacies. A number of
travel agents sold cheap tickets to Delhi and Amritsar. I felt
nostalgic for India.

Impulsively I went inside a supermarket to buy some spices.
The shelves were full of different kinds of ingredients, properly
graded and packed by importers. Some had come straight from
India in distinctive Indian wrappings. In India they looked ordinary but in Southall they stood out as exotic. A large woman in a

sari was buying bags of flour, a sack of rice, and a huge tin of cooking oil. I thought she ran a restaurant but when I asked her what she was going to do with all her purchases she told me in Hindi they were the groceries for her family for a week.

I was surprised how England had changed the attitude of Indians. Foodstuffs were clean and not adulterated; there was no bargaining either. In India adulteration is so common that even oil sealed in tins is suspected of being impure. I was told by a cardiologist friend that the painkiller supplied to him by the government was only distilled water.

When I saw the sweetmeat shop selling milk products an incident came to my mind. Large wagons of blotting paper were coming to a town in Orissa but nobody knew what was happening to them. The police became suspicious and investigated. It was found that the blotting paper was being used by a famous sweetmeat shop to thicken the cream in preparing 'ras malai', their most popular sweet.

We visited the house of the newspaper editor. He was from the Punjab, married with two sons. He had lived in Southall for fifteen years in a terraced house a little way away from the shopping centre. As we sat down, large plates of Indian snacks and sweets appeared on the table. His wife had gone to great trouble preparing them. Although we were not feeling hungry after our large Indian meal, we could not refuse. It is an Indian custom to offer food and refreshments to the guests. She sat beside us, putting more and more on our plates and encouraging us to eat. When I could not eat any more she said, 'Don't you like my cooking?'

Indian hosts always give food and drink to unexpected guests without asking them and it is considered impolite to refuse. But in England visitors are always asked, 'Have you eaten?' 'Would you like something to drink?' These questions put the guests into an embarrassing position. They do not want to cause inconvenience and usually reply, 'No'.

That evening I had invited some English friends to meet the politician. As they started arriving I asked one of them, 'How are you?'

'Not too bad', he replied.

At dinner when I asked them what they thought of the wine, one of them said, 'It's not bad at all.'

The expressions 'It's not so bad', 'It couldn't be better' are often used while describing food or even a person's health. Instead of making a positive statement 'I am well', or 'I am unwell' or 'It is good', English people make statements which are ambiguous. 'Not' is negative; 'bad' is also negative.

It is not bad, but is it good? No, it is in-between, neither bad nor good; it is indifferent. In India we make positive statements.

It took me a long time to get used to these strange expressions, including, 'I doubt it', 'I am not sure', 'I don't think so'. I also learned to read between the lines: 'We will get in touch with you', 'Let us meet some time', 'I hope it will be possible for us to meet soon', 'I would love to see you, but . . .'

People have little time to be honest with each other or even to themselves. The statements are expressions of detachment and non-commitment. But for an outsider it is difficult to understand what they really mean.

When my English friends left, one of them asked, 'How long is the politician going to stay?'

'I don't know. We don't ask such questions', I replied.

In my village guests arrive at any time of the day or night and they are always welcomed. Nobody asks, 'Why have you come?' 'How long are you going to stay?' They become a part of the family. In England these questions are openly discussed so that the hosts can arrange their plans accordingly. People lead their own lives and there is very little flexibility in fitting in unexpected visitors.

I had to learn not to overstay my welcome when invited to English homes. If I was invited for lunch I was expected to leave before tea and if I was invited for tea I was not expected to stay for supper.

Many Indians living in Britain wanted to meet my politician friend. I went with him and saw how prosperous Indian businessmen lived in north London. Their homes were filled with gadgets: huge television sets with large collections of Hindi films on video, electronically-controlled curtains, and even heated swimming pools. There was plenty of ostentatious modern furniture but not a single work of contemporary art. When I asked a businessman if he was interested in art, he replied, 'The only art I'm interested in is the art of making money.'

My friend wanted to buy some presents for his relatives and

friends and I took him to Oxford Street. He had never been to a
large department store before. There were so many items to
choose from that he was unable to decide. 'You select for me', he
said. He had not bought anything in Europe, because in India
the label 'Made in Britain' is more prestigious. But most of the
items we bought turned out to be manufactured in Hongkong or
Korea.

We made so many purchases that we decided to take a taxi.
Outside the store a taxi stopped, some passengers got down, and
we got in. When I asked the driver to take us to Pimlico, he
refused. He wanted to take an English girl who approached him
shortly after us. 'We were first', I said.

The taxi driver put his indicator off and said he was not for
hire. We got out and I wrote down the number of the taxi. The
driver made a U-turn to the other side of the road. He spoke to
a policeman who beckoned us. We thought the taxi driver was
going to take us after all and crossed over to the other side.

The policeman asked me if I could understand English. When
I said 'Yes', he shouted, 'This taxi is not for hire.' The taxi driver
immediately left. I told the policeman the taxi driver wanted to
take another passenger instead of us, but he again shouted, 'I say
the taxi is not for hire.' I suggested to the policeman he should
have investigated the matter.

'I'll arrest you', he threatened.

'Why?'

'You're obstructing the highway.'

My friend had been quietly listening. 'Strange you should call
him over here and then accuse him of blocking the highway.'

'I don't care,' the policeman said.

'He is a well-known politician from India. What opinion do
you think he is going to have of the London police?' I said.

'Bloody hell, I don't care.' He took a pad from his pocket and
asked me for my name and address.

'Take me to your police station and I will give my name and
address to your superior officer,' I said.

'If you behave like that you should be in a psychiatric ward.'
He went on scribbling on the pad, looking at me from time to
time as if he was noting down my description. He was still writing
when we walked away.

My friend was very disturbed by the incident. 'If the police treat educated Indians in that way in the West End, how do they behave towards uneducated Indians in other parts of London?' He complained to the Home Secretary. Weeks later in India he received a reply setting out the various addresses he should write to if he wanted to pursue the matter.

I thought how the image of the London police had changed since I first arrived. What had happened to the friendly Dixon of Dock Green? There is a saying in my village, 'If the protector becomes the oppressor, even God cannot help.'

While my friend was staying with me it was difficult to paint and I was feeling restless. After he left I spent long hours painting, working with colours and forms, expressing my emotions. It was like being in a state of love and I felt at peace with myself.

Sometimes I sat by the window staring at the grey sky, looking for a patch of blue. The sun came out and I walked to St James's Park. It looked glorious in the autumn light. An old man sat alone on a bench observing life around him. He told me his wife had died eight years ago and he lived alone in a flat. Every day he went from park to park to see people and enjoy the scenery. He had a routine. First he would sit in the park, then go to a favourite pub before returning to his lonely flat.

Nearby a young man painted in water-colours. Children offered bread to the birds and the pelicans flapped their wings. The grass was covered with yellow leaves which were falling like raindrops. I spread my coat and sat down in a quiet place to write a letter to my parents.

As I was writing, three young people, two boys and a girl, came and sat a few yards away. A flower fell on my letter and I looked up. One of the boys was lying on top of the girl and the other boy was sitting next to them, holding a bunch of flowers. He must have picked them from the flowerbed. I continued writing. Another flower fell. I looked up again.

'Are you writing a poem?' the youth, a skinhead, asked.

'No, a letter.'

Suddenly he snatched it away from me and started to dance, waving the letter and chanting, 'He's writing a love letter. He's writing a love letter.'

I asked him to return it, but he still went on dancing.

'Give it back to him,' the girl shouted.

The youth crumpled the letter in his hand and threw it at me. 'Go away, you Paki bastard.'

The beautiful park had suddenly become a place of menace. I picked the letter up and quickly walked away towards the lake. I looked at the children feeding the birds. They were so innocent. I wondered how they could grow up to become such aggressive youths. What sort of education do they receive at home and at school which does not teach them to treat a stranger as a friend.

I left Wapping because I no longer felt safe in the East End. Now I felt threatened in the most respectable part of London.

When I first arrived, London was a safe place to live in. Gradually violence had become a natural part of life.

The incident in the park was so disturbing that whenever I saw a group of youths a feeling of panic went through my body. I tried to get over this by walking to the centre of London to see films and plays, but I was careful not to travel alone at night.

In February 1979 I read in the *Guardian* about an Indian woman teacher being subjected to a virginity test on her arrival at Heathrow. She had come with her fiancé, an Indian who worked in London and lived in Southall. She was examined by a male doctor to find out if she was a virgin. The Home Office admitted that the examination was carried out to ascertain if the woman was a genuine fiancée. If she was a virgin she would be unmarried and hence a fiancée. If not, she would be a married woman.

The woman teacher told the reporter than soon after her arrival at Heathrow she was sent for a medical examination by the immigration officials. A woman interpreter spoke to her in Hindi and asked her to undress.

'Then a man doctor came in. I asked for a dressing-gown, but it was not provided. I was most reluctant to have the examination but I did not know whether it was the normal practice here. The doctor said, through the nurse-interpreter, that he thought I had been pregnant before. I said that before marriage no Indian lady would do that sort of thing.'

The interpreter then translated the consent form for her and she signed it.

'I was frightened that otherwise they would send me back.'

The doctor then began to examine her.

'He was wearing rubber gloves and took some medicine out of

a tube and put it on some cotton and inserted it into me. He said
he was deciding whether I was pregnant now or had been pregnant before. I said he could see that without doing anything to
me. But he said there was no need to get shy. I have been feeling
very bad mentally ever since. I was very embarrassed and upset. I
had never had a gynaecological examination before.'

The Commission for Racial Equality protested. The Home
Secretary wrote them a letter expressing his concern and
confirming that immigration officers had been instructed not to
ask the medical officer to examine passengers with a view to
establishing whether they had borne children or had had sexual
relations. Identical instructions were issued by the Foreign and
Commonwealth Office to British posts overseas. He revealed that
in 1977 some 45,000 medical examinations were carried out at
ports in the context of immigration control.

Virginity tests had been carried out on Indian women for over
ten years, both in Britain and in India, but the women had been
too embarrassed and frightened to complain in case they were
refused entry into Britain. The incident at Heathrow, reported in
the *Guardian*, brought the matter for the first time to the notice
of the public. The Indian Government protested and the Indian
press demanded reciprocal action.

In April that year the National Front decided to hold a meeting
in Southall where many Indians live. The Indian residents
believed the National Front was being deliberately provocative.
The meeting took place in the Town Hall, heavily guarded by the
police, as an anti-National Front demonstration was planned.
Some 2,700 police equipped with riot shields and backed up by
dogs, horses, and units of the Special Patrol Group protected the
National Front from the demonstrators. Violence broke out, 345
people were arrested, and Blair Peach, a thirty-one-year-old
schoolteacher, lost his life.

Against this background of humiliation and violence, the
Festival of India was being planned to celebrate the relationship
between India and Britain. High level committees were formed
and to my surprise I was asked to join the Festival of India
Committee in Britain.

When I attended my first committee meeting in 1980 I discovered that everything had already been decided by the two governments. There was nothing about contemporary India and the

festival events stopped at the time the British left. Modern art, literature, theatre, music, and, above all, village and tribal art had been forgotten. The Indian community living in Britain had also been ignored. I hoped the festival would give an opportunity to analyse what had happened to the culture of Indians living here, related to India's present and past. The involvement of the Indian community with its artists, writers, and creative people could have given the festival a real sense of participation. When I suggested an exhibition of contemporary Indian art a senior member of the committee remarked that the British public would not be interested.

'Have you asked them?' I said.

There was laughter among the committee members, but that was all.

The Indian High Commission invited Indian businessmen to contribute to the festival. They were pleased to be asked and gave money generously. It was ironic; their money was readily accepted, but the Indian artists living in Britain were not recognized as Indians for the purpose of the festival.

The Indian community wanted to participate by arranging their own events. A committee was set up but there was always the problem of money and space for venues. With modest means a number of items was planned and I was asked by the co-ordinator to work with the children in a multi-racial school in London to present a dance on the day of the opening of the festival. It was like being back in the school in the East End. There were Indian, African, and British children, both boys and girls. They painted and danced together and there was a great feeling of friendship. But the headmistress told me about her problems. Some of the children came from homes which supported the National Front and the children brought those attitudes to school. On the opening day when I was preparing the children to present their tiger dance outside the Royal Festival Hall, a well-dressed, middle-aged man came up to me, gave a Nazi salute, and walked on.

At the opening of an exhibition at the Science Museum I found myself in the VIP enclosure by mistake. Mrs Thatcher was standing alone, waiting patiently to receive the Indian prime minister. It was very cold. When the British prime minister saw me she came up to me, shook my hand, and smiled.

'Can I stand beside you?' she said. 'It's so draughty there.'

Before we had a chance to talk to each other she was quickly taken away by the Foreign Office staff. I had often heard her described as the Iron Lady but this briefest of encounters made me realize she was a real human being. In India ministers expect to be treated like gods and goddesses.

The Arts Council, responsible for promoting contemporary art in Britain, had devoted both its galleries to old Indian sculptures and crafts. I tried to get other public galleries in London interested in presenting an exhibition of works by Indian artists living in India and Britain. But nobody showed any interest. The President of the Royal Academy, also a member of the Festival of India Committee, was sympathetic and offered space in one of his galleries. But the exhibition was organized by a committee in Delhi set up by the Indian Government and the Indian artists in Britain were excluded. However, they managed to hold their own exhibition at the Barbican Arts Centre. The President of the Royal Academy, who had been unable to provide them with space in his galleries, came to open it. The title of the exhibition was 'Between Two Cultures' and had a mixed reception. National Front supporters showed an unexpected interest in art. Several of the exhibits were disfigured with racist slogans.

I arranged an exhibition of my own paintings at the Commonwealth Institute, giving performances of my 'Dancing Hands', relating movement to painting. I wanted to reach the children who visited the Institute on conducted tours from their schools.

The audiences joined in and the children loved to use their hands, imitating me. I felt as if I was back in Leeds or in the primary school in the East End.

During one of my performances I saw a little English boy of about three moving his hands, following me. He was accompanied by his grandmother. When I asked him to join me he shyly gave his own interpretation.

A young West Indian girl pointed at a painting and asked me what it meant.

'What does it mean to you?' I replied.

'It looks like a womb, but I'm not sure. I will have to bring my mother to see it,' she said.

How strange, I thought. A few years ago I displayed a painting with some of my books at an international book fair in Delhi. The painting had a red oval form with a blue surround and a red point in the middle, with patches of light coming through. One morning a holy man came, looked at the painting for some time, brought his disciples, and told them the painting was meditative. At lunchtime a Westernized Indian said it reminded him of an embryo. In the afternoon a small boy came with his father. He pointed at the picture excitedly and said, 'Chanda Mama, Uncle Moon.'

One painting meant three different things to three different people who tried to relate it to their own experiences.

But the English and Indian visitors could not relate their experiences to the images of gods and goddesses in the exhibitions of traditional art. The Indians seemed confused at the huge number of exhibits displayed out of their religious context. The British visitors were puzzled because they could not understand the Indian iconography.

At the Hayward Gallery an Englishman came up to me and asked a series of questions—'What is the name of the goddess who eats people?' 'Is Shiva man or a woman?' 'Do you worship sex?'

'Kali is the Goddess of Destruction. Shiva is the God of Creation; he's phallic, he dances and creates. Hindus worship sex; sex is the source of life,' I tried to explain.

He and his woman companion grinned with embarrassment and left.

Groups of musicians and artists were picked from their villages in India and brought to London to dance and sing. No time was given to them to adjust and they looked bewildered. Some tribal dancers arrived one day, appeared before the press the next morning, and that evening gave their first performance. It was both classical and modern, with a unique combination of dance, mime, music, and painting. In their village they danced on the soft earth but in London they had to leap and jump on a concrete floor. Some injured their knees. After three days they were taken back to their villages with their 'souvenirs'—transistors and tape recorders.

The Festival of India 1982 lasted for eight months. At openings and receptions I usually met the same people, a small group interested in Indian art, culture, and mysticism. Several had spent many months in ashrams in India, trying to find themselves. But the festival did not seem to reach the ordinary British public, who tend not to visit museums and art galleries.

Shortly before the end of the festival I was returning home from Piccadilly after a committee meeting at the Arts Council. It was raining and I waited for a bus. Many buses drove past without stopping and a long queue formed behind me in the meantime. After an hour a bus stopped and there was a rush to get on. The seats on the lower deck were full and I stood with several other passengers. The woman conductor came down from the upper deck, counted the standing passengers, and told me to get off. When I said that I was the first in the queue, she replied, 'There's no queue here.' She stopped the bus and threatened to call the police while the other passengers grumbled about the delay. I was the only Indian and felt embarrassed. An Englishwoman came down from the upper deck and said there was an empty seat upstairs. I went up and sat down. When the conductor came to collect the fare she said loudly for everybody to hear, 'You're not coming in my bus again.'

The next morning while shopping I asked a local Indian grocer if he had been to any of the Festival of India events. He laughed. 'We work until midnight every day. Where is the time?'

I wanted to go to Germany to arrange an exhibition of my paintings. I was told I needed a visa and it took twenty-four hours to get it. The previous arrangements between the Governments of India and Germany had been cancelled. With an Indian passport I need visas for practically every country in the world, except Scandinavia. Getting them was quite easy when I first arrived, but as successive governments in Britain introduced legislation controlling immigration and the politicians and the media debated the future of the immigrants, I found it more and more difficult.

My plan was to go by train via Ostend and I needed a transit visa for Belgium. When I telephoned the Belgian Consulate I was told I could get the visa the same morning. I was not feeling well and an English friend offered to take me there by car. When I reported at the visa counter with my application the officer would not accept it. He wanted to see my train ticket, my bank account, etc, which I had not carried with me. When I told my friend I could not get a visa to my surprise he asked to see a superior officer at the consulate. After we had waited for about half an hour a man appeared with a couple of pieces of paper in his hand. He came up to my friend and enquired, 'Do you want to buy a car in Ostend?' 'No, I want to know why my Indian friend cannot get a visa. He wants to visit Germany, not to live in your country. Why do you have such restrictions?' 'You have the same restrictions for Indians', the officer replied. Then he looked at me for a while, took my passport, and arranged for me to get a visa immediately.

Every time I want to go abroad I have to wait in queues for hours and face embarrassing questions from the immigration officers. It is humiliating.

When I returned to my studio I remembered the words of my Irish friend in Surbiton. 'Prafulla, you are an artist. You belong to the whole world.'

I have held exhibitions of my paintings in Europe, America, Japan, and Scandinavia, which gave me an opportunity to visit those places. But I only feel at home in India and England. When I am in England I want to go back to India and when I am in India I want to return to England. But as soon as I arrive at London Airport I am made to feel an outsider when the immigration officer checks my passport and asks, 'Do you live here?' But London provides me with the solitude and isolation necessary for my work. I have learned to live alone with myself in a dream world surrounded by violence and racial tension. As I paint, write, arrange exhibitions, meet friends, go to theatres and cinemas, and from time to time watch a little television, I become involved with life in England.

I had wanted to make a film to show people the beauty and simplicity of life in my village. By chance, in the summer of 1980, I met a BBC producer in the house of a friend. A few days later he telephoned to say that he had enjoyed reading my book, *My Village, My Life*, and thought it would make an excellent film for television. We met a number of times to discuss the project.

During my annual visit to the village in the spring of 1981, the producer came there to do research and make preliminary arrangements for the film. I spent several days looking after him, introducing him to the villagers and government officials in Delhi and Orissa.

Foreign film-makers are required to sign an undertaking to observe certain regulations laid down by the Government of India. First, the script must be approved by the Government of India. Second, a liaison officer, appointed by the Government of India, must be present during the entire duration of filming in India and the team must agree 'to abide by his advice regarding the filming of any particular scene.' The team must also 'meet the expenses for the travel and stay of the liaison officer'. 'Failure to abide by the liaison officer's advice regarding shooting of any particular scene may result in the immediate stoppage of any further filming and confiscation of the exposed film.' Third, a final rough cut of the film must be shown 'to a representative of the Government of India at least two weeks before final telecasting screening, also furnishing in advance a full translation in England of the commentary, and further agreement to abide by such advice as may be given by the representative with regard to alteration in or excision of such parts of the film and the commentary as may affect a balanced and accurate presentation of the theme of the film'.

The producer's script was not accepted by the government of India because it did not give a balanced view. He came to me for help and showed me a letter which he had received from Delhi: 'In our opinion the portrayal of the village in your script is rather static and it does not show in any way how more than thirty years of development planning initiated by the Government has transformed the village. To that extent the portrait lacks balance and we would like you to restore this balance after due consultations with Mr Mohanti.'

The producer said that the BBC had invited me to make this film about my village through my eyes, based on my book. The BBC would provide me with all the facilities and help me to realize my vision of the village. The film would be the BBC's contribution to the Festival of India, and apart from being shown on television, it would also be shown at the National Film Theatre. He also said he did not want a liaison officer and asked me to write a letter to the Government of India.

I hoped the film would help the villagers and by showing it I would be able to collect money for my village development project. So I wrote a letter to the Government of India. In it I said: '(The producer) wants the film to be about myself and my village, seen through my eyes. It will show what the village means to me and to the other villagers; the family life and human relationships, the sense of belonging to a community, the dignity of the individual, the arts and crafts, and above all the beauty of village life. The development since 1947 will be unavoidable— electricity, improved farming methods, and the express highway which has connected the village with the outside world. By describing my childhood and showing the village how it is today the film will reveal the developments which have taken place since Independence. For example, I received a loan scholarship from the Orissa Government to study architecture in Bombay in 1955. This changed my life and would have been unthinkable during the British Raj. Cholera and smallpox are under control and modern drugs have reduced suffering and raised the expect- ancy of life. But I have to be careful not to appear to make government propaganda or give too romantic a view of my vil- lage. That would lower the quality and importance of the film.

'(The producer) is one of the most sensitive film-makers I have met here. I can communicate with him. He came to my village last March and spent one week there. He liked the village and the villagers liked him and accepted him as a friend. He believes that the village helped him to understand the importance of basic things in life and that it has a lot to offer to the West. I would like to assure you that the film will give a positive and perceptive picture of Indian village life although the film is only about one particular village.

'I understand that it is usual for a liaison officer from the Ministry of External Affairs to be attached to a foreign film unit. As I will be present throughout the making of this film in India I wonder if a liaison officer is really necessary. The presence of a government official could easily inhibit the villagers and make them self-conscious. As you know, I love my village and would not allow anything to be done which would offend the villagers.'

I received a prompt reply from the Government of India saying they would do their best to reconcile my sensitivities with their procedural requirements.

On the strength of my letter all the necessary permissions were given without the usual bureaucratic delay and my request not to have a liaison officer was granted. My friends in government departments went out of their way to help by making arrangements for accommodation and transport of the BBC team.

No money was discussed, although I had worked on the project for over one year without a formal contract. I had not asked for payment and nor had the BBC offered me any. But I believed the BBC paid its contributors in a fair way. I was brought up in a tradition where, if you invited somebody, you looked after him in every way.

After I had made all the arrangements for the film, which spread over nearly fifteen months, I suddenly received a telephone call from a woman in the BBC Contracts Division.

'I understand you want to make a film and you don't have an agent.'

'Yes.'

'We will offer you a fee of £1,600.' She outlined the work I would have to do.

I said I would think about it and let her know. After discussions with friends who had worked in television, I thought £2,000 and the rights to show the film in cinemas would be adequate.

When I phoned her she said she would have to talk to the producer.

'Why? Has he suggested an amount?' I asked.

She giggled.

'I have been meeting him frequently. Why didn't he tell me about it himself?'

'That's how it is done inside the BBC,' she said.

I considered the producer as a friend. 'If he thinks it is the right amount, that's all right by me,' I said.

The next day the producer took me to lunch at a fashionable restaurant. When I told him what the Contracts Division had said he denied having suggested an amount.

A friend introduced me to an agent who said it was not a fair contract. But the BBC argued that I had already accepted its offer on the phone and threatened to withdraw the project. I found it most embarrassing as the film was planned to be shown during the Festival of India and all the arrangements had been made. I volunteered to give my services free if it would help my village.

The executive producer came to see me. He was an extremely

sensitive person and had made a film in India before. He persuaded me to accept the offer with certain amendments to the contract. He also promised to give me any help I needed in the making of the film. I was assured that the villagers would be paid for their contribution.

I had an exhibition of my paintings in Tokyo. On the way I stopped in Delhi for ten days, getting all the government clearances for the film and making final arrangements for the travel and accommodation of the crew, so that when they arrived they would not face any problems.

Unfortunately, a week after my arrival in Tokyo I was taken ill, an after-effect of my attack in Wapping. I was advised complete rest by the doctors but I wanted to make the film and kept my original arrangements with the BBC.

When we arrived in the village with all the government clearances and no liaison officer, the producer handed me a script and a schedule and demanded that I organize the villagers to act accordingly. The film was going to be a portrait of my village through his eyes, not mine. The BBC was doing me, my village, and India a favour by making this film, I was told. He wanted the film to show me arriving in the village by bus, being greeted by the villagers, taking off my Western clothes, putting on Indian dress, and then going round introducing the village and the villagers—in other words, a typical BBC documentary. I wanted the film to be an honest and authentic portrait of the village without me standing between it and the viewers, giving them an opportunity to get into its heart.

I saw the film as a work of art, depicting aspects of the village which have influenced me as an artist and writer, showing both its beauty and its problems.

I ignored the producer's orders and tried to direct the film, but he started threatening me, saying he would return to England with the crew.

I was feeling extremely tired after my illness in Japan and had the sole responsibility of organizing the villagers for filming. They do not allow non-Hindus near the sacred places and into their homes. But the BBC team was accepted by the villagers because they thought they were my friends.

After a young woman was filmed, her husband was bitten by a snake. Luckily the snake was not poisonous but the villagers

thought the BBC had brought bad luck. I spent long hours
persuading them and got their full co-operation. But I found it
difficult to get the help and understanding of the producer.
When it came to paying the villagers he started bargaining, even
refusing to pay ten rupees to the taxi driver for his meal. A
seventy-year-old Brahmin, who spent three days in the river
being filmed, was offered £6 for his remuneration. Yet the
producer and the crew drank fifty bottles of beer a night, costing
at least £50, and a man was employed at £20 a day to ferry the beer
by taxi from a town sixty miles away.

I tried to explain the village customs to the producer and how
you can offend people by offering them less than they deserve. 'I
haven't got the time to understand your village,' he said. The
next day the taxi driver delivered a letter to me at my house. It
was from the producer withdrawing the project.

I had promised the executive producer that I would complete
the film and did so with the help of the crew. The villagers
decided not to accept any money from the producer and autho-
rized me to act on their behalf. When the team left after two
weeks the villagers gave them a farewell reception and the children produced a play.

I got the film cleared through the government officials in
Orissa and the BBC crew returned to England. Then I received a
letter from a friend in London saying that the BBC had the right
to show the film the way it wanted to without consulting me.
There were twelve hours of filming and I was concerned that if
any aspect of life in my village was shown out of context it would
give a distorted image. So I wrote a letter to the Government of
India who made it a condition that I should be present at the
preview to the Indian High Commission.

In London I met the executive producer to discuss the shape of
the film. He said he had known the producer for twenty-five years
and had a sense of loyalty towards him. But he agreed to listen to
both our views and then decide.

Surprisingly, the executive producer agreed to all my
suggestions as against those of the producer, who gradually with-
drew. I spent two months editing the film, giving it a shape,
selecting the music, and writing and narrating the commentary.
The executive producer was like a teacher, helping me patiently
at every stage. When I discussed the payment of the villagers with

him I received a letter from the BBC saying that all financial matters should be settled between my agent and the Contracts Division.

A press preview was promised but it was withdrawn. The absence of a producer and editor on the credit titles would give bad publicity to the BBC, I was told. On my insistence a preview was arranged only a day before the broadcast. Nobody noticed the omissions. The film was shown on BBC 2 on 25 March 1982 during the first week of the Festival of India, and was highly-praised by the critics and the viewers.

Soon afterwards I received a letter from my agent telling me that the BBC Contracts Division did not want to get involved with the fees to the villagers and the Head of the Arts Department was looking after it. When I took the matter up with him I received a letter saying that the BBC's representative in Delhi had verified that the villagers had already been paid. I knew it was not true and wrote a letter to the Chairman of the BBC on 23 July. Instead of receiving a reply from him I got a letter from the BBC solicitor.

A few days later I received a letter from a friend in the village. It said that on 27 July a BBC official arrived in the village with an interpreter and another Indian, who was presented to the villagers as the District Collector. They told the villagers that I had sent money for them and distributed 950 rupees (£55) among a few contributors who were present and took their receipts. When I wrote back saying the money had not come from me the villagers returned it to the BBC and asked for their receipts. When my agent discussed payment for my extra work the BBC pointed out that my contract read, 'For all work necessary to complete a fifty minute film', and when I wanted to show the film to the villagers the BBC said I would have to buy a copy and quoted £1,250 plus VAT for a 16-mm film and £380 plus VAT for a video cassette.

Two months later I was intrigued to read an article in *The Times* headed, 'Brideshead repainted, thanks to Granada.' It said, 'Castle Howard, the architect Vanbrugh's first masterpiece, was used as Brideshead in Granada television's dramatization of Evelyn Waugh's novel. The fee which George Howard, chairman of the BBC, squeezed out of his commercial rivals for lending his house has provided the finance to realize a dream of creating new rooms.'

But my dream of helping the village through the film did not come true. I sat in my studio reflecting on the film. For the BBC it was only one of many films it makes every year. For me it was the most important. I had kept all my promises to the BBC in spite of immense difficulties. I was brought up in a culture where the spoken word is as important as the written word. I felt all the problems I had faced were worthwhile when people came up to me in the street and said how much they had enjoyed my film. Several teachers wrote to me saying that they wanted to show the film to their students to help them understand India. Tears came to my eyes when I read what the *Daily Telegraph* critic had written: 'Never before, in my fallible memory of television past, has the audience been able to see a remote primitive Indian village through the eyes of one of its sons; one who regards it, even when he is in England, especially when he is in England, as the home he can never leave.'

I watched the tree in the yard change through the seasons. In the winter, without leaves, it looked sad, but with the coming of spring, buds gradually opened out like flowers and turned into leaves. In the summer the tree was full again and as autumn approached the leaves turned yellow and brown and started to fall. It was a resting place for all kinds of birds who filled the air with their songs. Pigeons danced on the slate roof and when it rained and water cascaded, they took shelter on the drainpipe outside my neighbour's house. The back wall in summer was covered by a creeper which turned into deep red in the autumn. But the first wind of the winter proved too strong for the delicate leaves. Suddenly the wall was bare again. It was time for me to leave for India.

India is a beautiful country with kind and friendly people. You can find everything—blue skies and golden sun, miles of sandy beaches, snow-covered mountains, green paddy fields, lakes, rivers, and streams with clear blue water, caves and temples with ancient sculptures, forests with tigers, elephants, and dancing peacocks. I believed what I said to my English friends and longed to go back.

Travelling by Air-India, India began at Heathrow, with graceful hostesses, curries, and Hindi movies. But as soon as I arrived at Delhi airport my romantic vision of India disappeared. It was past midnight and I stood for an hour to get through immigration. The officers checked every passport slowly as they gossiped among themselves.

I joined a long queue of foreign tourists. When my turn came a man appeared from nowhere with a bunch of passports in his hand. He gave it to the officer who ignored me and attended to him. I protested but the immigration officer took no notice. After stamping the passports he looked at me and said, 'He's a big officer. In India we have to attend to them first. Why are you in a hurry? You'll have to wait there.' He pointed at the crowded customs enclosure.

'Where's your health certificate?'

'I was told it is no longer necessary.'

He was not convinced. He talked to his colleagues who agreed with me. He stamped my passport and said, 'It is better you get inoculated against cholera.'

I thanked him and proceeded to collect my baggage. His words reminded me that I should be careful about drinking water, even in cities. I tried to remember where I had put my water-purifying tablets.

I waited for a long time for my baggage in an atmosphere of chaos and confusion. When it arrived I put it on a trolley. It did not move and I noticed it had no wheels. I dragged it through the crowded space and joined another queue for customs examination. The officer treated me like a thief and searched each bag thoroughly. I felt like protesting but knew from previous experiences it would only make matters worse. Once, because I protested, a customs officer was so thorough in searching that he not only tore the lining of my case but completely spoilt a box of chocolates which I was carefully carrying for my mother by emptying the contents on the counter. 'He was only carrying out his duty,' I was told by his superior.

I looked around and saw other people being examined. An Indian woman was asked to take all her jewellery out and put it on the table for evaluation. I had spoken to her on the plane. She was from a village near Madras and worked as a nurse in America. Her mother was seriously ill and she was anxious to see her. 'We can get everything in America, but not the dust of our village street and the love of our mothers.'

After an hour the customs officer cleared my bags. He entered the details of my camera and tape recorder in my passport. I was worried there might not be any space left for my visas. I felt relieved as I came out of the airless space.

It was already three o'clock in the morning and I did not want to disturb my friends I had arranged to stay with. I thought of spending the night in a hotel. All I wanted was a clean bed and a clean bathroom. But cleanliness in India costs money and I have never understood why. Five-star hotels are beyond my reach and permission is required to stay at a government guest house or a YMCA hostel. There, too, prices are high for India, so I decided to knock on the door of my friends. He and his wife welcomed me with pleasure and we spent the rest of the night talking and drinking tea.

I watched the sun rise and listened to the birds. Dew drops glistened on the leaves. I had already forgotten the harassment at the airport.

I telephoned a friend. He told me there was an opening of an exhibition at the National Gallery of Modern Art that morning and we arranged to meet there. On the way I noticed that Delhi had undergone an enormous change. There were new buildings, flyovers, stadiums, fountains, and flowerbeds. I met all my artist friends and the atmosphere on the gallery lawn under the blue sky was one of joy and celebration.

In the evening I went to Old Delhi to collect some paintings. I had stacked them on the pavement outside the framer's shop and was waiting for a taxi. It was very cold. A young man came up to me and said, 'Why have you put these paintings here?' He was thin, shabbily dressed, and looked worried.

'Why not?' I asked.

'This is my place; I sleep here.'

I noticed along the pavement other families preparing for the night.

'I'm only waiting for a taxi,' I replied. He looked relieved.

Later in the evening I went to a party given by an Indian businessman. When I arrived I found a modern house in a smart residential area set in a large garden guarded by a darwan. It was full of guests, mainly smartly dressed Indian intellectuals. The hosts were charming and hospitable.

There was plenty of foreign liquor—whisky, gin, vodka, and brandy. I heard English being spoken in polished accents and the conversation consisted of malicious attacks on artists, writers, and politicians. The drinks continued to flow and the atmosphere vibrated with excitement. Suddenly I felt as if I were watching a Pasolini film. The whole place had turned into a vomitorium. I thanked my hosts and left. I kept thinking of the young man in Old Delhi and tried to relate him to the party I had just left.

It was already past eleven and there was no direct bus to my friend's house. It was too cold to go by auto-rickshaw and it was a long way to walk. I went to the nearby taxi stand but the taxi drivers were all asleep in their taxis, wrapped in blankets. I tried to wake them but they ignored me.

At last a driver woke up and agreed to take me. He was an old man, fragile and wearing a turban. The taxi looked ancient. I got in and as he drove the taxi shook and the doors rattled. A cold wind whistled through the gaps in the door frames.

'It is such an old taxi. Why don't you get a new one?' I asked.

'If you don't like my taxi I'll drop you here.' He stopped. The road was lonely and dark.

'Please forgive me.'

He drove on, lecturing me. 'Will you throw your father away because he's old? This taxi is like my father. I have been driving it for the last thirty years and it provides me with a regular income. It has looked after me and I have to look after it.'

I listened to him quietly and eventually we reached my friend's house. As I paid the fare he put his hand on my shoulder and said, 'Son, my old taxi got you here or not?' His eyes smiled in triumph.

When I arrived in the village everybody was in despair. The crops had been damaged again by severe cyclones and floods. People had no money or food and many were ill. Friends I had seen smiling the previous year had turned into skeletons.

The Chief Minister of the state was an educated man and I thought I would discuss my village development plan with him. I made an appointment to see him at his government residence at nine o'clock one morning.

When I got there the huge iron gate was closed and a crowd had gathered outside. Among them was a group of holy men in saffron robes. Three men were standing inside guarding the gate.

'I have an appointment with the Chief Minister,' I said.

'Where is the letter?'

I looked for it but could not find it among my papers. By mistake I had left it behind in the village.

'You must have a record of my appointment,' I said.

'His secretary is inside.'

I asked to talk to him but there was no telephone. I wrote down my name and message on a piece of paper and asked one of the men to take it to him, but he refused.

'It's not my job. I'm not the messenger.'

'Where is he?'

'Inside.'

After a few minutes a man in shabby clothes appeared. He was the messenger and took my note to the secretary.

I asked if there was anywhere for me to wait and was directed to a shed where a couple of wooden benches were placed. The holy men came and joined me.

'Why have you come to see the Chief Minister?' I asked them.

'To forecast his future.'

The messenger returned and asked me to go inside the house with him. As we walked up the driveway I admired the carefully laid-out gardens with flowering shrubs and trees.

I was taken to a room where two middle-aged clerks were sitting at a table facing each other.

'Have you an appointment with the Chief Minister?' one of them asked.

'Yes.'

'Where is the letter?'

I apologized for having left it at home.

'You say you have come to see the Chief Minister, but where is the proof that he wants to see you?

'His secretary must have a record of my appointment. Can I see him?'

'He is inside the living quarters.'

'Can you send my note to him? If the Chief Minister doesn't want to see me I'll leave.'

He sent my note but the Chief Minister was having his bath. Half-an-hour passed. In the meantime several people came and talked to the clerk about contracts, promotions, and transfers.

It was now ten o'clock and I was told the Chief Minister was worshipping his gods.

'But he asked me to come at nine.'

'If you talk like that your work won't be done,' they threatened me.

I kept quiet. At ten-thirty I was told the Chief Minister had completed his morning rituals, eaten his breakfast, and was ready to receive visitors.

At eleven I was called to see the Chief Minister. He was sitting alone on a chair which looked like a throne in the corner of a large luxuriously furnished room. As soon as he saw me he said, 'I'm going to attend the Assembly. There is no time to discuss. Make another appointment.' He got up and left.

A group of people were waiting outside. They greeted him by joining their hands and bowing down. The Minister was well-fed, with a round face, wearing freshly-laundered Indian clothes. He looked like a bridegroom or a god.

That evening the young people in the village had arranged a musical competition. A young boy sang a devotional song in praise of Lord Jagannath.

'I walked a hundred miles along a muddy path; I crawled part of the way. I climbed up the twenty-two steps and was harassed by your attendants.

'But when I stood in front of you for a second and received your darshan, it was enough. I achieved my salvation.'

I thought of my meeting with the Chief Minister.

After the music the villagers discussed their problems. 'Dishonesty is the norm and honest people cannot survive.'

A female journalist in Orissa was raped and murdered because she and her husband wrote about the corrupt practices of a businessman.

'This is Kaliyug, the Age of Destruction,' an old Brahmin said.

'A labourer was ploughing a field and found a pair of gold bracelets. He called the owner of the land and offered them to him. The owner refused to accept them.

"You found them, they are yours," he said.

"I was only ploughing the field. The land belongs to you, so the bracelets are yours," the labourer replied.

'They continued to argue and went to the king, Parikhit, to

decide for them. The king listened to both of them and declared
that the bracelets belonged to the treasury.

'A few days later the king went hunting in the jungle and lost
his way. He came across a sage and went up to him for help. But
the sage was in deep meditation and the king was unable to wake
him up. He was so annoyed that he killed a snake and put it
around the neck of the sage.

'The son of the sage returned. When he found his father
humiliated he made a curse. "Whoever has put this dead snake
around my father's neck will die of a snake bite within seven
days."

'When the sage woke up his son showed him the snake.

' "No harm is done," the sage replied, "but why should
anybody do this to me?"

' "Whoever it is, I have cursed him to die of a snake bite."

'Through meditation they found out that king Parikhit was
responsible. He was a pious and benevolent king and they
wanted him to live.

'They prayed to the gods for the divine herbalist to come from
heaven to heal the king when the snake bit him. They called all
the holy men together to sit round the king for seven days,
protecting him.

'Dharmayug, the Age of Truth, was passing and Kaliyug, the
Age of Destruction, was coming in.

'The snake was coming to kill the king and the herbalist was
coming to cure him. They met on the way. They were surprised to
see each other.

' "I'm going to kill the king," the snake said.

' "But I have come to cure him."

' "Let us test our skills," the snake said. "I'll bite a tree and I
challenge you to bring it back to life."

'The snake bit a tree. A man was sitting on one of its branches,
cutting wood. The tree and the man turned into ashes.

'The divine herbalist sprinkled water on the heap of ashes and
immediately the tree and the man came back to life again.

'The snake thought to himself, "What is the point of my
going all that way to kill the king if the herbalist can cure him?"

'He said to the divine herbalist, "I'll give you the money you
have been promised for healing the king. Why not go back? Why
should you walk all that way?"

'The snake gave him gold and silver and the herbalist went back, happy.

'When the snake arrived at the palace he found the king guarded by the holy men and he could not enter.

'He saw a man carrying a basket of fruit for the king. The snake gave him some money and asked him to carry a fruit. The man took the fruit and the snake hid inside it. It was the most colourful and attractive fruit in the basket and as soon as the king saw it he picked it up to eat.

'The snake bit him. The king died instantly, turning into ashes.'